TRANSITION AND REVOLUTION

TRANSITION
AND
REVOLUTION

Problems and Issues
of European Renaissance
and Reformation History

EDITED BY

Robert M. Kingdon
UNIVERSITY OF WISCONSIN, MADISON

BURGESS PUBLISHING COMPANY ● MINNEAPOLIS, MINNESOTA

Contents

ROBERT M. KINGDON

General Introduction

THE RENAISSANCE AND THE REFORMATION in Europe are probably best remembered as movements of great importance in the history of culture. The Renaissance, beginning in the city-state of Florence and spreading first to other parts of Italy and then all over Europe, witnessed tremendous advances in the culture of an educated elite. Particularly in the fields of art and literature, there were cultural achievements in this period which have seldom been matched in the entire span of human history. Most authorities would agree that only Greece in its golden age, the fourth and fifth centuries B.C., was as creative in the arts as Europe in the Renaissance. The Reformation, beginning in the principality of Saxony and spreading first to other parts of Germany and then all over Europe, witnessed profound changes in the culture of the entire population, including many in the lower classes who had not been touched directly by the Renaissance. Above all in the field of religion, ideas were developed which shattered irrevocably the unity of Western Europe, a unity which had been given institutional shape by the Roman Catholic Church. These ideas led to the creation of entirely new Reformed Churches, unconnected to Rome, in many parts of northern Europe. They also helped stimulate the formation of militant new religious orders and other reforming groups within the community still obedient to Rome, largely in southern Europe. These dramatic changes both in

1

ecclesiastical institutions and in the religious ideas which called them into being, forced further social, economic, and political adjustments. Customs and institutions had to be modified within thousands of local communities, within entire nations, and even on the international plane.

Most students of this period, in consequence, are particularly interested in cultural topics. A culture is such a large and complex entity, however, that its study can easily attract the interest and talents of many different types of specialists. That has certainly happened in scholarly study of the Renaissance and Reformation. Many specialists on the period simply want to understand more fully and precisely the nature of its culture, since it forms such an important part of our modern heritage. This desire has led them to focus their energies on the study of particular writers or artists and the works of thought or art they produced—on great literary figures like Dante, Rabelais, Shakespeare; on profound thinkers like Erasmus, Luther, Calvin, and Montaigne; on superb artists like Leonardo da Vinci, Michelangelo, Raphael, and Dürer. Not all of these scholars would regard themselves primarily as historians; many would instead call themselves specialists in literature, arts, philosophy, or theology.

Other specialists want to explore the connections between the Renaissance and the Reformation. To some extent the two movements overlapped, both in time and in place. While the Renaissance first sprouted in Italy early in the fourteenth century and reached its finest bloom there late in the fifteenth century, it did not penetrate much of northern Europe very deeply until the sixteenth century. It became important in Germany and France just before the Protestant Reformation got started; it blossomed in England even later, after Protestantism had been pretty well established. These overlaps pose some intriguing problems. For example, they lead some scholars to ask how the arts and religion are related; they lead others to consider how the culture of an elite and the culture of a general population affect each other. Most scholars with this type of interest would probably regard themselves as historians, specializing in cultural, intellectual, or perhaps social history.

Still other specialists want to investigate the society within which these two movements developed. While this was not a period of great change in the economy and in those facets of a society controlled by the economy, like the Industrial Revolution of the eighteenth and nineteenth centuries, it was a period of significant changes in political structures and in some types of technology. These changes are interesting in themselves. They also pose intriguing problems of the relations between society and culture. For example, they lead some scholars to study whether any one type of government, any single method of distributing property, or any particular family structure is likely to encourage great artistic achievement or spark a general religious revival. Most scholars with this type of interest would regard themselves as historians, specializing in political, economic, or social history.

The six essays which make up this book represent a cross section of work currently being done by professional historians on the Renaissance and Reformation. It would have been possible to draw on the work of scholars in many other disciplines, but that would have made for a rather diffuse collection. It would have also been possible to make quite a different selection of work by historians. This one seems reasonably representative to me, however. It runs the full gamut of types of history, including examples of current work on political, social, intellectual, cultural, and economic history. It contains a considerable geographic spread, reflecting intensive research in several different parts of Europe. Its authors draw on several different allied fields of scholarly inquiry, illustrating the possibilities of interdisciplinary history. All six essays were written by American specialists on the period, scholars currently at work on the frontiers of knowledge, whose publications have won recognition and respect for their discoveries and insights from the international community of scholars. Five of these essays were written specifically for this volume; the sixth is presented here for the first time in English. All but one are supported by a collection of the sources used by the essayist in his research. Many of the documents are here translated into English for the first time.

The combination of essays with selections of documents is an unusual and important feature of this book and of the series in which it appears. It sets this book apart from both collections of scholarly essays, which leave all critical judgment to the reader, and collections of documents, which leave all evaluation to the reader. The combination should have some distinct advantages for the student who has not as yet gone deeply into the field. It should make it easier for him to appreciate the working methods of a professional historian. He will find together in a chapter devoted to a single topic both relevant documentary raw material and professional conclusions drawn from that material.

Important additional lessons should flow from the collection in one volume of essay-document combinations dealing with several different types of history. This collection should illustrate clearly the fact that different types of history can require quite different kinds of documentation, which in turn pose different technical problems, and demand different research skills. For example, political history of this period is often based on state papers while intellectual history is often based on philosophical treatises; state papers were often written in vernacular languages, philosophical treatises were usually written in Latin; correct interpretation of a state paper may well require some study of law, correct interpretation of a philosophical treatise often requires knowledge of theology. Specialists on political and intellectual history may thus need quite different linguistic skills and auxiliary training. There are striking examples of these and other differences in this book.

It has long been a tradition to begin books on the Renaissance and Reformation with an analysis of the state. The tradition goes back at least to Jakob Burckhardt, the great nineteenth-century Swiss historian, who began his seminal study of *The Civilization of the Renaissance in Italy* with a chapter on "The State as a Work of Art." There are solid logical reasons for maintaining this tradition, since political structures in any period provide an important part of the shape and definition of a society. Accordingly this volume begins with an essay on the state, by Gordon Griffiths. Professor Griffiths is particularly interested in exploring the common idea that in this period monarchic states became absolute and hence more modern. He examines a number of these states, in Italy, Spain, the Low Countries, and France, and demonstrates that in every single case the power of the ruler was checked by institutions which mediated the wishes of other elements in the population. These institutions varied, to be sure, from city governments to purely provincial estates to national representative assemblies, but in every case the royal authority, even of the most powerful monarch, was significantly limited. This demonstration requires a close analysis of several types of state papers: constitutions, treaties, bills, and laws, all of which are illustrated in the selection of documents. It also provides, and this is probably its greatest novelty, an interesting and valuable use of the comparative method. Much work on political history has tended to deal with only one government. Many historians focus their attention on the history of their own country; those who do specialize on other countries often acquire the linguistic tools to work on only one other area. However, work focused on one government cannot provide complete explanations, for it fails to see what is unique to that government and what features it shares with others. It has proved to be extremely revealing to break with tradition and compare different governments with each other, even though this can be very difficult, involving as it does research on materials in several different languages reflecting rather different legal and political traditions. Professor Griffiths is a leading member of an organization devoted to just this kind of comparative history, the *International Commission for the History of Representative and Parliamentary Institutions*. His essay is an extremely valuable introduction to the type of work sponsored by that body.

My own essay deals not with political structures, but with political and social change, of the most profound and far-reaching sort, which we now label revolutionary. This is a phenomenon which interests a great many people today, including those who want to provoke revolution because they despair of resolving acute social problems in any other way, and those who want to avoid revolution because they fear it would demolish essential values proved by time, and even those who only want to observe revolution because it affects their own lives. I argue that the Protestant Reformation provoked change of the type that is commonly called revolutionary because it drove from power a ruling class, the Catholic clergy. My argument requires a careful definition of the term "revolution," some general consideration of the role of the clergy in pre-Reformation European society, and a close study of the actual changes involved in the establishment of Protestant regimes. I illustrate this argument with one extreme case study—the Reformation in the city-state of Geneva. Before the Reformation this city was an episcopal principality, allied to the duchy of Savoy, and an intellectual and cultural backwater; afterwards it became a secular state, allied to the Swiss cantons, and the international headquarters of the Protestant movement created by John Calvin. My case study is based on two types of documents: laws and chronicles. The laws reveal the final institutional shape given to Reformation changes in Geneva, as decided by the government which seized control of the city at that time. The chronicles contain narratives, year by year and sometimes day by day, by contemporary observers, of the changes which finally made these laws necessary. These chronicles also contain some passages of analysis, prepared by the same contemporaries at somewhat later periods, when they could reflect on the history they had witnessed. To ensure that my presentation of contemporary opinion is reasonably fair and complete, I have presented excerpts from the accounts of three very different witnesses. One was a Catholic sister, Jeanne de Jussie, who was forced by the Reformation to leave her convent, along with almost all of her religious community, and move to another city. Another was a prior, François de Bonivard, who defied his superiors, was thrown into jail, and finally won release and permission to lead an honorable life as a lay gentleman, thanks to the Reformation. A third was a sober and talented civil servant and magistrate, Michel Roset, whose father was in the group of lay citizens who engineered the Genevan Reformation and who himself rose to great power and prominence within the city as a result. These chronicles pose for the historian problems in reconciling different viewpoints and piecing together different perceptions into a single plausible account. They also contain insights, which can be recovered in no other way, into what the political and social and religious changes of the Reformation really meant to contemporary participants.

The drastic and often painful changes provoked by the Reformation were justified, in the minds of their exponents, by a set of radical new religious ideas. Of the many thinkers who developed and expressed these ideas, the most important was clearly Martin Luther. His significance has been so great and so obvious since his lifetime that for centuries his career and his ideas have attracted a tremendous amount of scholarly study. This study has grown so voluminous and so substantial that a scholar could now spend all of his time simply keeping abreast of it. In fact, there is a book-sized periodical published annually which does nothing but list all of the year's studies of Luther. Other leading Protestant Reformers, like John Calvin, also continue to attract a very great amount of scholarly study. The very quantity of this work leads some to despair of ever finding anything new to say about these men, to conclude that every modern study must either be unoriginal or false. This temptation to despair has been brilliantly dispelled in recent years by an international group of scholars, many of whom have been trained and stimulated by Heiko Oberman, formerly of Harvard University and now of the University of Tübingen. These experts have concentrated their attention on the thought of the Catholic theologians of the fourteenth and fifteenth centuries, the period immediately preceding the Reformation. It was against these theologians that Luther and many of the other leading Protestant thinkers were reacting. A study of their thought thus makes it possible to recreate an important part of the intellectual context out of which Protestantism developed. But this body of thought is extremely complex. It uses a special technical vocabulary and categories of thought unfamiliar to most historians. The study of it is thus very demanding. Only a scholar with unusually thorough training in the history of theology is equipped to understand these ideas and connect them to the ideas of the Reformation.

Of the scholars who have acquired this necessary background, one of the ablest is Steven Ozment. His essay in this volume is based on an extremely intensive study of Luther's earliest writings, of treatises he prepared before the posting of his Ninety-Five Theses in 1517 attracted international publicity and launched the Reformation. In these treatises, Professor Ozment finds germinating the fundamental idea with which Luther created Reformation theology, the doctrine of justification by faith alone. He finds this idea developing in Luther's reactions to two types of late medieval theologians: mystical theologians, notably Tauler and Gerson, whose theory of human nature and the human soul Luther rejected, and rational theologians, notably Ockham and Biel, whose theory of man's role in his own salvation Luther rejected. Professor Ozment's documents present examples of all these reactions. They deserve very close reading.

Luther's theological insights could never have conquered half a continent and remained influential down to the present without the conversion of an intellectual elite and the creation of a set of educational and ecclesiastical institutions designed to preserve these ideas and pass them on to the general population. A part of this process is the subject of Lewis Spitz's essay. Professor Spitz has long been interested in humanism, the most pervasive and fundamental ideology of the Renaissance. He has become one of the world's leading authorities on how humanism spread from Italy into Germany and on how it was connected to the Reformation. His many able students have further helped to expand our knowledge of these developments.

Humanism was a complex and protean movement. Experts still argue about its exact nature. They seem to agree, however, that an essential part of it was an attempt to recover from classical antiquity a set of educational disciplines, the humanities, including what we would now call literature, history, and communications skills. This attempt could obviously lead to the reform of educational institutions. Many humanists did in fact become prominent as teachers and educational administrators, reforming the curricula and staffing of older schools and universities or building entirely new ones. Often these humanists developed strong interests in religious reform. Some of them tried to revitalize the Catholic Church from within; others joined the Protestant Reformation. There was an interesting generational split involved in this choice, which Professor Spitz has discussed at greater length elsewhere. Humanists of Luther's own age or older, like Erasmus, tended to remain Catholic; humanists of the next generation, like Calvin, often joined the Protestant camp. Among the most prominent who turned Protestant are two whom Professor Spitz examines at length in this essay: Melanchthon, Luther's most influential disciple, and Beza, Calvin's most influential follower. Both devoted much of their careers to developing a new kind of education, Melanchthon in the young University of Wittenberg where he was a teacher and in other German communities where he acted as a consultant, Beza in the new Academy of Geneva which he served as presiding rector.

Another important facet of humanism was its rejection of the life-style of intellectuals who remained, like many medieval theologians, in an ivory tower, developing and refining speculative ideas only for other specialists. The humanists wanted intellectuals to enter the real world of secular and ecclesiastical politics, and use their skills to make society better. These attitudes drew inspiration from the example of ancient rhetoricians, notably Demosthenes, who influenced Athenian politics, and Cicero, who dominated the Roman Senate. The genre which reveals both of these men at their most characteristic is the oration. It is thus very significant that several of the documents upon which Professor Spitz builds his case are sixteenth-century orations, modeled quite closely on the orations of antiquity. They are quite different in tone and content from the technical treatises in which the young Luther had first developed his ideas.

It would be a mistake to assume that Luther and the humanist intellectuals, both in his own camp and in the opposition, dominated all thought during the period of the Renaissance and Reformation. In any society, the ideas of the most respected intellectual leaders rarely win the support or even the understanding of everyone. Indeed, they are often resisted by significant elements in the population, who sometimes see in these ideas an attempt to manipulate them and keep them under control. This resistance often finds its most interesting expression in elements of the culture of the lower classes. Lower-class culture in any society is very difficult to study Ordinary people seldom record their ideas and feelings in writing, and yet historians are trained to quarry most of their evidence from written records. Such study becomes particularly difficult for the historian of premodern societies, in which most ordinary people could neither read nor write. However, more and more scholars are convinced that it is necessary to try, that cultural history must not be viewed solely as the creation of an intellectual elite, that it must also be studied from "underneath," from the point of view of the common people. Anthropologists and psychologists have worked at developing techniques for doing this, and historians have learned from them. Historians have also become adept at drawing evidence of lower-class culture indirectly, from upper-class comment on the rest of society. This requires great sensitivity and critical skill.

One index to popular culture at the time of the Renaissance and Reformation, which is currently attracting a great deal of scholarly talent and attention, is to be found in ideas about witchcraft. Witchcraft, or at least the fear of witchcraft, became endemic in much of Europe toward the end of the Reformation, particularly in rural areas and among the uneducated. Erik Midelfort is a pioneer in the study of this phenomenon, especially as it developed in southwestern Germany. In his essay he grapples with the problem of whether groups of witches actually met to engage in worship of the devil and plot harm to their neighbors. He lays bare a wide gamut of contemporary views on witchcraft and of alternative attempts to understand and manipulate the supernatural. His documents reveal the great delicacy of this line of research, for not one of them comes from a witch or from a writer claiming personal familiarity with witches. The nearest approach to this sort of record is a dramatic popular account of the terrible activities of witches operating in certain German villages in 1580. Even this record is clearly very hostile to witches. So are most of the rest of his documents. So are almost all of the surviving records of witchcraft. They were typically written by clergymen who saw in witchcraft a terrible competitor to true Christian faith, by lawyers who saw in it a serious threat to social order, by doctors who saw in it a severe form of illness. They include laws which proscribe witches and records of trials in which accused witches were closely examined. By their very nature, these records make it easier for us to examine the reactions of articulate society against witches than witchcraft itself. To penetrate through to the reality behind these records requires all the critical skills and extreme care which Professor Midelfort displays so admirably.

Any culture, elitist or popular, requires media of communication for its spread and development. The Europe of the Renaissance and Reformation acquired an extremely important new medium—the printed page. It was made possible by a technological breakthrough, movable metal type as used in the printing press. It was made significant by the rapid development of an entire new industry commanding important material and human resources, the publishing industry. Simply because printing was so novel, it had much of the shock effect that television has had on twentieth-century society. Since it controlled so much of the communication of thought, it came to influence in profound and subtle ways both the content of ideas and society itself.

Elizabeth Eisenstein, a historian who began as a specialist on modern French topics, has become fascinated in recent years by the impact of printing on European society of the Renaissance and Reformation period. In a series of brilliantly suggestive essays, she has sketched many of the possible ramifications of this impact. One of these essays, first published in the leading French journal for the interdisciplinary study of history, is now presented in this book for the first time in English. It examines the relations between the development of printing and the Reformation. That there was some relation between the two was obvious from the beginning, as Professor Eisenstein makes clear with quotations from Luther, Foxe, and others. But she argues that the full dimensions of this relationship have not as yet been appreciated, and proceeds to sketch a number of lines upon which further study should prove fruitful. This type of argument is not easily susceptible to the documentary demonstration which supports the other chapters in this book. Accordingly, there are no documents attached to this essay. However, there are a great number of footnotes. They make it clear that this essay is partly a synthesis of the views of many other scholars, including specialists on the history of printing, general historians familiar with the entire period, and experts from such other disciplines as sociology, anthropology, and psychology. But the essay is even more an exercise in intuition, pointing out with great ingenuity a variety of possible and plausible connections between printing and other phenomena. It is the kind of scholarly study which may well prove to be a starting point for many more intensive and highly focused research projects.

Taken all together, these essays reveal how experts on one important historical period are proceeding with their work. They should make readers appreciate more fully the ways in which historical research is defined and developed, of how it depends on a solid documentary foundation, and yet draws on many other disciplines to explain fully the meaning of its documents. Perhaps they may even inspire some readers to try for themselves to do research on the fascinating and important period of the Renaissance and Reformation.

GORDON GRIFFITHS

The State: Absolute or Limited?

THE RENAISSANCE FOUND its expression in the State as well as in Arts and Letters. So we are told by some distinguished historians. The first part of Burckhardt's *Civilization of the Renaissance in Italy* is entitled "The State as a Work of Art." Burckhardt argued that both aspects of the modern State, despotic and republican, were first developed in the Italian Renaissance. Baron speaks of an "underlying general affinity between the texture of political life in Renaissance Italy and the structure of the modern state."[1] Major uses the term "Renaissance Monarchy."[2] For Pollard, one of the chief factors in Modern History was "The New Monarchy."[3] Rice uses both terms: "Renaissance Monarchy" and "New Monarchy."[4] The first of Lord Acton's "Lectures on Modern History," now published under the title of *Renaissance to Revolution,* was entitled "Beginning of the Modern State."[5]

Such terms are used to convey the notion that the State had

[1] Hans Baron, "Towards a more positive evaluation of the fifteenth-century Renaissance," *Journal of the History of Ideas*, 4 (1943): 26.

[2] J. Russell Major, *Representative Institutions in Renaissance France, 1421-1559* (Madison: University of Wisconsin Press, 1960), especially pp. 3-5.

[3] A.F. Pollard, *Factors in Modern History* (London: 1907; republished, Constable, 1921.)

[4] Eugene R. Rice, Jr., *The Foundations of Early Modern Europe, 1460-1559,* pp. 105-6.

[5] The lectures were delivered at Cambridge between 1899 and 1901, and first published by Macmillan in 1906. Schocken Books have produced a paperback edition (New York, 1961).

entered upon a new stage of development during the period in question. The variation in terminology reflects, however, an important difference of opinion as to what that period was. Authors who talk about "the rise of the Modern State" are thinking of an institution lasting into their own time, or at least until the French Revolution. Those who talk about a "Renaissance Monarchy" imply that it was peculiar to a period which they label "Renaissance." Let us consider the broader concept first.

We are asked to recognize the appearance of the "Modern State" by certain manifest signs: its size, its unity, and its constitution (whether the monarch is absolute or limited by representative institutions).

The importance of size does seem obvious when we consider what happened to the Italian states at the hands of France and Spain. During the fifteenth century, five Italian cities—Florence, Venice, Rome, Naples, and Milan—had been the centers of wealth and of the culture of the Renaissance. Yet they were unable to resist the power of France and Spain, which in the course of the "Italian wars" (1494-1530) made themselves the dominant powers in Europe.

But size is an inadequate sign of power, else the German Empire, or Poland-Lithuania, would rank ahead of the western monarchies. England, usually mentioned as an example of the "new monarchy," could hardly be ranked with France and Spain if size were the test. We must look for other factors.

"It was obvious," according to Lord Acton in his lecture on the beginning of the modern state, "that the countries newly strengthened, the countries growing in unity and concentration and superfluous forces, would encroach upon the demoralized" and weak.[6] As evidence of Spanish unification, Acton cited the marriage of Ferdinand and Isabella and the conquest of Granada; of French unification the expulsion of the English, the institution of a permanent army, the acquisition of frontier provinces, and the destruction of centrifugal forces of feudalism. From the documents to follow, however, it will be possible to see how little unity was attained in Spain, and even in France, during the sixteenth century. Aragon and Castile might acquire common rulers, Provence and Brittany might come into the possession of the King of France, but what did such provinces have in common besides a common ruler?

The degree of unity in a State can only be discerned by examining its constitutional structure. This was to be, for the

[6] *Op. cit.*, Schocken ed., p. 37.

"modern" State, absolute monarchy, or so at least we are assured by many authors. Sabine, the author of a standard history of political theory, says that:

By the opening years of the sixteenth century, . . . absolute monarchy either had become, or was rapidly becoming, the prevailing type of government in western Europe . . . . Absolute monarchy overturned feudal constitutionalism and the free city-states, on which medieval civilization had largely depended.[7]

Elton, in his *Renaissance and Reformation,* speaks of "monarchic power approximating to absolutism," and of "the elimination of rival authorities like the Church, assemblies of estates, free cities," etc.[8] In a very recent assessment, Eugene Rice reaches the following conclusion:

By 1560 in the key monarchies of western Europe giant steps had been taken toward territorial unification, administrative centralization, and the magnification of royal power. The rapid accumulation of exclusive prerogatives by the central governments of France, Spain, and England—to make laws, to govern through legal, financial, and administrative officers, to tax, to declare war and make peace, to exercise ultimate jurisdiction, and to coin money—defines their transformation from feudal monarchies into sovereign territorial states. Thus we call them the new monarchies not because they broke abruptly with the past or because all feudal remnants had disappeared . . . but because their structures were sufficiently novel to mark a new period in the history of European political institutions. On these foundations were built the great sovereign monarchies of the seventeenth and eighteenth centuries.[9]

Rice has qualified his statements more carefully than Sabine or Elton. He believes that there was something "new" about monarchy in the sixteenth century, and that it laid the foundations for the monarchy of the seventeenth and eighteenth centuries. But by using the term "Renaissance Monarchy" he suggests that this was only a preliminary stage in the process, and not to be confused with the fully developed absolutism of a later era.

The notion that absolutism was already established in the sixteenth century is further shaken when one turns to Bodin, who made the study of constitutions his lifework, and who was able as an eyewitness to observe how the State of the sixteenth century actually worked. He believed that government, to be effective,

---

[7] George H. Sabine, *A History of Political Theory,* p. 333.

[8] G. R. Elton, *Renaissance and Reformation* (New York: Macmillan, 1968), p. 90.

[9] Rice, *loc. cit.* The chapter is entitled "The Formation of the Early Modern State." *Cf.* Joseph Strayer, *On the Medieval Origins of the Modern State* (Princeton, 1970), p. 100: "Well into the seventeenth century the best-organized states were in a sense only federations of counties or provinces . . . Early modern Europe was not ready for real centralization."

must be absolute, and that the best form of government was monarchical. But, search as he might, he confessed that he could not find any monarchy that even approached his prescription except the French.[10]

The idea of a "national State" in the sixteenth century is, according to J. F. Hexter, a "myth." Attacking Pollard, he asks whether the national state was "quite so predominant in power, quite so pre-eminent among the loyalties of men, *in the sixteenth century* [his emphasis], as Pollard supposed." "To both these questions," Hexter says, "the answer of most present-day historians probably would be 'No'."[11]

If Hexter's majority is correct in thinking that absolutism hardly became established before the seventeenth century, the question remains whether the preceding age produced some other characteristic form of State. Some would answer that the principal institutions of the French and English and Spanish monarchies remained much as they had been since the beginning of the fourteenth century, and should be thought of as products of the later Middle Ages. Others have introduced the term "Renaissance Monarchy." To answer the question, we should have to examine the ways in which the monarchy and representative institutions functioned in the fourteenth and fifteenth, as well as in the sixteenth, centuries and we can hardly attempt that in the space available.

Instead, we have looked for documents that might indicate how far the most powerful princely dynasties—the Habsburgs in Spain and the Low Countries; the Valois in France—were able to go in the direction of absolutism in the sixteenth century, and how far they were still limited by obligations to consult representative institutions. We have omitted the Tudors on the ground that so many collections of English constitutional documents are accessible.

For some, the term "Renaissance Monarchy" means something more than a form of monarchy characteristic of the sixteenth century. In their view, there was a model for the northern "Renaissance" monarch in the Italian "Renaissance" prince of the fourteenth and fifteenth centuries. We shall therefore begin with an example of an Italian princely State.

---

[10]R.W. and A.J. Carlyle, *A History of Mediaeval Political Theory in the West* (New York: Barnes and Noble), Vol. VI (1936), p. 426, citing Bodin's *De Republica*, I:8.

[11]J. H. Hexter, "Factors in Modern History," in *Reappraisals in History* (New York: Harper Torchbook, 1961), p. 29.

ITALY

Many historians have thought that the model of the modern State was to be found in the Italy of the Renaissance. They have pointed particularly to the despots of northern Italy who already in the fourteenth century were reducing the self-governing communes to subjection. It was easy to see in this process the surrender of republicanism to absolutism, and of the city-state (or commune) to the centralized territorial State.

The most successful of the despots were the Visconti of Milan. One Visconti ruler, Gian Galeazzo, managed to conquer so much of northern and central Italy that, before his death in 1402, a kingdom of Italy was almost within his grasp. The Republic of Florence, in central Italy, continued to resist, but Gian Galeazzo had managed to gain control of the most powerful cities surrounding Florence. One of these was the Republic of Siena, which came under his dominion in 1399. This event is often described as the climax of a process of surrender of freedom to despotism, and of self-government to the centralized State.

Source 1 (see Sources at the end of this essay) is in itself evidence that the surrender of Siena was not unconditional. In the preamble, Gian Galeazzo would have the world believe that the twenty-nine Articles were a unilateral gift, but we know that they were based on the thirty-two Articles drawn up by the General Council of Siena for submission to the Duke. In words, the representatives of Siena spoke of "freely transferring the dominion of the city, jurisdiction, county and district of Siena to the person of Giovan Galeazzo Visconti," but in fact he received their submission on the terms agreed in the twenty-nine Articles.[12] Nowhere are these referred to as a contract; only as *patti* (agreements) or *capitoli* (articles). But they amounted in fact to a contract, or to what in later centuries would be called a constitution. Gian Galeazzo's authority over Siena was thus not to be absolute, but limited by a written constitution.

The Articles show how much the Duke of Milan yielded to the demands of the Sienese. Their traditional form of government was to be preserved, particularly its executive (Article I) and administrative (Article III) officers, and its constitution and laws (Article VI). The Duke was not to impose new taxes, nor to raise existing ones (Article XVIII). He undertook not only to defend Sienese territory but also to maintain the Sienese in possession of

---

[12] Orlando Malavolti, *Historia di Siena*, Part II, fol. 185ro.

their surrounding subject towns and lands (Article XX). They could even look forward to preserving their monopoly over positions in the Church throughout the territory traditionally governed by Siena.

On the other hand, Gian Galeazzo gained power over the things that really mattered to him. No action could henceforth be taken, in either domestic or foreign affairs, by the government of Siena without the signature of the Duke's Chancellor (Article III). The Duke's representative (Lieutenant) had the right to take part, and vote in all city councils (Article XII). Another ducal official was assigned to watch over the collection and disbursement of revenue (Article XIV). In order to defend Sienese territory, the Duke had to be granted the right to appoint the captains of local fortifications and castles. With control over defense, finance, and foreign policy, Gian Galeazzo could afford to let the Sienese take care of local matters. Some Sienese must have expressed fear that under the twenty-nine Articles the agents of the Duke might behave in a tyrannical way, for a few weeks after putting his signature to these, he agreed to an additional seventeen Articles.

The additional Articles limit the Duke's Lieutenant. Article II undertakes to protect the citizens' freedom of speech against him. By Article XII, he undertakes to see to it that the constitution and laws of Siena are not violated. Articles VII, VIII, and XIII forbid the kinds of petty tyranny that must have been common. By Article IX, the Lieutenant promises not to interfere in criminal cases, except where these affect "the State."

Article III makes a similar reservation on behalf of "the State" (*lo stato*). The promise to respect local self-government, except in matters affecting "the State," was of course no sure guarantee against abuse, but it is evidence of a considerable degree of political sophistication when so clear a distinction is made between those matters that could be left to local government and those that were to be reserved to the central government.

The fact that Gian Galeazzo forbade his Lieutenant to behave like a tyrant of course tells us nothing about how his lieutenants in this and other cities did in fact behave, but it does indicate that Gian Galeazzo cannot be dismissed as the kind of tyrant who was unaware of the problem.

How far is it legitimate to generalize about the Viscontean State on the basis of the Sienese Articles? Siena was no doubt a special case, but so were the other towns conquered by Gian Galeazzo in central and northern Italy. This is true even of the fourteen towns in his original dominion. Each of these, and each of the six he added to his dominion, proclaimed him its lord (*dominus*). Each, like Siena, agreed as part of their contract with him that he might be represented by a Lieutenant. But Gian Galeazzo was the only institution they had in common. The twenty cities were never fused into a political unity. The Viscontean dominions, old and new, were a collection of cities rather than a State in the modern sense. Gian Galeazzo did have a ducal chancery, and he did establish certain councils with competence over more than one city. These administrative institutions may be regarded as embryonic elements of the modern centralized territorial State, but the Sienese Articles are a fair indication of the limits of centralization. Gian Galeazzo never dreamed, like a Napoleon, of giving his dominions a common legal code, or of conferring on the citizens of his twenty cities a common citizenship. To find his legislation, in fact, it is necessary to go through each city's collection of statutes. For an act of Gian Galeazzo was not enacted by any State-wide institution with jurisdiction throughout his dominions; it had to be enacted and registered in the statute-book of each city in turn.[13]

The common description of Gian Galeazzo Visconti as the builder of a centralized, absolute State must therefore be abandoned. It would be rather misleading to go to the other extreme and describe him as a constitutional monarch presiding over a federation. He was an aggressive conqueror who deprived Siena and other cities of their independence and threatened to destroy the independence, and in this sense the freedom, of the rest of Italy. But the system he was in the process of imposing, and which may have served as a model for later trans-Alpine states, was a federal rather than a centralized system.

SPAIN

It is commonly asserted that the Spanish monarchy acquired absolute power by the sixteenth century; in support of this assertion it is maintained that the kings were no longer checked as they had been during the later Middle Ages by the representative bodies called the *Córtes.*

After speaking of a "general recession of representative institutions," Sabine begins his picture of the general growth of absolute

[13] F. Cognasso, "Lo stato di Gian Galeazzo," chapter XXXI of his book on *I Visconti* (Milan, 1966); see also his "Istituzioni Comunali e Signorili" in *Storia di Milano* Vol. VI, Part III (Milan: Fondazione Treccani degli Alfieri, 1955).

monarchy with Spain by saying that "the uniting of Aragon and
Castile by the marriage of Ferdinand and Isabella began the
formation of an absolute monarchy."[14] Elton says that, while
England "never abandoned her representative institutions, the
Spanish *Córtes* gradually died, so that Philip II could complete the
structure of a bureaucratic royal absolutism."[15] How do such
statements stand up in the face of the documents?

First of all, Spanish *Córtes* continued to meet throughout the
sixteenth century, which included the reigns of Charles V and
Philip II. In the case of Castile, there were at least thirty-five
sessions. The proceedings of these have survived and have been
published.[16] Were the representatives who attended these meetings simply acting out parts in a pageant to bemuse the public or
did they have some real power? If so, on whose behalf did they
exercise it?

Some of the questions about the power of the *Córtes* of Castile
can be answered by reading the petitions submitted by the
representatives who met in the *Córtes* in 1506. Petition 6
(Source 2) emphasizes the diversity of the realms and provinces of which "Spain" was composed. After all that Isabella had
done to unify the country, the representatives petition her
successors (Juana and her husband Philip I) to recognize that it
would be inappropriate to attempt to impose uniform laws.

One of the purposes of the *Córtes,* according to Petition 6, was
precisely to protect provincial diversity against the tendency,
natural in the executive councils of the monarchy, to promote
equality and uniformity. Thus the machinery of representative
government is associated with the protection of provincial rights,
which, it is claimed, have been jeopardized by the arbitrary
decrees of a royal council acting without the advice of those
knowing the local situation.

The representatives speak in their petition of "realms" (*reynos*)
in the plural. Throughout the century, they continue to refer to
the *Córtes* of Castile as representing several realms. If the *Córtes*
represented diversity within Castile, they made no pretense at all of
representing the wider unity of Spain. Other realms had their

---

[14] Sabine, *op. cit.,* p. 334.
[15] Elton, *op. cit.,* pp. 89-90.
[16] In *Córtes de los antiguos reinos de Leon y de Castilla* (Madrid: Real Academia de
la Historia), Vol. IV (1882): 1476-1537; Vol. V (1903): 1538-1559; and in *Actas de las
Córtes de Castilla* (Madrid: Congreso de los Diputados, 1861-1925): for the period
1563-1627. See Griffiths, *Representative Government,* pp. 1-75, for a selection of texts,
in Spanish with English translation, commentary, and bibliography.

separate *Córtes:* Aragon, Valencia, and Catalonia. Occasionally the last three were convened in *Córtes Generales* under the crown of Aragon, but no such institution existed in the sixteenth century for Spain as a whole, comparable to the Estates General for France. The king had to deal with the *Córtes* of each realm separately, if he was to obtain their assent. The unity of Spain supposedly brought about by the marriage between Ferdinand of Aragon and Isabella of Castile was confined to the institution of the monarchy itself and to that of the Inquisition; it did not extend to other institutions such as the *Córtes.*

Petition No. 6 of 1506 may, on the other hand, be read to sustain an argument that Spain was already becoming absolute and united. The Petition was after all a protest against these tendencies. Should we read it as evidence that the process was about to be completed? The advice of a royal councillor in the following century shows how far from completion it was, even in his time:

The most important task that confronts Your Majesty [he told Philip IV] is to make yourself King of Spain; by which I mean, Sir, that Your Majesty should not rest content with the titles of King of Portugal, King of Aragon, King of Valencia, and Count of Barcelona, but that Your Majesty should labor and plan, with careful and secret consideration, to reduce all these realms of which Spain is now composed, to the fashion and laws of Castile, without any difference.[17]

Petition 33 of the *Córtes* of 1506 (Source 3) answers the question about the constituencies they represented. The representatives (*procuradores*) did not represent population or countryside; they represented towns, and only those eighteen towns that by law and custom had the privilege of being represented in the *Córtes.* They guarded the privilege jealously, as the petition shows, and they professed no understanding of the argument that other towns ought also to be represented. This proposal they dismissed as if it were merely a demand for an increase of offices.

The relationship between crown and *Córtes* may be glimpsed by the differing reception given to these two petitions by the king. To the first (the request that he observe the law to make no laws except with the advice of the *Córtes*), his response was evasive, but he found no difficulty in consenting to the other, that the eighteen cities should retain their exclusive privilege.

Source 4 recites a fundamental claim of the Castilian *Córtes:*

[17]A passage quoted by J. Russell Major, in "The Limitations of Absolutism in the 'New Monarchies,' " in *The "New Monarchies" and Representative Assemblies,* ed. Arthur J. Slavin (Heath, *Problems in European Civilization,* 1964), p. 84.

the right to present petitions (what in English usage would be called "bills"). Bills drawn up in *Córtes,* Parliament, or Congress are, however, of no effect until signed into law by the executive. Source 4 records such an event. What began as Petition No. 6 of the *Córtes* meeting in Toledo in 1525 found its way into the great codification of law published under Philip II in 1567. The language is not, indeed, that of the original petition, but of the king's response; we cannot say that the *Córtes* could control the ultimate language of the law (in this respect they lacked the power eventually acquired by the English Parliament and the American Congress), but we can recognize that the king was bound under this law to give some kind of response to every one of the *Córtes'* petitions, and to do so before the end of the session. The *Córtes* thus had a share in legislation, recognized by Charles V (who was king in 1525) and by Philip II (under whom this law was included in the published code). Countless other laws in the code acknowledge the legislative power of the *Córtes* by reference to the number of the Petition and the date of the *Córtes* which originated it.

Only a share, however. The king controlled the language of his response, which could be a disguised negative. Even if it was positive, who could be certain that the "necessary provisions" to execute it would be adequate? On the other hand, he could not under this law exercise a veto. He must respond before the end of the session, and was thus deprived of the option of a "pocket veto." Nor did the language of this law permit an outright veto, for the king was obliged to "comply" with the petitions, "in accordance with Justice" (*las cumplir de justicia*). Compliance in accordance with Justice nevertheless allowed the king considerable freedom of interpretation.

Why did the *Córtes* present this petition in the first place? Its necessity is indication that the king had not been responding to their petitions. Through the reign of Philip II, *Córtes* after *Córtes* make the same complaint, indicating that the law of 1525, though recognized in theory, was often disregarded in fact. Nevertheless, so long as *Córtes* continued to meet, and succeeded in getting some of their petitions enacted into law, we cannot say that the *Córtes* were dead or that the king was absolute.

The *Córtes* made what was perhaps their most severe challenge to the monarchy in the session that opened in December 1566 and was not concluded until the middle of the following June. The very length of the session is evidence that Philip II was not able to treat them as a rubber stamp. On the contrary, he badly needed the revenues which he asked them to vote him. Here was the opportunity for the *Córtes* to use the power of the purse to secure their long sought demand that the King answer their petitions before dissolving the *Córtes*.

The Book of Laws and Decrees (Source 5), published immediately after the conclusion of the *Córtes*, acknowledges in its very title the role of the *Córtes* in the legislative process. In the preamble, the King proclaims that he has responded to the petitions within the time requested. His responses were not, however, always favorable.

Taxation was always a principal concern of the *Córtes*. Their principle, that no new laws should be made without their consent, applied above all to legislation regarding taxation. Petition No. 3 of 1567 proclaims the principle that no new taxes should be imposed without the consent of the *Córtes*. The issue had been debated for months. Most of the representatives had come to the *Córtes* under instruction from their constituent towns to protest the new taxes which had been imposed by the Crown. They protested on the ground that they could no longer afford to pay, but also on the constitutional ground that the new taxes had been devised outside the *Córtes* (*fuera de Córtes*).

For many weeks the representatives said that they would not grant the aid (*servicio*) demanded by the King until after he had relieved their grievances, one of which was the imposition of the new taxes without their consent. Eventually, however, the *Córtes* were persuaded to accept a compromise. They voted the aid on the promise that some recognition would be given to their grievances. The final text of their petition (Source 5) and the King's response show the outcome. The King had successfully argued that their principle must yield to the urgent needs of State. He had explained what these were: the defense of Christendom and of his various States.

Could the *Córtes* have challenged Philip's argument? In theory, there was nothing to prevent their challenging the wisdom of plunging Spain into the wars which Charles V and Philip II had waged for the protection of their Italian and Netherlandish possessions against France, or the commitment of resources to the defense of the Roman Church against the Reformers in Germany, France, and the Netherlands. In 1566 Philip was preparing for a showdown with the Netherlands; in 1567 he despatched the Duke of Alva with a Spanish army to overawe the opposition by force.

That opposition had become too strong in the Estates of those countries for Philip to be willing any longer to risk attempting to govern with their assent (see section on the Low Countries). Members of the *Córtes* might have regarded their opposite numbers in the Netherlands as allies in the defense of freedom and representative government against the common threat of arbitrary monarchy.

The representatives in the *Córtes* were not unaware of the developing struggle in the Netherlands (what they called *Flandes*). The proof of this is in the record of their proceedings for 18 March 1567 (Source 6). They were protesting the non-parliamentary imposition of the new taxes. "Several times" they had asked the King to stop this practice. What had stood in the way of the satisfaction of their demands? The pressure of business, the problems of Christianity and of the Estates of Flanders so obviously required remedy and assistance that he had peremptorily ordered them not to treat of this matter any more for the time being, nor even to discuss it in the *Córtes*!

We might conclude from this that Philip's determination to crush the religious and political opposition in the Low Countries led to the crushing of the *Córtes* in Spain as well. The King did succeed in getting the *Córtes* to vote him an aid (*servicio*) before he had responded to their grievances. Nevertheless, despite his effort to silence them, they insisted on going on to declare that they did not consent to any new taxes without the consent of the *Córtes*.

Philip II obtained the substance—the aid—but at the cost of having published, for all Castile to know, the Petition expressing the opposition of the realm to any new taxation without the consent of the *Córtes*. The monarchy could evade this principle, but it could not eliminate it from public consciousness. For the remainder of the century and beyond, it remained available to any who might wish to use it to resist the expansion of royal power.

THE LOW COUNTRIES

Charles V and Philip II were rulers of the Low Countries as well as of Spain and other countries. The documents selected to illustrate their relations with the Estates of the Low Countries supply additional evidence on the question of the extent of unity and of absolutism achieved by the Habsburgs in the sixteenth century.

Source 7, reciting the efforts of the imperial Regent, Margaret of Austria, to obtain a grant of revenue from the Estates of Brabant, shows on the face of it that it was to the Estates of a Province that the Habsburg rulers had to appeal, rather than to the Estates General that might purport to represent a wider unity. On this occasion, in 1528, the Estates of Brabant proved to be more resistant than usual to the government's demands, which were only satisfied in the end over the protest of the Chancellor. In the course of his protest, he recited what was the normal and constitutional procedure, namely, that a tax must have the consent of all three Estates: prelates, nobles, and townsmen, the latter being representative of the four towns privileged to be represented, *viz.*, Brussels, Antwerp, Bois-le-Duc, and Louvain. The refusal of any one of these was enough to block a proposal. This was the constitutional obstacle confronting the government, and which Margaret sought to avoid by contriving a new "union," omitting the two troublesome towns of Brussels and Louvain. Nothing came of her proposed union between Holland and Brabant. The Chancellor's defense of the constitution was, on the other hand, not forgotten. In 1561, another Margaret, Regent on behalf of Philip II, was having similar troubles with the Estates of Brabant. In a letter dated 16 July (Source 8) she reported to Philip that the Chancellor was being asked to refuse to seal any decree unless it had been approved by the Estates.

The constitution to which the Estates of Brabant appealed was embodied in a document called the *Blijde Inkomst*, or in French the *Joyeuse Entrée*. The term refers to the reception of each new sovereign, granted upon his confirmation of the traditional privileges of the province. The first *Joyeuse Entrée* was agreed to in 1356 by Johanna and Wenceslas; subsequent versions were granted by their successors as the condition of being received as rulers of the duchy. The *Joyeuse Entrée* to which Charles agreed in 1515 included sixty-four articles; these were reduced to fifty-eight in the document to which Philip subscribed in 1549, but the Estates on that occasion resisted efforts to introduce important changes in the text. The article referring to the consent and privileges of the Estates was identical in 1515 and 1549 (Source 9).

The correspondence between Philip II and Margaret of Parma (Regent of the Netherlands from 1559 to 1567) reveals more of the real opinions of these rulers about Estates than most official documents. Her letter of 13 June 1562 (Source 10) expresses the opinion that aid and not advice were what a prince should ask

of his Estates, that the common people (literally the "little
people," *menu peuple*) were not qualified to understand problems
of State, and that it was too much trouble getting the large
number of people involved in the machinery of Estates to agree
(or, as she put it, to get such a large number of heads under one
bonnet).

Margaret's letter gives a good picture of the way the Estates
worked. She points out that the representatives came to the
Estates with only limited powers. They were responsible to their
respective constituencies. In the case of the Third Estate, its
members were responsible to the towns which had elected them—
not, of course, to the whole population, but to the town councils.
She explains that there were in each town council three members:
the magistrates, the notables, and a third member, composed of
"deans," "nations," and "little people." The deans (*doyens*) were
officers of the guilds. The guilds met in the groups called
"nations," of which in Brussels there were nine.

A new tax had to have the assent not only of the assembled
three Estates but also of the constituencies to which they were
responsible. It could be blocked by one of the three members of
one of the towns of one of the provinces of the Low Countries.

The "nine-year Aid" mentioned in Source 10 refers to what
was granted by the Estates General which met in 1558-59. Instead
of remembering that grant with gratitude, Margaret reminds Philip
of the political lessons of that assembly. It was an assembly which
included the newly conquered as well as the older provinces of the
Low Countries, and so symbolized a greater unity of the Low
Countries than had heretofore been achieved. But it offered
opportunity for all to concert their arguments in the face of the
king's demands. Ever afterward, Philip insisted that the Estates
General should be summoned, if at all, in accordance with the
"old" rather than with the "new" way (*le viel chemin et non pas
le nouveau*), that is, in such a way as to prevent concerted unity
against him.

The conflict between the Regent and the Estates eventually led
Philip to remove her from her position and, in 1567, to send the
duke of Alva at the head of a Spanish army. He is generally
remembered for acts of tyrannical cruelty, but what is specifically
relevant to our discussion of constitutional development is that he
attempted to devise a permanent tax that would free the king of
the necessity of consulting the Estates each year. Here at last we
encounter an actual attempt to lay down the foundations of an
absolute government. But though the attempt was made on behalf

of a Spanish king, it should be noted that it was undertaken not in Spain but in the Low Countries, and, above all, that this most serious attempt to establish absolutism in the sixteenth century was a failure. The reaction to it was the Revolt of the Netherlands, led by the Prince of Orange. That Revolt aimed partly at Dutch independence of Spain and partly at protecting Protestantism against the Counter Reformation, but it was also a struggle between opposing principles of government, in defense of representative, constitutional principles against absolutism. This conception of the struggle is expressed in some of the most eloquent paragraphs of the *Apology* of William of Orange (Source 11). It is his response to the sentence of Philip II which had declared William an outlaw and had announced a reward for his assassination. William's response, addressed not to Philip but to the Estates, is an indictment of Philip for violating the constitution and attempting to replace it by absolute rule.

The ultimate outcome of the Revolt of the Netherlands was a Dutch Republic. It lasted, like the older Venetian Republic, until the French Revolution. More powerful than the republican Swiss cantons, longer-lasting than the English Commonwealth (1649-1660), the Dutch Republic defied the conception that absolute monarchy was the inevitable form of the modern state.

Did the Dutch Republic constitute the model of a new form of State? It was a model that was indeed considered by the authors of the American Constitution, but more as one to be avoided than to be imitated. They perceived the dangers of a system which had reduced the executive to impotence. Indeed, William of Orange, however much he might extoll the Estates in his *Apology*, was already aware, as his letters[18] show, of the need to create a new executive to take the place of Philip II. Neither Orange nor the Estates had in mind the creation of a republic without a monarch. It was only after they had failed to find a suitable ruler in the brother of the King of France, or in Queen Elizabeth, that they came to accept a government without a king. Their ideal, as expressed in the *Joyeuse Entrée* and throughout the conflict with Philip II, had been the limited, constitutional monarchy, in which the executive function would remain the responsibility of the ruler, but of a ruler who would perform his duties only with the advice and consent of the Estates.

When the Estates, after 1576, found themselves obliged by

---

[18] See for example his Remonstrance of 9 January 1580 to the Estates General, reproduced as Document XLIV of my *Representative Government*, pp. 469-76.

default of a ruler to undertake many of the functions of the executive, they may be regarded as anticipating the parliamentary governments of the nineteenth century. But they did so without any conscious notion of innovation. They sought rather to maintain the corporative, communal, and parliamentary institutions which they had inherited from the later Middle Ages, and which in their view had been threatened by the innovations of Philip II. Whether these institutions, as applied to the conditions of the seventeenth century, should be designated as "medieval" or "modern" is perhaps a meaningless question.[19] In any case, an examination of them would require a study of administrative intricacies beyond the scope of this inquiry.

FRANCE

The address of Michel L'Hospital, the Chancellor of France, before the opening session of the Estates General which met at Orleans on 13 December 1560 (Source 12) enables us to see our problem in the perspective of a contemporary statesman. He points out that the Estates had not been convened for about eighty years (not, in fact, since the beginning of the reign of Charles VIII in 1484). He implies that the subsequent failure of the kings to consult their subjects was a departure from custom and detrimental to both king and people.

L'Hospital offers his audience, and us, his conception of the function of Estates. His conception is imbued with a generous confidence in the people and their representatives that was evidently not shared by those who had advised the king against holding Estates (the Guises). L'Hospital's conception is nevertheless a limited one. As a jurist, he thinks of the Estates as a court of justice, distinguished from the *Parlement* only insofar as the latter was concerned with private and particular cases, while the Estates were concerned with public and general ones. He does not claim for them the function of making the law. He attempts to counter the argument that the Estates would tend to reduce the king's power. He does not go so far as to say that they should serve as a limitation upon the executive.

The Chancellor's hope that goodwill would prevail and that France would henceforth be governed with the assistance of regularly assembled Estates General was not to be realized.

[19]For the debate on this question, see my "Revolutionary Character of the Revolt of the Netherlands," *Comparative Studies in Society and History*, 2 (1960): 458-59.

Instead, France was torn by a civil and religious war between irreconcilable parties for the balance of the century. The king summoned the Estates General again only four times (1561, 1576, 1588, and 1614) in the period between 1560 and 1615, and thereafter not again until 1789. The infrequency of assemblies of the Estates General, even in the sixteenth century, has led some historians to conclude that the monarchy had already become absolute, well before the seventeenth century. Even the few meetings between 1560 and 1615 have been explained away as aberrant phenomena of a period of civil war.

The Letter Patent of Henry II (Source 13) shows that Estates were being held, before 1560, despite L'Hospital's testimony. The Estates referred to in Source 13 are, however, not the Estates General of the whole realm of France, but the Estates of the country and duchy of Burgundy. These, the document tells us, met every three years (other provincial Estates, those of Languedoc, for example, met annually, throughout the century).

One of the privileges cherished by the Estates of Burgundy, according to Source 13, was that no taxation could be imposed upon Burgundy without their consent. Far from being absolute, the king was thus obliged to bargain with the Estates over revenue, and, we may assume, to offer to redress some of their grievances as his part of the bargain. From other documents, we could show that this was indeed what did take place. The Estates of Burgundy (and of other regions possessing Estates, such as Normandy, Brittany, Dauphiny, Provence, and Languedoc) thus had a share in the legislative and administrative as well as the fiscal process of government. Indeed, it has been said that these provincial Estates were never more powerful than they became in the course of the sixteenth century[20] (when, by other accounts, the kings of France had already become absolute).

But let us examine the king's letter more closely. After recognizing the principle of no taxation without the consent of the Estates, the king goes on to say that the disposition of his subjects' property is within the authority of the Estates. That he should have conceded such authority to them may at first sight seem surprising. But even Jean Bodin, the proponent of absolute sovereignty, said that the king must consult the Estates before imposing taxes, and argued thus on the ground that the natural law conferred the right to hold property. The taking of any part of

[20] See Henri Prentout's essay in comparative history of the provincial Estates of France, in Vol. II of his *Etats provinciaux de Normandie* (1925).

that property, whether by taxes or in any other way, without the consent of the owner was therefore a violation of natural law.

The king's reason for conceding to the Estates authority over his subjects' property had, however, a practical purpose, for, as his letter explains, such authority would include the power to bind and obligate the subjects to pay whatever the Estates had voted.

The actual assessment of taxes was left, between sessions of the Estates, to officials elected by them and called the Elect (*élus*). Certain persons had been challenging the decisions of the Elect, and had appealed these decisions to the court of *Parlement*. The royal government could hardly continue to function if every taxpayer could challenge his assessment in the courts. Accordingly, the king came to the defense of the Estates and of their delegated Elect.

The purpose of the king's letter is now evident. It was to stop taxpayers from taking their assessments to court; if an error had been made, redress was evidently to be sought only from the Estates at their next meeting.

The letter also proclaimed the immunity of the Estates from the interference of the courts. Even the *Parlement* of Dijon, which was the supreme court of Burgundy, was forbidden to assume jurisdiction or to take cognizance of the matter—taxation—which the king had assigned to the Estates and to their delegated agents, the Elect. The royal government was thus in fact lending support to the principle of the separation of powers. But the effect was not to limit the executive in the face of the legislative, but rather to strengthen the executive by securing its most vital resource: a continuous, dependable flow of revenue. A government constructed along fully absolute lines would aim to provide such a reliable flow of revenue, but Absolutism had a different method of assuring this flow. A Duke of Alva believed it necessary to deprive the Estates of control over taxation, and thus to free his master of any need to cater to them. Richelieu, in the following century, would have liked to get rid of the Estates altogether. In the sixteenth century, the usual method was for the king to attempt to use the Estates as vehicles for the extension of royal control and for the sustenance of royal power.

Thus the mere fact that provincial Estates survived and continued to function through the sixteenth century does not in itself disprove the assertion of those who have argued that the monarchy was laying the foundations of absolutism. Besides the formal institutions of representation, we must take account of other important departments of government: administrative, fiscal, and judicial.[21] In these departments, the French king in the sixteenth century was able to extend the reach of royal influence, and to promote the process of centralization. But the advocates of premature absolutism go wrong when they ascribe to the sixteenth century the methods of the seventeenth century, when kings did free themselves of Estates, and thus became truly absolute. In the sixteenth century, however, the almost universal practice of monarchs was to promote their power not by destroying but by using provincial Estates. Russell Major is right in insisting on a term for the sixteenth-century monarchy that will differentiate it from the Absolute Monarchy of a later period. The sixteenth century has been called the century "of the Renaissance," and so, although Estates had nothing inherently to do with the Renaissance, Major's use of the term "Renaissance Monarch" can be justified as having a fairly well-defined meaning.

FOR FURTHER READING

Allen, J.W. *A History of Political Thought in the Sixteenth Century.* London: Methuen, 1928; New York: Barnes and Noble (University Paperbacks), 1960.

Carlyle, R.W., and A.J. Carlyle. *A History of Mediaeval Political Theory in the West.* London, 6 vols.; Vol. VI ("Political Theory from 1300 to 1600"), 1936; later impressions, New York; Barnes and Noble, no date.

Cassirer, Ernst. *The Myth of the State.* Yale, 1946; Garden City, N.Y.: Doubleday Anchor, 1955.

Figgis, J.N. *Studies of Political Thought from Gerson to Grotius, 1414-1625.* Cambridge University Press, 1907; 2nd ed., 1916 and several times reprinted.

Griffiths, Gordon. *Representative Government in Western Europe in the Sixteenth Century: Commentary and Documents for the Study of Comparative Constitutional History.* Oxford: Clarendon Press, 1968.

Guenée, Bernard. "The History of the State in France at the End of the Middle Ages, as Seen by French Historians in the Last Hundred Years," in Peter Lewis, ed., *The Recovery of France in the Fifteenth Century.* London: Macmillan, 1971.

Koenigsberger, H. G., and George Mosse. *Europe in the Sixteenth Century.* New York: Holt, Rinehart and Winston, 1968.

[21] Bernard Guenée, "L'Historiographie de l'Etat en France . . . vue par les historiens français depuis cent ans," *Revue Historique,* CCXXXII (1964). This article is a valuable criticism of the traditional French emphasis on the rise of the national State and monarchy. He believes, however, that Major's insistence that the "Renaissance" Monarchy was limited and decentralized cannot be sustained on the basis of evidence of the continued functioning of Estates without taking account of the role of other institutions. There is an English translation of Guenée's article in *The Recovery of France in the Fifteenth Century,* Peter Lewis, ed. (London: Macmillan, 1971).

Major, J. Russell. *The Age of the Renaissance and Reformation.* New York: Lippincott, 1970. Chapters on "The Renaissance State" and "The Constitutional Crisis."

Mattingly, Garrett. *Renaissance Diplomacy.* Boston: Houghton Mifflin, 1955; Penguin Books, 1964.

Rice, Eugene F. *The Foundations of Early Modern Europe, 1460-1559.* New York: Norton, 1970.

Sabine, George H. *A History of Political Theory.* New York: Holt, 1937.

Slavin, Arthur J., ed. *The "New Monarchies" and Representative Assemblies: Medieval Constitutionalism or Modern Absolutism?* Problems in European Civilization Series. Lexington, Mass.: Heath, 1964.

THE ESSAYIST'S SOURCES

1

Articles Agreed to by Gian Galeazzo Visconti for the Administration of Siena

SOURCE: The twenty-nine Articles of the original agreement were dated Pavia, 11 December 1399, and ratified by the General Council of Siena on 26 December by a vote of 347 to 102. The seventeen additional articles were contained in a letter addressed to the Sienese by the Duke of Milan and dated Pavia, 17 March 1400. They were transcribed from the original by Orlando Malavolti and printed in his *Historia di Siena*, Venice, 1599, Part II, fols. 186ro-190ro. This work was photographically reprinted by Forni Editore, Bologna, 1968. Translated by Gordon Griffiths.

ARTICLE I

First, that the city of Siena shall retain its Priors, Governors and Captain of the People, who are required to be present to carry out the business of the Commune. These Priors and Captain shall reside in the customary palace, and shall have the same powers that they possessed before the transfer of dominion (executed in accordance with their orders), except for the article below regarding the Lieutenant, and save for the above-said transfer of dominion.

ARTICLE III

That the aforesaid Priors, Governors and Captain of the People, or rather the city of Siena, shall retain their accustomed Chancellors and Notaries, and at their accustomed salaries, and another Chancellor for His Lordship the Duke of Milan, who shall be required to sign the letters and decrees drawn up by the Priors, Governors and Captain of the People.

ARTICLE VI

That the provisions, *riformagioni*, and statutes of the city shall be observed in accordance with the judgments handed down in the palace of the Senator and *podestà*, particularly those regarding merchants and the *mercanzia,* the Wool Guild, that of the judges, notaries and other guilds, and the statutes on the minting of money; and all those concerning outlaws, exiles and rebels; and the provisions and statutes on the building, repair and fortification of castles and houses; and all other provision, *riformagioni* and statutes of the city, without changing anything in them.

ARTICLE XII

That his ducal Lordship may appoint and assign a Lieutenant to the city of Siena, when it seems expedient to him to do so. This Lieutenant may and must be present at communal functions, alongside the aforesaid Priors, Governors and the Captain of the People, and in all the Councils of the city, whenever they take place; to these Councils the Lieutenant must be invited. In all the business conducted by the said Priors, Governors and Captain, Councils and boards of the city, the Lieutenant shall have two votes only, in such wise that his two votes count for no more than two of the votes of the said Priors, Governors and Captain of the People. . . .

ARTICLE XIV

That his ducal Lordship may assign an official, who, alongside the officials of the commune of Siena, that is, the Chamberlain and four officials of the treasury (*provisori della Biccherna*), may and must be present and keep record of all the revenues and expenditures of the commune, so that all receipts and payments of money may be carried out in the proper manner, and pass through the hands of the said official as well as through those of the said officials of the commune of Siena.

ARTICLE XVIII

Furthermore, the said Duke, and his descendants, may not and shall not impose upon the citizens, peasants, or inhabitants of the district of the city of Siena, or raise any tax or loan or collection, beyond what the community now receives, nor may they devise any gabelle, or levy any other tax, whether in the form of loan or collection, nor permit such to be levied.

ARTICLE XX

That His ducal Lordship shall be expected to and must preserve, defend and maintain all the lands, castles and places in the county and district of Siena presently obedient to Siena in obedience and reverence to him and to the city of Siena; and indeed he should expand the city to its rightful position of power, jurisdiction, and authority. He may not sell, nor in any manner transfer, nor release from his hands and dominion, this city of Siena, its county or district, its lands, castles, or above-mentioned places, to any Prince, government, or individual, of whatever preeminence, for any reason or under any color or title. And should it come to pass that the said Lord Duke of Milan should wish to abandon the city of Siena, its county, territory, lands, castles or other possessions, or to divest himself of them, the said Lord Duke promises to leave the said city of Siena, its county and district in the hands of the governing bodies of the city, and in accordance with the form, jurisdiction and system presently observed by the city and its governing boards, and as they were before the transfer of dominion to the present Lord Duke.

ARTICLE XXIV

That offices in the Church, or benefices, that are vacant or which may become vacant in the cities of Siena, Massa, Grosseto and their dioceses and districts should be given to Sienese and not to others. His ducal Lordship undertakes to write on their behalf to the Roman court. . . .

ADDITIONAL ARTICLES

I

First, that the Lieutenant shall be present at all Councils held in our city of Siena.

II

When propositions are being considered in these Councils, he shall be the last to offer his counsel; because, if he were the first, the citizens might out of fear or respect for him refrain from saying what they wished or really thought.

III

In matters affecting the Commune and the City, and not the State, he shall let the citizens do as they wish in accordance with their own ordinances and customs.

VI

He shall show respect for the citizens according to their rank.

VII-VIII

[He will not interfere in civil suits or in the enforcement of regulations concerning merchants.]

IX

He will not interfere in criminal cases which do not affect the State, nor suspend criminal trials in such cases; rather he will let them be decided in accordance with the ordinances and statutes of the city by the criminal judges and other appropriate officials.

XII

He will take care not to permit actions contrary to the ordinances, statutes, provisions and customs of the city.

XIII

He will not require citizens or inhabitants of the district or anybody else to supply wood, hay, straw, wine, grain, or anything else; and he must not accept these things for himself, or through any third person, directly or indirectly.

XIV

The Lieutenant shall pay the gabelles he owes, just as everybody else has to; and likewise the other officials and soldiers shall be obliged to pay.

2

Petition 6 of the Castilian *Córtes* of 1506: The King Not to Make Laws Except in *Córtes*

SOURCE: Spanish text in Gordon Griffiths, *Representative Government in Western Europe in the Sixteenth Century: Commentary and Documents for the Study of Comparative Constitutional History* (Oxford: Clarendon Press, 1968), p. 14, from *Córtes*, IV:225.*

It has been written and said by the wise men of old that the wealth of a province comes from within, and for this reason laws and ordinances should suit the needs of their provinces, and cannot be equal and uniform for all countries. For this reason the kings decided that, when they had to make laws, to be sure that they would be beneficial to their realms, and to each province in particular, the *Córtes* and representatives should be summoned and an understanding reached with them, and for this reason the law was established that laws should not be made or revoked except in *Córtes*.

They therefore beg Your Highnesses** that from now forward this law should be kept and observed, and that when laws have to be made, Your Highnesses should summon their realms and their representatives, in order to be much better informed by them about such laws, and for your realms to be provided for in accordance with Justice and Right.

And whereas many decrees have been made outside this regulation, and

---

*Translations of Sources 2 through 13 are by Gordon Griffiths from the original language texts found in *Representative Government*, though, in the case of the Spanish documents, based on the translation made by Dr. D. W. Lomax for the book.

**Editor's Note: Philip the Fair and Joanna.

your realms consider that they have suffered on this account, they beg you to order such decrees to be reviewed, and to investigate and remedy the suffering that these decrees have introduced.

Response: If it should prove necessary, His Highness will order provision to be made in such a way as to take account of this petition.

3

Petition 33 of the Castilian *Córtes* of 1506: On Representation in the *Córtes*

SOURCE: Spanish text in Gordon Griffiths, *Representative Government in Western Europe in the Sixteenth Century* (Oxford: Clarendon Press, 1968), p. 15, from *Córtes*, IV:233.

Older is best

In accordance with certain laws and immemorial custom it is established that eighteen cities and towns of these realms have the vote through their representatives in *Córtes,* and not more; and yet it is said that certain cities and towns are negotiating, or are trying to negotiate for the privilege that they should have the vote through representatives in *Córtes.* Because this increase would result in great damage to the cities which now possess the votes, and would lead to confusion, we beg Your Highnesses not to allow the said number of votes to be increased, since any increase in the number of offices with votes is forbidden by the laws of these realms.

Response: So it will be done.

4

The King's Response to Petition 6 of the Castilian *Córtes* of 1525: On His Obligation to Respond to Their Petitions

---

SOURCE: Spanish text in Gordon Griffiths, *Representative Government in Western Europe in the Sixteenth Century* (Oxford: Clarendon Press, 1968), p. 41, from *Novísima Recopilación de las leyes de España* (Madrid, 6 vols., 1805-1829), Lib. III, Tit. VIII, Ley VIII, reproducing what was designated in Philip II's *Recopilación* of 1567 as Lib. VI, Tit. VII. Ley VIII.

Whereas the Representatives in *Córtes,* summoned by our mandate, provide aid to us and promote the welfare of our Realms, we are bound to hear them benevolently and to receive their petitions, both general and particular, and to respond to them, and to comply with them in accordance with Justice. We are ready to do this, as our royal ancestors have ordained, and we order that, before the dissolution of the *Córtes,* response shall be given to all the articles, general and particular, which shall have been submitted by the Realm, and that the necessary provisions be taken that will contribute to our aid and to the profit of our Realms.

5

From the Book of the Laws and Decrees That His Majesty King Philip Ordered Made in the *Córtes* Which He Held in the Town of Madrid in the Year One Thousand Five Hundred and Sixty Seven

---

SOURCE: Spanish text in Gordon Griffiths, *Representative Government in Western Europe in the Sixteenth Century* (Oxford: Clarendon Press, 1968), pp. 53-55, from *Actas*, II.

Philip, by the grace of God, King of Castile, of Leon, of Aragon, . . . (to all officials and any other subjects), greeting and grace.

Know that in the *Córtes* which we ordered to be held in the town of Madrid, which began in the past year of 1566, and concluded in this present year of 1567, we were given certain petitions and general articles by the representatives in *Córtes* of the cities and towns of our said Realms, who had met together in *Córtes* by our mandate; that, with the agreement of our Council, we responded to the said petitions and articles; the tenor of which, and of our responses, was as follows:

. . . .

PETITION 3

And whereas Your Majesty's royal predecessors of glorious memory ordered by laws made in *Córtes* that no new taxes, imposts, dues, monies or other tributes, whether particular or general, should be created or collected without an assembly of the Realm in *Córtes,* and without the grant of its representatives, as it says in the Ordinance of King Alfonso;

And whereas recently, because of certain needs which have faced Your Majesty, some new taxes and dues have been created and imposed outside the system (above-described), and others have been increased, such as those on salt, in the customs of wool, new ports, and other things, which have resulted in such a burden to these Realms, and such a shortage of the necessities of life, that there are very few who can live without great labor, since the damage that has been suffered as a result of the said new taxes has been greater than the benefit obtained from them;

We beg that Your Majesty be pleased to consider this with his accustomed clemency, and that he relieve his Realms of the said new taxes and increases, and as for the future, that he grant them the favor [*merced*] that there should be reserved to them what had been long established, in accordance with the said law which is proof of this;

For it is just that Your Majesty's subjects, when they are called upon to relieve the needs that may arise, should hear what they are and should choose the least inconvenient means and system of relieving them, and it is certain that they will do so, in conformity with the love and ancient loyalty with which they have served, and continue to serve Your Majesty.

To this we respond, that, as you already know and have many times been informed, because of the great and urgent needs, and of the wars and enterprises with which my lord the King-Emperor, who is in glory, and I have been confronted, in defense of the public cause of religion and Christendom and these Realms and our other states, our patrimony and the old royal revenues [*rentas*] have been so consumed and encumbered, that, not having the means or any way of being able to provide what was necessary for the support of the royal estate, it has been impossible to avoid using the arbitrary expedients and impositions and increases to which you refer in your petition; but, when these necessities cease or other and better means of providing for them are available, we shall be very pleased to alleviate and relieve these Realms, and to show them in this and in every way the favor that we wish to show and know is proper.

With regard to what you say next, we shall be pleased, as needs present themselves, to have the advice and opinion of the Realm, and to obtain its aid and assistance, considering (as we do consider) it a sure thing what you say, that they will continue to serve us with the ancient loyalty and love that they have always shown in our service and in that of our royal predecessors . . . .

6

From the Proceedings
of the Castilian *Córtes* of 1567

SOURCE: Spanish text in Gordon Griffiths, *Representative Government in Western Europe in the Sixteenth Century*

(Oxford: Clarendon Press, 1968), pp. 48-49, from *Actas de las Córtes de Castilla*, Vol. II.

18 MARCH 1567

Then all the gentlemen representatives present (those absent being listed by name) said that whereas over a period of years certain new taxes had been created, ordered and actually levied, certain dues had been increased and other new and unaccustomed ones had been collected, and the price of salt had suffered a general increase, and dues had been added to it in certain places; and whereas all this had been done without convocation or assembly of the Realm in *Córtes,* nor any grant on the part of its representatives in accordance with the laws of these Realms and the custom always observed in them; and whereas, for the above reasons, and also because of the harm which such practices have caused and are causing to the service of His Majesty and to the well-being of these Realms, they have several times, since the opening of this assembly of the *Córtes,* asked His Majesty to order a stop to these practices, both because of the way they were introduced and because of the grave damage which the Realm has suffered as a result of them; and whereas the *Córtes* had been persevering and insistent in its request that His Majesty be pleased to grant them this grace, yet pressure of business and the problems of Christianity and of the Estates of Flanders so obviously required remedy and assistance that he had peremptorily ordered them not to treat of this matter any more for the time being, nor even to discuss it in *Córtes,* and they, as always obedient to their duty, have not pursued their request any further;

They nevertheless declare and proclaim in the name of these Realms that they have not granted nor consented, nor do they grant or consent either tacitly or expressly, to any new tax or new dues, nor to any increase in them, nor to any increase in the price of salt, nor to the way in which this matter is being administered, nor to the dues added to it in certain places in Andalusia and other parts of these Realms, nor to any other due, local or general, which has been or may be created or levied in these Realms outside the *Córtes* and without the consent of the representatives of the Realm;

On the contrary, they have asked and do ask His Majesty to order all such practices abolished and stopped, and that henceforth the law be observed which lays down the way in which His Majesty is supposed to seek the aid of these Realms, and likewise the custom which has always been followed for the provision of such aid; and they charge the representatives of these Realms who in future assemble in *Córtes* to speak for these Realms, always to press upon His Majesty the request for this grace, as a matter of such importance for his service and for the general welfare of his Realms, being confident, as they are confident, in the goodness and clemency of His Majesty, that he will, when the times are more opportune, grant them this grace; and they asked to be supplied with a testimonial of what they had above said, declared, and agreed.

7

Record of the Imposition of an Aid Upon Brabant by the Regent of the Low Countries, 27 June 1528

SOURCE: French text in Gordon Griffiths, *Representative Government in Western Europe in the Sixteenth Century* (Oxford: Clarendon Press, 1968), pp. 351-52, originally published by L.P. Gachard in the Belgian *Bulletin de la Commission Royale d'Histoire*, 2nd ser., XII, pp. 399-403.

My dread Lady, the archduchess of Austria, duchess and countess of Burgundy, *etc.*, aunt of the Emperor and Regent on his behalf of the Low Countries, had an announcement made to the Estates of Brabant, assembled at her residence in Malines on 27 June 1528. Because of the length of their deliberations, the delays and changes made in their proposals, and the opposition she had encountered among them, particularly the prelates and the representatives of Louvain and Brussels, regarding the means she had suggested to them for raising the Aid she had asked of them on behalf of the Emperor, to be used to pay the troops he had seen fit to raise for the defense of Brabant against the warlike acts which Charles of Gelderland had taken and was still taking against the country; she had decided, for the sake of the honor and reputation of the Emperor, and for the preservation, security and safety of Brabant and of themselves and their property, to depart from the ordinary and accustomed course in Brabant and to organize a union between the nobles and towns of Antwerp and Bois-le-Duc and their districts on the one hand, and of the Estates of Holland on the other (a record of this action has already been made), and furthermore to draw up an order to the chancellor and to the imperial accounting officers in Brabant to assess a tax on the country of 102,000 pounds (40 groat), to be employed as set forth above.

To relieve the chancellor and accounting officers and receivers of Brabant, who would be levying the said taxes, of responsibility, she had despatched the appropriate orders, and so that they should not claim ignorance of these, she wanted them to be informed by a reading of the aforesaid record and orders, which was done in her presence. After which My Lady ordered Mr. Jerome vander Noot, knight, the chancellor of Brabant, to seal the said orders.

The chancellor insisted in all humility and reverence that what he was about to say was not meant to be in disobedience to the Emperor nor to her who was acting on his behalf, nor to delay the business of His Majesty, whose most humble servant and unworthy chancellor he was, and who had always been obedient and was determined to continue so; but he remonstrated to My Lady that for the period of thirteen or fourteen years that he had held the position of chancellor and had been the guardian of His Majesty's Brabantine seal, . . . he had never seen, known or heard that an Aid or money had been levied, nor any tax or assessment imposed on the country, by chancellor, accounting officers or anybody else, nor that any order had been given to them to do so, except for such Aids as had been jointly and uniformly consented to and granted by the Estates of Brabant. Such a grant was always certified in a record signed by the prelates and nobles (or some of them), and by the representatives of the four principal towns of the country. The *Joyeuse Entrée* of Brabant, to which he as chancellor, at the Emperor's command, had sworn, expressly required that it was to be done in this way. The regulations prescribing the proper procedure were in the possession of the Estates. He could not contravene them without being guilty of perjury, and he hoped My Lady would not bring pressure upon him to do so. With these and other arguments, the chancellor begged My Lady to accept his remonstrances and excuses in good part, and to relieve him of the obligation of sealing the above orders, and not to be displeased with him.

Whereupon My Lady, in the presence of the Estates and the representatives of all save Brussels, declared to the chancellor that he was aware, from what had been said in the various Estates and councils, of the effort she had made on the Emperor's behalf to explain to the Estates the state of affairs and of the war, and what was needed for the defense of the country, themselves and their property; that he was also aware of the trouble she had taken personally and through her representatives to persuade the Estates to do their duty. She had always wished, and wished now to maintain the privileges and customs of the country. He knew that it was their diversity of opinions and the opposition of some of them that had put her in the position where she must either lose the confidence of the Emperor and of the country which had been committed to her charge (she would do everything in her power to avoid that), or resort to the orders now before them. Furthermore he knew that she had decided, in a perfectly proper fashion, to see that he, the accounting officers, receivers and other officers of the Emperor were not held responsible for what, upon her orders, they would be doing, and all to accomplish a great good and to avoid a great evil. Nevertheless, if the chancellor objected to sealing the above orders, he should give her the Emperor's seal, and she would seal them herself.

Whereupon the chancellor delivered the Emperor's Brabantine seal to My Lady, and she, in the presence of the Estates, had the orders sealed. To relieve himself of responsibility, the chancellor requested that a record be drawn up, which My Lady granted to him, dated in Malines, on the aforesaid day and year, in her Council, at which the cardinal of Liège [*et al.;* six listed by name] and others were present. Subscribed and signed: In my presence: Du Blioul.

8

Letter from Margaret of Parma, Regent of the Low Countries, to Philip II, 16 July 1561

SOURCE: French text in Gordon Griffiths, *Representative Government in Western Europe in the Sixteenth Century* (Oxford: Clarendon Press, 1968), p. 383, from L. P. Gachard, *La Correspondance de Marguérite d'Autriche, duchesse de Parme, avec Philippe II (1559-1565)*, Brussels, 1867-1881, 3 vols., Vol. I, pp. 510-11.

...The Estates of Brabant are putting up opposition to this, as Your Majesty knows, and will add it to their list of grievances, although none of the towns' representatives was authorized to go that far and some of the prelates did not want to sign. But they have a certain Wellemans, pensionary of the Estates of Brabant, who, whether from his malign nature or at the instigation of others, makes it his business to uncover and to put forward many things to the disservice of Your Majesty. Recently he has presented a request to the Chancellor of Brabant in which he demands, in the name of the Estates, that the seal be affixed to no decree in Brabant unless it has had a hearing (before the Estates). ...

9

Article 3 of the *Joyeuse Entrée* of Brabant, in the Text Agreed to by Charles V in 1515 and by Philip II in 1549

SOURCE: Gordon Griffiths, *Representative Government in Western Europe in the Sixteenth Century* (Oxford: Clarendon Press, 1968), p. 346, for the Dutch text, taken from Jeanne Mennes, "De Staten van Brabant en de Blijde Inkomst van Kroonprins Filips in 1549," *Standen en Landen*, XVIII (1959).

That, as Duke of Brabant and Limburg, we shall never enter into any undertaking affecting the lordship of these countries, to make war or to raise or force loans upon anyone, except with the counsel, will and consent of our cities and the country of Brabant. And that we shall not give our pledge or seal to any other act by which our countries, boundaries, or cities, or any of their inhabitants, or any of their rights, liberties, or privileges might be injured or diminished or our countries and subjects damaged in any way.

10

From a Letter from Margaret to Philip, 13 June 1562, on the Function and Composition of the Estates of the Low Countries

---

SOURCE: Gordon Griffiths, *Representative Government in Western Europe in the Sixteenth Century* (Oxford: Clarendon Press, 1968), pp. 388-89, for the French text, from L. P.

Gachard, *La Correspondance de Marguérite d'Autriche duchesse de Parme, avec Philippe II (1559-1565)*, Brussels, 1867-1881, 3 vols., Vol. II, pp. 242-43.

Some advocated summoning the Estates, putting everything before them and asking their advice, with the idea that they would accept the burden of producing the ordinary revenue, despite the fact that there was little hope offered of ever getting anything from them. I gave it as my opinion that aid and not advice was what a prince should ask of the Estates, because it is so difficult for them to reach decisions. This is because the persons sent to the Estates by their constituencies have no authority to do more than listen and report back, and those from the towns, before reaching a decision, must first communicate with the magistrates, then the notables, and finally the deans, nations and common people, who have neither the capacity nor the experience to grasp the problem properly; by this method we were more likely to fall into confusion than to find a remedy; we had seen what the result was of the negotiations for the nine-year Aid, and the resulting conflicts still raging to this day among certain Estates, and the difficulty of putting so many heads under one bonnet. I also told them that Your Majesty had ordered me, if it came to the point of summoning the Estates, to do so by the old and not by the new way. . . .

11

From the Apology of William of Orange, 13 December 1580

SOURCE: Gordon Griffiths, *Representative Government in Western Europe in the Sixteenth Century* (Oxford: Clarendon Press, 1968), pp. 525-27, for the French text of selected passages, taken from Jean Dumont, *Corps Universel Diplomatique du Droit des Gens* (Amsterdam, 1726-1731), 8 vols, Vol. V, part i.

You know, gentlemen, what he [Philip II] has promised, and that he does not have the authority to do whatever he pleases, as he does in the Indies. For under the Privileges of Brabant he cannot oblige a single one of his subjects by force to do anything, except in accord with the customary laws of their place of residence. He cannot by any Ordinance or Decree alter the constitution of the country in any way. He must rest content with his ordinary revenues. He cannot levy or exact any other taxes, without the express consent of the country, and in accord with its Privileges. He cannot bring soldiers into the country without its consent. He cannot tamper with the value of money without the consent of the Estates of the country. He cannot have any subject arrested, without a warrant from the local magistrate. He cannot have the arrested man removed from the country.

Do you not see, gentlemen, from this mere summary, that if the barons and nobles of the country, who owe their preeminent position to the fact that they have the responsibility of bearing arms, do not resist when these Articles are, not only violated, but tyrannically and contemptuously trodden underfoot; when not just one Article, but all of them are annulled or corrupted, and not just once, but a million times, and not just by the Duke, but by barbarians—if, I say, the nobles, in obedience to their oath and duty, do not require the Duke to recognize the country's rights, should not they themselves be condemned for perjury, disloyalty, and rebellion against the Estates of the country?

. . . .

I shall say nothing of the acts of violence or of the exactions of ransom and other exactions committed by the Spaniards; I shall mention only the most important point: you have never been able to have a free assembly of the Estates General. Your enemy knows very well that to prevent their convocation is to cut the tree of your Privileges at its roots, and to poison the source of your liberty. For of what use is it to a people to have Privileges on beautiful parchment locked up in a coffer, if they are not maintained by means of the Estates, and if their benefits cannot be felt?

12

The Address of Michel L'Hospital, Chancellor of France, at the Opening Session of the Estates General at Orléans, 13 December 1560 (Excerpts)

SOURCE: French text in Gordon Griffiths, *Representative Government in Western Europe in the Sixteenth Century* (Oxford: Clarendon Press, 1968), pp. 146-47, from the *Oeuvres Complètes de Michel L'Hospital*, I (Paris, 1824).

So, gentlemen, since we are renewing our former custom of holding Estates, which has been abandoned for eighty years or thereabouts, but which goes back beyond the memory of man; I shall explain briefly what holding Estates means, the reason for their assembly, the procedure and the question of who presides over them, what benefits they bring to the king, what benefits to the people, and whether indeed it is useful to hold Estates or not.

Certain it is that the kings of former times were accustomed to hold Estates often, that is, assemblies of all their subjects, or of their representatives. When we say "holding of Estates" we mean essentially that the king is communicating with his subjects about his most important business, taking their advice and counsel, hearing their complaints and grievances, and taking care of them as far as he can. This process used to be called holding a *parlement*, the word still used in England and Scotland.

But, since kings take cognizance of many general complaints, affecting the public as a whole, while private and particular complaints are considered by courts of judges established by the king, which are called *parlements;* the public and general hearings, which the king has reserved to himself, have come to be known as Estates. Estates would be assembled for diverse causes, and as times and situations demanded: to obtain aid in men and money, or to put the judiciary or the military into order, or to attend to the *apanages* of the king's sons, as happened in the time of Louis XI, or to provide for the better government of the realm, and for other causes. . . .

There is no doubt but that the Estates are of great benefit to the people; for they have this opportunity to approach the person of their king, to present him with their complaints and requests, and to obtain the necessary remedies and provisions.

There are some who have doubted whether it was useful or profitable for the king to hold Estates; they say that the king's power is somehow reduced by seeking the advice and counsel of his subjects when he is not obliged or required to do so. And also, that he makes himself too familiar to them, which breeds contempt and lowers the royal dignity and majesty. This opinion seems to me to have little justification. First, because I say that there is no action so worthy, and so proper to him, as the holding of his Estates, and giving a general hearing to his subjects, and rendering justice to all. Kings were chosen in the first place to do justice; doing justice is a more royal act than making war. For tyrants and wicked men can make war as well as kings, and very often the wicked man is better at it than the good man. . . .

13

Henry II, Letter Patent, Regarding the Estates of Burgundy

SOURCE: French text in Gordon Griffiths, *Representative Government in Western Europe in the Sixteenth Century* (Oxford: Clarendon Press, 1968), pp. 223-25; from M. Varenne, *Mémoire pour les Elus-Généraux des Etats du Duché de Bourgogne contre le Parlement-Cour des Aydes de Dijon,* 2e ed. (Paris, 1772), pp. 335-60.

Henry, by the Grace of God King of France, to all who see these presents, Greeting. The members of the three Estates of our country and Duchy of

Burgundy have through their Delegates reminded us that, since the kings and dukes of Burgundy who have preceded us, out of regard for the great fidelity, loyalty and prompt obedience always demonstrated by our subjects in the said country and Duchy of Burgundy and adjacent territory, have granted, among other Privileges which we have confirmed, in accordance with the ancient and immemorial constitution of the said countries, to the members of the three Estates that no aid or subsidy should be levied on the said country or its adjacent territory, for the benefit of ourselves or of anybody else, without the consent of the members of the said three Estates, duly assembled by virtue of our letters, on whom is thus devolved the total and entire disposition of the property of our subjects and inhabitants of the said countries, including the authority to bind and oblige them, with the consent of these Estates, to (make good) the gifts, subsidies, and grants thus accorded us;

And since the said Estates ordinarily meet only every three years, which means that it is not possible to settle the matters that come up every day between one assembly and the next, they have by the same privilege been permitted to elect from among themselves certain persons, to wit, from the Estate of the Church a Bishop, Abbot or Dean (in turn as is customary), from the Estate of the Nobility one of the principal gentlemen, and from the Estate of the towns a Mayor and Councillors [*echevins*] from the most ancient and notable towns of the said country, together with the Viscount Mayor of our town of Dijon who shall always be one of the Elect (*Elus*);

And these Elect, after the dissolution of the Estates, are empowered to apportion and equalize the incidence upon our subjects by hearth and parish of all the taxes granted us as well as all others voted by the Estates for the business of the said country, to commission and appoint collectors to collect the said taxes, *etc.* . . .

Yet certain private persons in our country and Duchy of Burgundy, to prevent the execution of these decisions, though it was no more their business as private persons than that of any other of our subjects in the said country, and without waiting to see whether the Estates would or would not endorse the decisions of the said Elect, are appealing the said decisions to our Court of Parlement of Dijon, and are harrassing the said Elect by litigation . . .

[After putting this matter before our Privy Council, we declare] that everything done or that may henceforth be done, concluded, decided, deliberated or executed by the Elect and Delegates of the said three Estates, during the term of their appointment and administration, in matters regarding the general welfare, shall be carried out and executed fully and entirely, at least provisionally, until the next assembly of the said Estates, opposition or appeals to the contrary notwithstanding . . .

And we forbid . . . private persons of whatever estate to go to court or to make countersuits, and we forbid our Court of Parlement of Dijon and all other officials and judges to claim jurisdiction or to take cognizance of them in any way or manner whatsoever . . .

We command by these presents our beloved and faithful members of our said Court of Parlement, the members of our *Chambre des Comptes* at Dijon, the Bailiff of the said place or his Lieutenant, and all our other judges and officials to have this ordinance ... read, published and registered wherever it should be, and that they observe and maintain ... it in all particulars, according to its form and content; and that they allow the members of the three Estates of our said country and Duchy of Burgundy and adjacent territory, their Delegates and Elect, to make full and undisturbed use of its content, without permitting any judgment, trouble, disturbance or impeachment to be put in their way ...

Given at Fontainebleau, 10 May 1555 ...

ROBERT M. KINGDON

Was the Protestant Reformation a Revolution? The Case of Geneva

Was the Protestant Reformation a revolution? The question should be of interest to a number of different students. It should interest those who are attracted to the period of the Reformation, who want to understand as fully as possible just what happened in that movement and what its full significance was. It should interest those who are curious about the nature of violent social change and who want to know more about the origins of the revolutions which have been such an important part of recent world history. It may even interest those who regard themselves as spiritual descendants of the Protestant Reformers and who want a clearer idea of the precise nature of their heritage.

Before we can answer the question, however, we must establish a definition of the term "revolution." This is not an easy task. The word has been used in many ways and much of this use has been by men passionately committed either to the glorious triumph or the complete eradication of a revolution. The term has thus come to carry strong emotional connotations. It is not easy to discuss it objectively and to define it in a way most people can accept. Nevertheless we must try.

Very few men at the time of the Protestant Reformation would have called it a revolution. In those days the term did not have a

53

political or social meaning. It was basically a scientific term, used primarily by astronomers. Its best known usage was in the title of the famous treatise in which the Polish astronomer Nicolaus Copernicus advanced his radical new theory that the sun, not the earth, was the center of the solar system. This treatise was titled *On the Revolutions of the Heavenly Bodies* and was first published in 1543. In this context the term "revolution" referred to the motions of heavenly bodies in orbits around either the earth or sun. There are two aspects of these motions which we should note. They involved constant return, as each heavenly body, in describing its orbit, returns again to each place it has been before. They also involved inevitability, as each heavenly body moves without interruption or distraction along a path which can be predicted with complete confidence by a trained astronomer.

There are obvious ways in which this astronomers' term can be applied, by analogy, to certain political and social changes. One can find a few examples of such an application during the sixteenth century. For example, one observer in 1525 called the rebellion of the Communeros in Spain a "revolution of the people."[1] But this usage is rare and its precise meaning is often uncertain. One can find more examples of this application in the seventeenth century. For example, a prominent English historian in 1674 called the overthrow of the ruling Rump Parliament and the restoration of the Stuart monarchy in 1660 "the revolution." This particular application of the term is quite close to the original astronomers' meaning of the term. For 1660 witnessed a return to a form of government the English had challenged in 1640, with the meeting of the Puritan Long Parliament, and had abolished a few years later, following the English Civil War.[2] This application, however, is quite far from modern usage.

Only in the eighteenth century did the term "revolution" come to be used commonly in a way we would recognize. It was applied then to the two great upheavals which we know as the American and French Revolutions. It still contained some resonance of its original astronomers' meaning. Both American and French revolutionaries thought they were returning their governments to earlier and purer forms, found in a historic state of nature or in some government of classical antiquity. Their knowledge of classical

---

[1] Cited by J. H. Elliott, "Revolution and Continuity in Early Modern Europe," *Past and Present*, no. 42 (1969), p. 40.

[2] Noted by the *New Oxford English Dictionary* as meaning 8a of the word "revolution." Cf. the comments in Hannah Arendt, *On Revolution*, p. 36; Jacques Ellul, *Autopsy of Revolution*, p. 40.

political thought was impressively detailed. And their respect for classical political institutions, particularly those of republican Rome, is striking. It is reflected, for example, by the adoption of the Roman name "Senate" for the upper house of the American legislature. Both groups of revolutionaries also thought these returns to be inevitable and irresistible, part of an inexorable historical process, of which they were the destined leaders.

These men also conceived of their revolutions as being primarily political. The fundamental problem they saw facing their societies was the behavior of a form of government, monarchy, which they felt had become obsolete and tyrannical. They felt they could solve most of society's problems by creating a new form of government, a republic, which would be more sensitive to the needs and aspirations of the general population. Some later analysts, however, saw these same revolutions as fundamentally social. They involved the triumph of a rising new ruling class, the bourgeoisie, over a decadent old ruling class, the feudal nobility. In this view the political changes which are so obvious were relatively superficial. The two types of government, monarchic and republican, were institutions created by the two ruling classes to perpetuate their control. The best known and most influential of these analysts was Karl Marx. It is his view of revolution, involving explosive conflict between social classes and a consequent restructuring of economic as well as political institutions, which tends to prevail in the twentieth century. And the revolutions he forecast, in which another rising new class, the proletariat, would overthrow and replace the victors of the eighteenth-century upheavals, the bourgeoisie, have come to dominate modern thinking on the subject. In particular the Marxist revolutions which succeeded in reshaping Russia and China supply the type to which most modern usage of the term "revolution" refers.

Many contemporary thinkers have analyzed this modern view of revolution at length. Some have reduced their analysis to succinct definitions. One particularly useful definition is provided by Sigmund Neumann, an eminent political scientist who died not long ago. He defined revolution as involving "a sweeping, fundamental change in political organization, social structure, economic property control, and the predominant myth of a social order, thus indicating a major break in the continuity of development."[3] It seems to me that this formula sums up modern opinion

---

[3] Sigmund Neumann, "The International Civil War," *World Politics*, I (1948-1949), p. 333, n. 1, quoted and used by Lawrence Stone, in *The Causes of the English Revolution, 1529-1642*, p. 48.

successfully enough so that we can use it. Armed with Neumann's definition, we can now return to our original question.

Was the Protestant Reformation a revolution, in Neumann's sense of the word? At this point some scholars would object that to use the term "revolution" in speaking of the Reformation era is to adopt an anachronism. It forces phenomena from one period into a concept drawn from another period. Such forcing distorts both the phenomena and the concept and is thus the greatest sin any historian can commit. It seems to me that this objection is specious. In order to understand a period one need not restrict oneself to the language of that period. Indeed it is often possible to understand some aspects of a period in history even better than the men who lived through it, by use of concepts developed and refined since they died. Modern economic historians, for example, understand far more about the development of the European economy during the fifteenth and sixteenth centuries than did businessmen who participated in that development. Their superior understanding is based in part on the use of concepts derived from modern economics and mathematics, unknown to the Renaissance and Reformation. Modern scholars, for example, can construct price indexes which show exactly what prices increased or decreased during the fifteenth and sixteenth centuries and where and how. These indexes are most frequently derived from the accounts kept by convents, hospitals, and other institutions housing groups of people, of the prices these institutions paid for grain, wine, and other essentials they had to buy continuously year after year. Men of that period often complained bitterly of rising prices but not even the best educated of them would have been able to construct a price index. That does not prevent modern scholars from creating price indexes and then using them to explain many facets of the economic and social development of the period only imperfectly understood by contemporaries. These indexes, for example, help us to explain more fully than ever before many of the food riots of the fifteenth and sixteenth centuries. I would argue that the concept of revolution is like the concept of a price index. If it is used with care, by someone who knows both what it means and what happened in the earlier period, it can be enormously illuminating.

A far more weighty objection to the suggestion that the Protestant Reformation was a revolution comes from specialists in the period itself. Many of them would argue that the Reformation did not involve changes in political organization, social structure, economic property control, and social myths which were fundamental enough to be fairly labeled revolutionary. It was thus not a revolution in Neumann's sense. One thoughtful expression of this point of view can be found in the writing of Professor J. H. Elliott. He sums up his argument in these words:

> The sixteenth and seventeenth centuries did indeed see significant changes in the texture of European life, but these changes occurred inside the resilient framework of the aristocratic-monarchical state. Violent attempts were made at times to disrupt this framework from below, but without any lasting degree of success. The only effective challenge to state power and to the manner of its exercise, could come from within the political nation—from within a governing class whose vision scarcely reached beyond the idea of a traditional community possessed of traditional liberties.[4]

Professor Elliott, to be sure, advanced this argument in the course of a debate on the meaning of early seventeenth-century political uprisings. He is a great authority on uprisings in Spain, particularly the revolt of the Catalans from the Spanish government between 1598 and 1640. He has not considered with equal care the uprisings which accompanied the beginnings of the Protestant Reformation, early in the sixteenth century. Still, he seems to believe that his conclusions apply to the entire early modern period in European history.

I would argue that the conclusion of Professor Elliott and others who share his point of view is defective as an explanation of Reformation changes because it overlooks one crucial fact: it ignores the role of the clergy in pre-Reformation European society. A revolution does not need to be aimed at the power of kings and aristocrats to be a true revolution. It can also be aimed at other ruling classes. The class against which the Protestant Reformation was aimed was the Roman Catholic clergy. In most of Europe before the Reformation, the Catholic clergy did constitute an important element in most political organization and in social structure, did control a good deal of the property, and were custodians of the predominant social myth. A challenge to the clergy thus had to be a radical challenge, calling for a revolutionary change in European society. It is my contention that the Protestant Reformation was such a challenge.

The power of the Catholic clergy in pre-Reformation Europe was revealed in many ways. One way was in politics. A significant number of clergymen exercised direct political power. The pope was the prince of a large state in central Italy, the capital of which was Rome. This state was one of the five largest and most

[4] J. H. Elliott, *op. cit.,* p. 55.

powerful in the peninsula. To maintain and protect this state, the pope controlled all the mechanisms used by any of the leading princes of the period. He directed an army and navy. He supervised one of the largest and best diplomatic services in Europe. He collected taxes and administered justice. In other parts of Europe prince-bishops exercised similar powers. This was particularly true in Germany. There the three prince-archbishops of the Rhineland not only governed their own principalities but also sat in the upper chamber of the imperial Reichstag, the legislature which assisted the Emperor in ruling all of Germany. Other prince-bishops possessed similar if less extensive powers in other parts of Germany. In addition, many clergymen exercised considerable indirect power. There were powerful bishops and cardinals in the councils of practically every king in Western Europe. At times these clergymen gained a significant share of sovereign power in these monarchies. Thus Cardinal Ximenes de Cisneros served as regent of Spain during the minority of Charles V; Charles de Guise, the Cardinal of Lorraine, was a leading figure in the governments of Francis II, Charles IX, and Henry III in France; Cardinal Wolsey dominated the government of Henry VIII in England on the eve of the Reformation.

Another way in which clerical power was revealed in pre-Reformation Europe was in legal systems. Over the centuries the Roman Catholic Church had created a large body of law, called canon law. This law was enforced in a Europe-wide court system, reaching into every community and climaxing in the papal appellate courts in Rome itself. Much of this law was designed to control the internal operations of the Church. But much of it reached out to touch the lives of men who were not clergymen. Most cases involving marital problems, for example, were handled in church courts since marriage was a sacrament of the Church. And even many problems that we would never expect to see handled by clergymen were in fact controlled by church courts in this period. In the province of Franche-Comté, for example, many of the loan contracts were enforceable in church courts. Debtors who had defaulted were hauled before the courts of the archbishop, not the courts of the king, and could be punished with spiritual penalties like excommunication as well as by fines and imprisonment.[5]

[5] Lucien Febvre, "L'excommunication pour dettes en Franche-Comté," *Au coeur religieux du XVIe siècle* (Paris: SEVPEN, 1957), pp. 225 and ff.

These extensive political and legal powers were sustained by formidable economic power. The economy of Europe was still basically agrarian and the fundamental means of production was arable land. A substantial percentage of all the land in Europe was owned directly by clergymen. Parish priests in villages would control land which provided income for their support and for the maintenance of church buildings. Monasteries and other church corporations would control large estates which supported the work of their communities. Bishops and their more important assistants would also typically control a good deal of land.

This considerable economic power was justified in part by extensive social services. Education tended to be a monopoly of the clergy. In much of Europe all of the schools, from elementary grammar schools to universities, were controlled and largely staffed by clergymen. Charity also tended to be a monopoly of the clergy. In cities it was usually administered in "hospitals," all-purpose charitable institutions, staffed by clergymen, with priests or monks in actual residence. These hospitals did much more than take care of the sick. Indeed, those who came down with contagious diseases were more likely to be treated at home or segregated in special pestilential hospitals. The normal hospital took care of orphans and foundlings, of people too old to care for themselves, and of the chronically sick and handicapped. They often also provided hotel services for newcomers and visitors, as did certain other ecclesiastical establishments.

All of this power was justified by a widely accepted social myth, rooted in a version of Christian theology. Every man was held to possess an eternal soul, which could escape damnation and enter into eternal bliss only with the active assistance of the clergy. This assistance could be provided only by clergymen who had been properly trained and ordained and who accepted the direction of the pope and his appointees within the hierarchy of the Roman Catholic Church. Even the myth itself was monopolized by the clergy. Only clerical intellectuals could refine its meaning. Only clerical preachers could proclaim its essential message.

Of course, Protestants were not the only enemies to clerical power. In fact, much of the power of the clergy had been attacked and eroded in many parts of Europe well before the Reformation, during the Renaissance and even earlier. Emperors and kings had challenged the plenary powers claimed by popes; powerful aristocrats had challenged the less sweeping powers claimed by bishops;

petty noblemen had even challenged the local powers claimed by priests; cities had often secularized services previously supplied by the clergy. Furthermore, clerical power survived the Reformation in many areas and in many ways. In some instances it even grew in strength. However, Protestants, wherever they were active, invariably opposed the Catholic clergy, often with considerable vehemence and insistence. The Protestant Reformation can fairly be called, I believe, an anticlerical revolution.

To document this conclusion fully would require massive empirical studies of the growth and nature of anticlericalism all over Western Europe during the Reformation. That is clearly beyond the capacity of any one scholar or group of scholars. Some indication of the plausibility of this conclusion can be given, however, by case studies. I would like to present here one such case study. The case I have selected is of a European community in which I have lived and whose history I know particularly well, the canton of Geneva.

Before the Reformation Geneva was an episcopal city, part of an episcopal principality. Her temporal and spiritual ruler was a bishop. Occasionally, especially in the early Middle Ages, she had claimed to be a part of the Holy Empire, centered in Germany, but as an ecclesiastical principality rather than as a free imperial city. More important by the sixteenth century was the fact that she was then lodged securely in an orbit of the duchy of Savoy. This duchy, which straddled the Alps and included parts of modern Italy, France, and Switzerland, was the most powerful principality in the area. Almost all of the rural areas and villages surrounding Geneva belonged directly to Savoy. Many of them were controlled in the usual feudal manner, by noblemen who maintained fortified castles or houses for the defense of the area, and conceded allegiance to the duke of Savoy. For several decades before the Reformation the bishop of Geneva had always been closely connected to the court of Savoy. Often he had been a younger son or brother of the duke. Sometimes he had been consecrated in his office while still a child, and a vicar had to exercise all of his power. This arrangement had the advantage for Geneva of securing Savoyard support for the city. She could call on the ducal army for defense and her merchants could trade more freely throughout the duchy. It also meant, however, that the bishop was seldom in actual residence within the city. He had to spend a good deal of time in following the ducal court, in superintending other properties, or in handling yet other types of secular and ecclesiastical responsibilities within the duchy. Some of the bishops also acquired charges outside of Savoy. A few of them were called to Rome to work for the central administration of the Catholic Church. Many of them acquired ecclesiastical property with attendant responsibilities in neighboring France. Still, the power of the bishop was always felt within Geneva. That power was symbolized graphically by the large cathedral church on the top of the hill in the center of the old city. It had been splendidly rebuilt and redecorated in the course of the fifteenth century, when the commercial fairs for which the city was famous in that part of Europe were particularly flourishing. It was visible for miles around, even from the high mountains which enclose three sides of the city from a distance. It easily dominated the city physically.

Within Geneva, the bishop's power was exercised by an episcopal council. The most important members of this council carried the titles of vicar and "official." The vicar was the bishop's chief representative in the city and presided over the council in the bishop's absence. The "official" was a judicial officer, responsible for supervising the administration of all ecclesiastical justice, both civil and criminal. There were also certain other agents of the bishop who sat in the episcopal council. This council acted as both an administrative body and an ecclesiastical court. The bishop was further assisted in his rule of Geneva by a cathedral chapter of thirty-two canons. Almost all of them came from prominent Savoyard noble families. The chapter was thus a microcosm of the Savoyard ruling class, technically presided over by a member of its most prominent family, filled out by members of many of its lesser noble families. Each of the canons was assigned a luxurious house near the cathedral of Geneva. Vacancies in the chapter were filled by the canons themselves, through co-optation. Their most important single function was to elect a new bishop on the death or resignation of an incumbent. However, they often saw their choice set aside by the pope. He retained the right to confirm any election of a bishop, and in the case of Geneva he reserved to himself the right to make his own final selection. Both the chapter elections and the final papal selections reflected very heavy political pressure from neighboring secular authorities. This pressure came primarily from the dukes of Savoy but it could also come from the French royal house and the Swiss cantons.

For the exercise of his spiritual responsibilities, the bishop depended upon ordained clergymen. There were several hundred of them in pre-Reformation Geneva, out of a total population of about ten thousand. They included secular priests, most of whom were attached to one or another of seven city parishes. They also included regular clergy, mostly of the mendicant orders, housed in some seven convents. The newest of these convents had been built in the century before the Reformation for communities of Augustinian hermits and Poor Clare sisters.

For the exercise of his temporal responsibilities, the bishop delegated some of his powers to laymen. Justice for laymen, in both civil and criminal cases, was supervised by an officer with the unusual title of *vidomne*. Some time before the Reformation, the bishops of Geneva had ceded the right to choose this officer to the ducal government of Savoy. The *vidomne* and his staff lived in a castle on an island in the middle of the Rhone river which cuts Geneva in half. That castle symbolized graphically the power of Savoy within the city. The bishop further allowed the lay population of Geneva to elect certain other officers to share in local government. The most important of these elected officers were four syndics, chosen once a year by the entire body of male citizens in an assembly called the General Council. These syndics had the right to act as judges in the more important criminal trials initiated by the *vidomne*. That right, along with many others, had been spelled out in writing in a charter of liberties of the citizens of Geneva promulgated by a bishop in 1387. Every subsequent bishop was expected to swear to uphold these liberties at the time of his installation. The syndics also chose a Small or Ordinary Council, of twelve to twenty-five men, who met at least once a week to handle local civic problems. Both syndics and Council members were normally relatively well-to-do Genevan merchants. Some of them were professional men. They were often older men, well enough established so that younger members of the family or assistants could keep their businesses going. To these men were assigned a variety of matters of purely local concern. They had to see to it that the walls and moats which fortified the city were maintained in good condition, that adequate food supplies were regularly brought into the city and stored with care, that the streets were kept clean. They also had to direct the collection and expenditure of much of the city's money. And they supervised a variety of educational and charitable institutions.

At this last point ecclesiastical and temporal authority overlapped again, for most of the educational and charitable institutions were staffed by clergymen. The education of clergymen had been handled within the cathedral establishment for a long time.

In the fifteenth century, an independent school for laymen had been established. It was financed and supervised by the city Council, but normally staffed by clergymen. The city had been awarded the right to establish a university, but had never done so. Charity was handled primarily by seven "hospitals." Most of them had been founded by the gifts or legacies of wealthy individuals, to provide for both the repose of their own souls and assistance to the poor. A typical "hospital" would be located in a converted house, perhaps itself part of the original bequest. Resident in it would be a priest, who would be in charge and would say masses for the souls of the founder and his family. He would be assisted by a "hospitallier" or administrator, who would assist the poor. Usually there would be a dozen or so poor people also in residence, a mixture of orphans, the handicapped, and the very old. From the middle of the fifteenth century, many of these hospitals were supervised by a municipal foundation, controlled by the Council, which also had supplementary funds to assist the poor who could remain in their own homes. In addition, the city maintained a pestilential hospital, outside the walls and near the cemetery, for people with serious contagious diseases. It was staffed by a priest, a doctor, and several servants. The city also maintained two small leprosaria outside its walls for victims of leprosy.

The control of public morals should have been the responsibility of the bishop, but he was seldom interested. There were always a good number of prostitutes in pre-Reformation Geneva, to service both visiting merchants and clergymen unable to keep their vows of chastity. Seldom was any effort made to drive prostitutes from the city. Instead they were regulated by the city Council. At one point they were asked to organize themselves into a kind of guild and elect from their number a "queen" who would represent them in dealings with the government. The prostitutes were also expected to live within an assigned quarter of the city, wear distinctive kinds of clothing, and limit their solicitation to specified times and places. If a sexual or marital problem required legal intervention, of course, the courts were prepared to act. Most cases of this sort were handled by the court of the bishop.

Geneva's ecclesiastical establishment was supported materially from a variety of sources. Church property and taxes within the city provided some income. A great deal of additional income came from a patchwork of rural properties scattered over the countryside around Geneva and belonging directly to the bishop.

These were superintended by episcopal officers who saw to it that order was maintained in each rural village, that local priests served the spiritual needs of the peasants, and that all the rents and taxes due the bishop were regularly paid.

After the Reformation Geneva was a secular city-state. The bishop and all his officers had been evicted, including the ones appointed with his permission by the dukes of Savoy. The clergy had all been forced either to leave the city or to convert to Protestantism and abandon clerical careers. Almost all of the ecclesiastical property, both within the city and in the country-side, had been confiscated by the new government. Many of the social services provided by clergymen had been secularized. A new Reformed Church had been created to minister to the spiritual needs of the population, but it was completely under the control of the city government. All of this had been engineered by the lay merchants and professional men of Geneva, led by their elected syndics and Council members. These changes began in the 1520s, with the whittling away of the bishop's powers. They reached a climax in 1536, with a formal vote by the entire male population to adopt the Protestant Reformation. They were not fully consolidated until 1555, when John Calvin, the new director of Geneva's spiritual life, finally won a definitive triumph over all local opposition.

The Reformation in Geneva began as a rebellion against the government of the bishop and his Savoyard allies. Step by step the syndics and the city Council seized powers that had heretofore been held by the episcopal government as parts of its sovereign prerogatives, until finally nothing remained for the bishop. The first powers to go were those of control over foreign affairs. This crucial attribute of sovereignty had naturally been claimed by the bishop. As sovereign lord of Geneva he had traditionally directed its relations with other governments. When he became allied to the House of Savoy, its government could help speak for Geneva. Now, however, the syndics and city Council, on their own initiative, opened formal negotiations with other governments, particularly with those of the free city-states of the Swiss Confederation. These were states with which Genevans had long had commercial relations. Merchants who dealt with the Swiss tended to have interests different from those who dealt with Savoy. That fact helped split the population into pro-Savoyard and pro-Swiss factions. These two factions began struggling for control of the Council. When the pro-Swiss faction won the upper hand, it tried to consolidate its power by negotiating formal alliances with two of the more powerful neighboring Swiss city-states, Fribourg and Berne. After several false starts, an alliance which persisted was finally signed in 1526. Fribourg withdrew from the alliance several years later, after Berne turned Protestant and Geneva began considering Protestantism. But Berne remained as Geneva's staunchest ally and that alliance was important, for Berne was one of the greatest military powers in the area. This was the period of the zenith of Swiss military might. Crack troops of Swiss mercenary infantrymen were hired by royal governments all over Europe to fill in their own armies when really major military campaigns were planned. And Berne was an important recruiting point for the formation of these armies. That meant Berne could recruit for her own purposes a powerful army, powerful enough to defeat the ducal armies of Savoy, if that became necessary.

The Savoyards protested vehemently against this alliance, arguing that it amounted to usurpation by the Council of a sovereign power really belonging to the bishop. Pierre de la Baume, the incumbent bishop, however, did not back up this Savoyard protest. He had become alienated from the duke at that point, despite the years he had spent in the ducal entourage, and was trying to play an independent game. In the course of personal negotiations with the city Council, he fatefully conceded to that body the right to sign alliances. That occurred in 1527. He also tried to make himself a party to this particular alliance. The Bernese refused to admit the bishop to the alliance and the bishop tried to revoke his concession to the Geneva Council. But it was too late.

The next episcopal powers to be seized by the city Council were the rights to control justice, another crucial attribute of sovereignty. The syndics had already won much earlier, under the terms of the 1387 charter, the right to sit as judges in certain criminal trials. But the arrest and execution of lay criminals remained in the hands of the *vidomne* and his staff. Clergymen accused of crimes were tried by the "official" and tried in the bishop's court. All civil cases were handled by either the *vidomne* or the "official." And all decisions could be appealed to the bishop. The first of these powers to go was jurisdiction over civil cases. The Council persuaded the bishop to surrender it voluntarily in 1527, when he was eagerly trying to placate the city and win the Council's support. This meant that the bishop had surrendered some of the powers previously exercised by the *vidomne* and the

"official." The concession of the *vidomne's* powers made the
Savoyards furious, since he was appointed by their government.
Again the bishop changed his mind and tried to retract his
concession, but again he was too late. Instead the city Council
proceeded to take over more judicial powers. It blocked all appeals
to superior courts outside of Geneva. It transferred to the syndics
the right to execute criminal sentences. Finally a new elective
magistracy was created, the office of the lieutenant, charged with
supervising all criminal justice. By 1530 all the judicial powers once
belonging to the bishop and his agents had been transferred over
to the elective government of the city. Pierre de la Baume may
have been trying to win these powers back in 1533, when he
returned to the city in person, after a nasty religious riot in which
a prominent canon named Werli had been killed. The council was
quite prepared to bring the murderer to justice but unwilling to
discipline certain others whom the bishop thought deserving of
punishment. And it refused to grant the bishop any role in the
judicial proceedings. He then left the city for good. Before long he
transferred his entire court to the small neighboring town of Gex.
A number of canons also left Geneva during these years of turmoil
over judicial jurisdictions.

Meanwhile Protestantism had begun to penetrate Geneva. It was
introduced with powerful encouragement from Berne, which had
itself formally adopted Zwinglian Protestantism in 1528. The
leader of the campaign to convert Geneva to Protestantism was an
inflammatory French preacher named Guillaume Farel, who
repeatedly visited Geneva during these years in spite of fierce
opposition from the leading local clerics. Farel's impassioned
sermons and public appeals plunged the city into further turmoil.
Iconoclastic riots began, in which mobs of boys and young men
pulled down altars, smashed religious statues, desecrated relics,
destroyed stained glass windows. Catholic religious services were
repeatedly disrupted, with preachers being publicly challenged
on points of Bible interpretation in the middle of their homilies.
Protestants seized certain of the church buildings, most notably
the Franciscan convent, and began holding services and administering sacraments in them, in competition with the local priests.
Finally in 1535 a public debate was held between a group of
Protestant pastors and a few local priests. (Many of the Catholic
clergy boycotted it.) The Protestants claimed that the debate had
resulted in a decisive victory for them, and that the population
was now generally convinced of the truth of their point of view.
They demanded that the city adopt legislation to establish firmly a

truly Reformed service of worship. Many members of the Council seemed inclined to accept this claim, but the Council as a whole did not want to proceed too abruptly. It ordered a temporary suspension of the Catholic mass, until the problem could be fully resolved.

That step convinced most of the Catholic clergy who were still in the city that they could no longer remain. A number had already left Geneva, because of the constant popular turmoil and harassment or because they had been caught in intrigues involving the bishop. A few had abandoned their religious vocation, had publicly converted to Protestantism, had turned to secular occupations, and had even married. In 1535, after the great debate, practically all the remaining Catholic clergy left Geneva. This included the bishop's vicar, the remaining canons, most of the parish priests, and most of the friars and sisters. A handful of priests who tried to stick it out were ordered by the Council either to leave or to conform to the Protestant settlement and regularly listen to Protestant sermons. The few who remained were relieved of all clerical duties.

Once most of the clergy had left the city, the Council seized control over all church property, both within the city and in the country districts heretofore controlled by the bishop's officers. Some of this property was used to pay off a substantial debt contracted to Berne for armed defense against Savoy. The rest was allocated to charity. All the hospitals created during the Middle Ages to minister to the poor were closed down. A new Hospital-General was established in the building which had been the convent of the Poor Clare sisters. A civilian staff, including a "hospitallier" or administrator, a teacher, a doctor, and servants, was assembled and housed in the building. A special committee of the government was created to supervise the activity of this staff. The administration of charity was thus thoroughly laicized and rationalized in Geneva. Later Calvin was to give these laymen responsible for the Hospital-General, both on the supervisory committee and in the office of "hospitallier," the additional ecclesiastical title of deacon. But they remained laymen without any clerical ordination or special clerical training for their jobs.

As a final assertion of sovereignty, the city Council authorized and supervised the coining of money. The new coins carried a slogan, somewhat modified from an earlier slogan used by the episcopal government, which was to become a rallying cry of the Reformation. It was: *Post tenebras lux*, "after darkness light."

Naturally all of these changes increasingly alarmed the bishop, the ducal government of Savoy, and the Savoyard noble families of the area surrounding Geneva. The bishop could see his power and wealth evaporating, the duke could see his claim on the city withering away, the nobles could see their relatives among the canons insulted and exiled. Considerable military pressure was brought to bear upon Geneva to stop this course of events. Armed bands of Savoyard noblemen, encouraged by the duke and the bishop, ravaged the countryside, interdicting much of the trade so vital to the city's economy and making it hard for the city to gather in essential food on a regular basis. By 1535 the city was virtually under siege. Geneva appealed for help in several directions and finally persuaded its Bernese ally to act. A sizable Swiss army came pouring down from the great plain to the north. There was little the Savoyards could do to withstand it. The army commanded by the Bernese effectively conquered all the Savoyard and independent territory surrounding Geneva. It even tried to take over the city itself, but the Genevans were able to resist that pressure.

With a ring of Bernese dependencies around her, Geneva was now free to go all the way to Reformation. In a special meeting of the General Council held in May of 1536, the final step was taken. It was voted that the city would henceforth live by the Gospel and the Word of God as it had been preached in Geneva since the suspension of the mass. It was further voted that "masses, images, idols, and other papal abuses" would no longer be permitted in the city.

That decision ended the power of Catholic clergy in Geneva. But it did not immediately create a Reformed Church. It really only left a vacuum, which was unstable and dangerous in an age when almost all Europeans felt it necessary to build their lives and their communities around some form of religious ideology. Farel, the most prominent of the preachers who had persuaded Geneva to abandon Catholicism, desperately tried to fill this void. He had the great good luck to recruit as his principal assistant a brilliant young French humanist lawyer who happened to be passing through Geneva only a few months after its fateful decision to become Protestant. This was John Calvin. He had only recently converted to Protestantism and fled from religious persecution in his native country to Basel. There he had composed and published the *Institutes of the Christian Religion*, a book which was to become, in its later and expanded versions, the most important single summary of Protestant doctrine produced in the century.

Calvin had not planned to settle in Geneva, but Farel managed to persuade him that it was God's will that he should stay and help build a Reformed Church in this place. Calvin was appointed a public lecturer in theology. Even with this help, Farel found it very difficult to organize a Reformed Church. For two years they worked together to announce the Christian truth as they saw it and to give it reality in the community by developing Reformed services and ecclesiastical institutions. They found it harder to control behavior than to persuade men to their belief. Calvin himself later reported that when he first arrived in Geneva, "the Gospel was preached ... [but] things were very disorderly ... the Gospel consisted mostly of having broken idols ... there were many wicked people."[6] They were frustrated at every turn by the Genevans, who did not want to trade what they regarded as Catholic clerical tyranny for a new Protestant yoke. Finally Farel and Calvin were both rather unceremoniously ejected from the city.

Now Geneva was really drifting, without any clerical leadership it could respect. Some thought the city might return to Catholicism. The liberal Cardinal Sadoleto of the Roman curia wrote from his diocese in southern France to urge the Genevans to consider this possibility carefully. Others thought the city might drift into some wild and eccentric religious experiment. This period of indecision finally ended when Calvin, alone, was invited back to take charge. He had settled in German Strasbourg, where he had been named pastor of the French refugees' congregation, and he was reluctant to return to Geneva. He posed strict conditions, and they were accepted. Finally, in 1541, he came back. He remained in Geneva until his death in 1564, and created there a Reformed Church which proved to be a model for Protestants in much of Europe and America.

Calvin accomplished this feat solely by moral suasion. He never possessed even a fraction of the legal power of the deposed Catholic bishop. He never commanded even a fraction of the material resources owned by the bishop, or for that matter by any one of the Catholic cathedral canons. Political power remained solely within the hands of the elected Council and syndics. Calvin and the other pastors were only employees of the municipal government, living on salaries paid by the city, most of them in houses owned by the city. They were far fewer in number than the

---

[6] Baum, Cunitz, and Reuss, eds., *Calvini Opera*, XXI (Brunswick, 1879), p. 43.

Catholic clergy whose places they took. Altogether there were only nine pastors in 1542. The number had risen to only nineteen by 1564, the year of Calvin's death. In addition, a few men with Protestant theological training secured positions as chaplains, teachers, or tutors. But the total of all these men was far short of the hundreds of Catholic religious who had served Geneva under the bishop. Furthermore, none of these Protestant clergymen was allowed to become a full citizen of Geneva. The city had become so suspicious of foreign pressures that it granted citizenship, with full rights to vote and hold office, only to certain native-born residents. All the pastors were immigrants, most of them from France, like Calvin. No native Genevan had been able to secure the type of advanced education the Council now decided was essential for this position. A few of the pastors became "bourgeois" of Geneva, an intermediate status which gave a man many political and legal rights, but not full citizenship. Calvin was granted the status of "bourgeois," but only toward the end of his life, in 1559.

This does not mean that Calvin and the other pastors did not exercise considerable political power in Geneva. But it always had to be exercised indirectly, usually through preaching or consulting. Calvin used both means to win great power for himself. He became an eloquent preacher, who clearly commanded the respect, if not always the affection, of his audience. This was in marked contrast to many of his predecessors both in the Catholic clergy and among the earliest Protestant preachers. He also became an active and useful consultant to the city government. The Council found his skill as a trained lawyer and his first-hand knowledge of the greater world of international politics to be extremely useful. He was often called in for consultation and his advice was usually accepted.

One of the first things Calvin did on returning to Geneva in 1541 was to draft a set of ecclesiastical ordinances, to give institutional shape and legal standing to the newly Reformed Church. His right to do this had been part of the bargain that led to his return. After some discussion and a few minor amendments, these ordinances were enacted into law by the government. They organized the Genevan Church by creating four categories of ministers and then building institutions through which the work of each could be channelled. The categories were: (1) the pastors who were to preach the Word of God and administer the sacraments, (2) the doctors who were to study the Word of God and teach, (3) the elders who were to maintain discipline within the community, and (4) the deacons who were to supervise the administration of charity.

The pastors were distributed among the parishes created before the Reformation both within the city and in the country villages it controlled. There were seldom enough men and resources to staff all of these parishes fully, but arrangements were made so that everyone had access of some sort to a pastor. The pastors' job was to proclaim the Word of God, as it had been discovered by Calvin, from the parish pulpits. They also had to administer the two remaining sacraments which the Reformed Church acknowledged as genuine, baptism and communion. For organizational purposes the pastors were grouped into a Company, which met once a week to handle routine church business, to discuss theology, and to engage in criticism of themselves and their colleagues. Calvin served as Moderator, or presiding officer, of this Company until his death. That was his only position of preeminence in Geneva. He also served as one of the pastors in the cathedral parish of St. Pierre, and occasionally also preached in the nearby church of the Madeleine, where many of the city's merchants attended services. The pastors were all chosen by co-optation, with the existing Company deciding on any new appointment. No choice could become final, however, until the candidate had also been approved by the city Council and presented to the parish in which he was to serve. The Council reserved to itself the right to dismiss without notice any pastor who displeased its members. Over the years a number were in fact dismissed, most commonly because they had offended Council members by things they said in sermons.

In the beginning, Calvin was really the only doctor. In addition to his pastoral duties, he spent a good deal of time in writing and lecturing on the Bible. His lectures attracted hundreds of eager young intellectuals from all over Europe. This teaching did not get formal institutional shape, however, until 1559, fairly late in Calvin's life. In that year Geneva created a new Academy, providing both secondary and university-level training in theology. Calvin, of course, was the star of this faculty. He was joined by a number of his disciples who had been teaching in neighboring Lausanne but who had recently been driven out by Berne. The Bernese, who controlled Lausanne directly, had come to object to some of the disciplinary and dogmatic ideas taught by these men. Material support for Geneva's Academy was provided primarily from property confiscated by the Council from native Genevans

who had been driven out of the city in a number of internal
upheavals ending in 1555. These ejections had had the net effect
of eliminating all opposition within Geneva to Calvin and fully
consolidating his authority.

The other two orders of ministers, elders and deacons, were
laymen most of whom served in this capacity only on a part-time
basis. They were drawn from the same pool of wealthy merchants
and professional men who served in the city Council and on the
city's various governing committees. Near the beginning of every
year, a meeting of the General Council was called to elect the
syndics and Council members for the coming twelve months. At
the same time members of a number of governmental committees
were elected, from slates prepared by the outgoing government.
These committees included ones to maintain the city's fortifications, control its grain supply, keep the streets clean, act as courts
to judge certain legal cases. Calvin's ecclesiastical ordinances added
two new committees to the list: a committee to maintain Christian
discipline, staffed partly by elders; a committee to assist the poor,
staffed by deacons.

The committee upon which the elders sat was called the
Consistory. The pastors were also members of this body. It acted
as a kind of ecclesiastical court and met once a week. One of the
Syndics served as its presiding officer. The elders were chosen so as
to represent all of the "dizaine" districts into which the city was
divided. They reported to the Consistory names of residents whose
religious ideas were suspect, who still clung to Catholic practices,
and who did not behave properly. A high percentage of their cases
were of people accused of sex crimes—prostitution, fornication,
adultery, sodomy, rape. They examined each case. If the fault was
minor and the accused penitent, he might be let off with a scolding.
If the fault was more serious and the accused stubborn, he could be
excommunicated. This was a serious penalty in a population which
took its sacraments seriously, and could cause great distress. If the
accused had done something of a criminal nature that required
further punishment, he would be referred to the city Council.

This was the most controversial single institution established by
the Reformation in Geneva. Calvin insisted on its creation when he
returned in 1541, and threatened to resign when its power to
excommunicate was threatened in later years. Few Protestant
governments elsewhere in Europe were willing to grant judicial
powers of this kind to an ecclesiastical body of this type. But
Calvin ultimately had his way, the opponents of the Consistory

were discredited and driven out, and a moral "reign of terror" followed. All of this helped to create that particularly austere pattern of behavior which has come to be labeled "Puritan."

The deacons worked with the Hospital-General. Their positions had actually been created before Calvin's arrival, in the series of events which led up to the final break with Catholicism. Calvin simply made room for them in the Ecclesiastical Ordinances and found Biblical warrant for their assignments. In effect he sanctified this office, gave it a special religious character, and in so doing made it a more highly valued and respected feature of Genevan society.

The Ecclesiastical Ordinances required the Council to consult the pastors when it drew up its slates of nominations for elders and deacons before the annual elections. However, this rule was not followed invariably. It was followed more often in the choice of elders than of deacons, and was followed quite scrupulously in the selection of both after Calvin's power had been fully consolidated toward the end of his life.

This ecclesiastical structure was an outstanding success in consolidating the Reformation in Geneva. Much of it persists in that city down to the present. It helped win for the city the international reputation as a center of Reformed Protestantism which has accounted for much of Geneva's distinctive character over the centuries.

Taken all together, it seems obvious to me that the changes in Geneva between 1526 and 1559 constitute a genuine revolution. They meet every requirement of the definition of a revolution laid down by Neumann which we adopted earlier. There was a fundamental change in political organization: a government run by a bishop assisted by canons, chosen according to Church law, was overthrown; a new government run by a Council of local laymen elected by the people took its place. There was a fundamental change in social structure: several hundred Catholic clergymen, a number of Savoyard noblemen, and ordinary laymen hesitant to go all the way to Calvinism were all driven out of the city; their places were taken by hundreds of immigrants, most of whom were artisans and merchants and most of whom came from France, as had Calvin. There was a fundamental change in economic property control: large amounts of property were confiscated from the old Church and its supporters and in effect socialized, put at the disposition of the entire community as represented by its government, rather than being distributed to private individuals. All of these changes were justified and sanctified by the most obvious change of all, in the predominant myth of social order. Roman Catholic theology was brutally rejected and a new variety of Protestant theology was created to take its place.

There remains one final problem that must be explored, however, before we can answer our initial question satisfactorily. We must consider the extent to which the Reformation in Geneva was typical. Even if the Reformation clearly meant revolution in this particular city-state, it may not have had the same meaning elsewhere. Geneva may have been unique, and thus not a case upon which generalizations should be built.

To resolve this problem would require extensive comparative studies. Even some tentative and preliminary studies of this sort do make one thing clear: the Reformation in Geneva was obviously more radical than in many communities. In few places had the power of the Catholic clergy remained as strong and as pervasive as it was in pre-Reformation Geneva. Cities all over Europe had once been controlled directly by bishops. For example, in Germany most cities had been ruled by bishops back in the tenth century. Since that period, however, new secular cities had been founded and many old cities had broken loose from episcopal control. By the time of the Reformation only a few German cities remained under the effective direct control of bishops. Most of the cities of importance had become free imperial cities, acknowledging allegiance to only one sovereign—the Holy Roman Emperor. Remnants of episcopal power remained in most of these cities, but most temporal power was concentrated in elected city councils like those of Geneva.

Furthermore, in many cities services that had previously been performed by the clergy had been turned over to secular institutions well before the Reformation. This was particularly true of educational and charitable services. The move to secularization of these services was especially pronounced in the great Italian city-states of the late Middle Ages. In fact it can be argued that the celebrated culture of the Italian Renaissance was made possible by the creation of secular schools and academies supported by municipal governments and wealthy laymen in communities like Florence. Similarly the administration of charity had been laicized and rationalized in communities like Milan which built and endowed large municipal hospitals for this purpose. Clergymen still staffed some of these institutions. But clerical control was gone and clerical participation was reduced if not ended. It can thus be argued that Geneva in the sixteenth century was socially retarded and that she used the Reformation to catch up, to introduce changes which had already occurred in other communities.

It is also clear that in few places did the Reformation go as far as it did in Geneva. It was not common for the entire body of the clergy in a community to be deposed or ejected. More often Catholic parish priests were simply converted to Protestantism, with a greater or lesser appreciation of what that meant, and allowed to remain at their work. Only slowly was a body of clergymen fully trained in Protestant doctrine developed. This seems to have happened in most of the Lutheran principalities in Germany and in the kingdom of England. In England the changes must have been particularly bewildering. For there priests were expected to renounce the pope yet remain Catholic in doctrine under Henry VIII, become Protestant with permission to marry under Edward VI, return to Rome and put aside their wives under Mary, become Protestant again and remarry under Elizabeth I. A remarkable number of priests in England seemed to be able to make many of those changes.

However even if the changes accompanying the Reformation were seldom as abrupt and as far-reaching as in Geneva, there were always some changes. In every single instance, for one thing, a community adopting Protestantism rejected the authority of the pope and broke all ties with Rome. And this was not a trivial move. The papacy had long symbolized in a concrete institutional way the unity of all Western European civilization. Rejection of its power meant a move to some sort of particularism, often to some type of nationalism. This marked an extremely important shift in the most fundamental values held by Europeans, from one basic assumption about society to another. It was a shift which was to have tremendous consequences for the history of Europe for at least another four hundred years, until the middle of the twentieth century.

Another change that almost always came with the Reformation was the closing of all monastic communities and the confiscation of their often considerable property. On rare occasions convents or monasteries were simply walled up and not allowed to recruit new members, thus going out of existence when all existing members died. But more commonly all the monks and nuns, friars and sisters, were required either to leave or find new occupations. And they lost all of their community property. There is a good deal of debate as to how significant were the resulting massive transfers of property. In many areas wealthy noblemen who already controlled much of a monastery's activities no doubt were able now simply to control this property more directly. But changes of some sort had to occur. And often they were brutal and of far-reaching consequences.

Yet another change that almost always came with the Reformation was the collapse of the system of church law and church courts. Appeals to Rome, of course, were always stopped. So at least that element in the Catholic legal system invariably disappeared. But a good many further changes usually followed. Church courts were either abandoned completely or their powers and the range of their jurisdiction were sharply reduced. New Protestant ecclesiastical bodies were seldom given many legal functions. In at least one aspect of legal practice, most Protestant communities went further than Geneva. Before the Reformation cases involving marital and sexual problems were normally tried before church courts. Geneva assigned these cases to a semi-ecclesiastic court, the Consistory. This court did not, to be sure, use Catholic canon law to settle these cases, turning instead to civil law and the relevant parts of the Bible as interpreted by Calvin. But clergymen were at least involved in this part of the judicial process in Geneva. In most Protestant communities they were not granted this right, and jurisdiction over marital and sexual offenses was jealously reserved to secular courts. Both Catholic law and the Catholic type of court were abandoned.

Taken together, the renunciation of papal authority, the closing of the monasteries, and the dismantling of the Catholic legal system were significant changes. They required some modifications in political organization, in the social structure, and in the economic control of property. They reflected a profound change in the predominant myth of the community. It seems to me that these changes can fairly be called revolutionary. Their full implications, to be sure, become obvious only when one examines an extreme case like Geneva. But they were always present. I would therefore conclude that the Protestant Reformation was indeed a revolution.

FOR FURTHER READING

On Revolution

Hannah Arendt, *On Revolution.* New York: Viking, 1965.

J. H. Elliott, "Revolution and Continuity in Early Modern Europe," *Past and Present*, no. 42 (1969), pp. 35-56.

Jacques Ellul, *Autopsy of Revolution*. New York: Knopf, 1971.

Lawrence Stone, *The Causes of the English Revolution, 1529-1642*. New York: Harper & Row, 1972. The first chapter in this book is a particularly useful introduction to scholarly study of the phenomenon of revolution.

On Geneva

Histoire de Genève, des origines à 1798. Geneva: Jullien, 1951. This symposium volume is available only in French.

Robert M. Kingdon, "The Control of Morals in Calvin's Geneva," in Lawrence P. Buck and Jonathan W. Zophy, eds., *The Social History of the Reformation*. Columbus: Ohio State University Press, 1972.

Robert M. Kingdon, *Geneva and the Coming of the Wars of Religion in France, 1555-1563*. Geneva: Droz, 1956.

Robert M. Kingdon, "Social Welfare in Calvin's Geneva," *American Historical Review*, 76 (1971): 50-69.

John T. McNeill, *The History and Character of Calvinism*. New York: Oxford University Press, 1954.

E. William Monter, *Calvin's Geneva*. New York: John Wiley & Sons, 1967. This is the best introduction in English.

E. William Monter, *Studies in Genevan Government (1536-1605)*. Geneva: Droz, 1964.

THE ESSAYIST'S SOURCES

1

Michel Roset, *Chronicles of Geneva*

While Michel Roset (1534-1613) was too young to have had a personal knowledge of many of the events described in his *Chronicles*, his account of the Genevan Reformation is valuable in several respects. Roset composed the work during the early years of his career with the city government of Geneva and completed it by 1562. He evidently was permitted some access to official records for the account is, in general, factually accurate. At the same time, the *Chronicles* reflect Roset's commitment to the Reformation and his intense civic pride. His father was an early and active follower of Farel, the first Reformer of Geneva, as well as a fairly prominent official in the municipal government. Upon completion of his education at Zurich, Michel Roset received an appointment with the Genevan government. Within five years, in 1560, he was elected one of the four governing syndics. By the end of his life, he had served a total of forty-five years in the office of syndic. Roset was also an able diplomat, serving on missions to Germany, Italy, and the other Swiss cities. His greatest achievements were the Treaty of Soleure in 1579, and the *combourgeoisie* (alliance of cities) of 1584. Both pacts preserved Geneva's independence during the crucial years following Calvin's death and became the cornerstone of the republic's foreign policy for the next two centuries.

SOURCE: Michel Roset, *Les Chroniques de Genève*, edited by Henri Fazy (Geneva: Georg, 1894), translation by Raymond A. Mentzer, Jr. pp. 12-15; 174; 176; 176-77; 190; 195-96; 196-98; 200-202; 207; 210; 211; 212-13; 214-15; 227-28; 232-33; 238.

THE STRUCTURE OF THE CHURCH
IN PRE-REFORMATION GENEVA

Formerly there was a Bishop who was the spiritual and temporal prince; thirty-two canons who had their own jurisdiction and over whom a provost presided; eleven chaplains called Maccabees; six choir boys; seven curés and seven parishes: Saint Croix in the Saint Pierre quarter, Dame La Nove, Saint Germain, La Madeleine, Saint Gervais, Saint Légier and Saint Victor. There were also five monasteries, of the Franciscans in the Rive quarter, of the Poor Clares, of the Dominicans in the Plainpalais quarter, of the Augustinians at Notre Dame de Grace near the Arve river,* and of the monks of the Order of Cluny in the Saint Victor quarter. The Bishop had a Vicar, an Episcopal Council and an "Official" for ordinary justice. He also had a *vidomne,*** a judicial officer from whom one could appeal to the "Official."

For the civil government, there were four Syndics elected annually, their Council and the Assembly of the Citizens and Bourgeois which was called the General Council. The Syndics were the judges of criminal cases, the magistrates of the city, and the masters of the port, the artillery and the munitions.

*Editor's Note: Roset appears to have made a minor mistake at this point. It was the Dominicans who had their convent at Notre Dame de Grace, in the Plainpalais quarter. The Augustinian house was near the Arve river.

**Editor's Note: Although theoretically a part of the episcopal administration, the office of *vidomne* had long been controlled by the House of Savoy. The *vidomne* exercised criminal justice within Geneva.

They possessed a written charter of liberties which the Prince Bishop reaffirmed when he took possession of the Bishopric. When the sun set in the evening, they alone .had total jurisdiction and authority within the city. Some individuals claim that in years past the people elected the bishop as their leader. Because of his spiritual jurisdiction, he was confirmed by Rome. It is certain that the Syndics were elected by the people on the feast of Saint Martin. The four Syndics elected their own Council, each of them choosing five prominent citizens to be councilmen. They also elected a treasurer. The edicts or public proclamations were made on behalf of the Bishop, his *vidomne* and the men of experience and integrity of the city. When the *vidomne* and other episcopal officers captured a criminal, they delivered him to the Syndics within twenty-four hours and brought suit before them for judgment, from which there was no appeal. Only the bishop could grant pardon. They commanded the *vidomne* to execute their sentence. The *vidomne* delivered the criminal to the Castellan of Gaillard, an officer of the Count of the Genevois, dependent of the rear-fief of the bishopric. He executed the criminal near the city and within its franchise at a place called Champel where the gallows are still located today. Our ancestors have handed down to us the account that a certain bishop, in debt to the Prince of Savoy, mortgaged to the Prince the office of *vidomne* and the castle on the island in the Rhone river where it flows through Geneva. Later, the bishop, wishing to be free of the arrangement, met with a refusal from the princes of Savoy. The money was deposited at Rome where the dispute remained pending, although no one knew why or how. As a result, the bishops excommunicated the Dukes of Savoy as usurpers of the property of the Church. This much is certain, that still in the closing years of the papal reign in Geneva, when a church procession passed in front of this castle, they lowered the cross as a sign of interdict.

THE FINAL VISIT OF THE BISHOP OF GENEVA
PIERRE de la BAUME, JULY 1533

The Bishop, de la Baume, accompanied by his advisors and several lords from Fribourg, returned to Geneva on 1 July 1533. He was received with great honor. He had the priests held for the tumult which occurred in April released. And, having required the General Council to assemble, he asked the people if they accepted him as their Prince. They answered yes, subject to their liberties and customs, written and unwritten. Afterwards, he commanded the Syndics to judge the prisoners held in the death of Werli.* Otherwise, he would try them in the city and his men would provide protection. He was beseeched not to endorse such armed men in order not to have bands in the

---

*Editor's Note: Pierre Werli, a canon of the Cathedral of Saint Pierre, had been killed in the course of an armed clash between Catholics and Protestants on 4 May 1533.

city. The Bishop asked that his councillors assist at the trial with the Syndics. The Syndics said that this was in violation of their liberties.

THE FINAL DEPARTURE OF THE BISHOP OF GENEVA, PIERRE de la BAUME, 15 JULY 1533

In the midst of these troubles, there were some citizens who feared that the Bishop might have the prisoners, who had been given over to the Syndics for judgment, secretly taken from them. For this reason, these citizens took up arms and patrolled the city at night. As a result, the Bishop departed Geneva on 15 July 1533. It was commonly said that his departure was out of fear of the people who may have been irritated because of the afore-mentioned prisoners. He has not returned since.

APPEALS TO THE COURT OF THE BISHOP ARE DISCONTINUED, JULY 1535

The Bishop, upon his departure, left serious trouble between the Syndics and his officers, concerning whom the Syndics had requested action be taken. Some claimed this was especially necessary because the persons who exercised the episcopal offices were prejudiced against the people of the city. Mean-while, the trial of the prisoners took shape with suit being brought by the fisc of the Bishop. The syndics pronounced the sentence freeing the prisoners. The fisc then appealed the sentence. To this the Syndics responded: Because we have no superior, we do not admit your appeal. One of the prisoners, who confessed having struck Werli when he was fleeing down a back alley, was decapitated on August 6.

THE BISHOP MOVES HIS COURT FROM GENEVA TO GEX, SEPTEMBER 1534

At the end of September, the Bishop had his Episcopal Council, his Vicar and his officers moved from Geneva to Gex. The Syndics tried by prohibi-tions to prevent this, but the officers proceeded to Gex against the Syndics' will and were thus regarded as rebels. The Syndics protested to the Chapter of Geneva which they asked to elect new officers for the city and not to consent to the aforementioned undertaking. Finally, on 7 October, they appealed to Rome against the Bishop and his fugitive followers. They wished to show that he broke their liberties and took away their jurisdiction. But such an appeal was not sent, because of the great troubles which followed step by step from that time forth. Already, it was dangerous for Genevans to venture outside the city.

THE SUBURBS OF GENEVA ARE RAZED
FOR DEFENSE, MAY 1535

Already in the preceding year, some individuals from Geneva had advised that the suburbs of the city be destroyed. They estimated that the enemy could use them to surprise the city more easily. As the plan proceeded to execution, many murmured against it. Others, who had houses in these suburbs, opposed the idea in great numbers. However, after all considerations were weighed, it was decided to demolish them, except for the suburb of Saint Gervais which was fortified with ramparts and ditches. The final decree to leave nothing stand was given on 10 May 1535. It was afterwards executed little by little. The monasteries and churches of Saint Victor, Notre Dame de Grace of the Dominicans in the Plainpalais quarter, Saint Légier, and that of the Friars Minor in the city were also razed. The streets of the demolished suburbs measured 6,200 feet.

THE PUBLIC DISPUTATION
ON RELIGION, MAY 1535

Although the Council leaned heavily to the side of the Gospel, it could not adopt the change which many of the citizens requested, because there were still varying opinions. Meanwhile, idolatry and the abuses held sway as always among those who had not yet heard the truth of the Gospel. Among other things, the small children who died were carried to the Convent of Notre Dame de Grace to be resuscitated. At the convent, there were several old matrons who, by clever methods and pretenses, caused a feather which they placed on the mouths of the children to stir. And, by warming the children, they sometimes caused them to perspire or piss. Then they cried: "Miracle, miracle," and had the monks sound the bells. These miracles were judged to be false by the Council which on 11 May 1535 prohibited the monks from further action of this sort. Now, prior to this, Jacques Bernard, the guardian of the Franciscan convent in the Rive quarter and a citizen, who not long beforehand had been called to the knowledge of the Gospel, had presented to the Council five articles or propositions. These he, along with the other preachers, offered to maintain. On 20 May he obtained permission for publication of the propositions and Sunday, 30 May, was assigned as the day of open disputation with all those who wished to support the contrary of the propositions. The articles were printed and notice was sent to the priests and canons of Geneva and of the surrounding places as well as to Grenoble, Lyons and elsewhere, along with a declaration of assurance and safe-conduct for everyone wishing to debate. The disputations were publicly opened in the great auditorium of the convent in the Rive quarter on the designated Sunday. The delegates of the Council, in the company of four secretaries, were present to preserve order. The propositions maintained were, in summary: justification of men by Jesus Christ alone; the government of the Church depends on the Word of God alone; the adoration of a sole God who is sufficiently satisfied by way of atonement for our sins by the unique oblation made one time by Jesus Christ; Christ is the sole mediator between God and man, from which it follows that those who attribute to themselves some power, thinking to justify themselves through their works, are in error; the human and papal traditions which are called ecclesiastical are pernicious; it is idolatry and against God's wishes to adore with honor the Saints and statues; the mass does not contribute to our salvation, nor do prayers for the deceased; the Saints are not our intercessors. The disputations were continued for several days before a large audience. Among those in attendance were two persons who supported the party of the priests. One was named Caroli, a Doctor of the Sorbonne, the other Chappuisi, a citizen of the city and a monk of the convent in the Plainpalais quarter. Both were defeated and confessed to it, following which they have since themselves preached the Gospel.

THE REGULAR CLERGY ARE EJECTED FROM GENEVA
FOLLOWING A PUBLIC DEBATE, JULY-AUGUST 1535

After the disputations of July 1535, the Ministers and many of the citizens asked the Council for a declaration of judgment concerning these public debates. On the other hand, many persons protested that they wished to continue living like their fathers. The Council, which still hoped to avoid dangers and harmful consequences for humanitarian reasons, delayed, hoping to avoid trouble. On 23 July, it prohibited Farel from preaching at the church of the Madeleine, one of the largest parishes. He asked for an audience before the Council of Two Hundred, but he was denied the request. Nonetheless, on 8 August, he preached publicly at the church of Saint Pierre. As a result, he was reprimanded by the Council. On this same day, several citizens and small children entered the aforementioned church and broke the statues. From there, they went to the other churches. For this they too were summoned and reprimanded. However, they maintained that they had acted correctly. Their argument was so persuasive that the Council was unsure if it should chastise them. It did, however, suspend the destruction of that which remained until further and wiser deliberation. At the same time, it ordered a cessation of the mass and had the property of the convents inventoried because of the troubles. This was on 10 August 1535. Two days later, the leaders of the priests, the Vicar and the Canons, were questioned by the

Council with respect to the disputations. They were asked if they had anything more to add. Some of them answered that they were simple men who did not know how to respond, except to say that they were accustomed to living like their fathers. But the Vicar and the Canons said that they did not wish to hear anything more, nor listen to the aforementioned disputations, nor read the summaries of the disputations which had been presented them. Thus many of the clergy left the city, some out of fear of their enemies, others because of their devotion. In order to prevent this, the Council ordered on 13 August that those who wished to leave would have to renounce their right of bourgeoisie and that this would be recorded. Thus, three days later, many of them appeared before the Council and requested permission for three masses each day at the church of La Madeleine. The request was denied. The women known as the Sisters of Saint Clare obtained a place at Annecy. They withdrew to Annecy with their property at the end of August, after having asked the permission of the Council. Around this time, on 28 August, several companies of Peneysans and Savoyards approached Geneva in the vicinity of the pasture land called Eaux-Vives. Fear of these companies caused the alarm to be sounded in the city on that day. However, nothing more developed at that time. On 30 August, the Duke of Savoy prohibited, on pain of death, anyone seven years or older from consorting with the people of Geneva. If anyone from Geneva wished to withdraw to the lands of the Duke, and to live there as his subject, he would be welcomed. Because of these developments, the magistrates of Geneva maintained a more careful watch, for they feared their city would be depopulated. On 18 September, several citizens found a priest in the very act with a whore. On their own authority, they paraded him around the city on an ass and had the whore trail behind him as a lackey. Many similar excesses, under the cloak of the Gospel, greatly scandalized the papists.

THE SECULAR PRIESTS ARE SUSPENDED
FROM FUNCTIONING, OCTOBER 1535

On 15 October, the Syndics and the Council, having once again asked the priests if they wished to say anything more concerning the disputations, prohibited them from administering the sacraments further and from wearing their habits.

THE MUNICIPAL HOSPITAL IS ESTABLISHED,
NOVEMBER 1535

In the midst of these troubles, the Council pursued the reformation which had started. Already on 29 September, the members had advised the establishment of two hospitals in the city. They would be supported from the property of the churches. Because some of the priests refused to relinquish their rights, the entire matter was put before the people in the General Council on Sunday, 14 November 1535. There, it was ordered that there would be a large hospital for the poor in the convent from which the Sisters of Saint Clare had departed. The property of the churches would be used for its operation. And, they elected a *hospitallier** who afterwards in his will made the hospital heir to his property.

GENEVA ASSERTS THE RIGHT TO COIN MONEY, NOVEMBER 1535

The city of Geneva, surrounded by enemies who controlled the countryside, was drained of money as well as provisions of food. Therefore, the magistrates decided to mint the city's own money. This was decreed on 24 November 1535. They agreed among themselves that they could assert their right to coin money. To better establish this right, they searched among the funds of the merchants for old pieces minted with the stamp of the city. Because their ancient motto was *Post tenebras spero lucem* (After darkness hope for light), they had *Post tenebras lux* (After darkness light) put on one side of the coins. They removed *spero*, saying that they had attained light. On the other side of the coins, they put *Deus noster pugnat pro nobis, 1535* (Our God fights for us, 1535). The motto was ordered on 4 December 1535.

THE PRIESTS AND CANONS ARE FORCED TO CONFORM OR BE EJECTED, DECEMBER 1535

From the moment that priests were forbidden to celebrate the mass, they continually complained throughout the city. Many of the citizens, principally those who were responsible for keeping the peace and maintaining the watch, lamented. Thus, by ordinance of the Council, the priests were once again, on 12 and 19 November, summoned to the town hall and called upon to respond to the disputations. Again they were told that if they did not feel themselves capable of a proper response, they would be permitted to have a learned individual of their choice to uphold their cause and to assure that they would be heard. Otherwise, they were enjoined to attend the sermons of the preachers. None of this changed them at all. Finally, on 5 December 1535, those who still had not left were summoned and told that if they did not wish to follow the Word of God, they must leave the city, never to return. Only a

---

*Editor's Note: The *hospitallier*, invariably a layman selected and supervised by the city councils, directed the actual care of the poor in Geneva's General Hospital.

few priests remained in the city and they were pensioned until their death. The Canons also now withdrew to Annecy.

THE RELIGIOUS RELICS OF THE GENEVAN CHURCHES ARE EXPOSED, DECEMBER 1535

In December 1535, when the city was continually besieged, the citizens sought out the idols and relics in the churches in order to leave nothing. Among others, four notable things were found. At the church of Saint Pierre, there was the arm of Saint Antoine upon which the most solemn oaths had been given. They found that it was the parched genital member of a stag. The brain of Saint Pierre, which had been held in great veneration, was found to be a pumice-stone. At the church of Saint Gervais, the priests said that under the main altar were buried Saints Nazarien, Celse and Panthaléon, called the holy bodies. They asked that they be canonized, but this was not done. If one pressed his ear to the monument, he heard beneath it a sound like the indistinct voices of men talking. There was also a hole through which the devout put their rosaries which were then so strongly held that they were not able to pull them out. The secret of all this was that under the altar there were great pots or earthen pipes situated so that they resounded at the least breeze. And, there were hooks cleverly placed below the hole so that the rosaries were held firmly. At the Dominican convent in the Plainpalais quarter, they found a very old picture of a monster. It had seven heads and ten horns and was expelling the popes from its backside. Below the popes, there was a furnace or abyss, filled with bishops, priests, monks and hermits. These four things among others, when made known and manifest, made the papist profession more odious.

GENEVA FORCES ITS COUNTRY DEPENDENCIES TO ADOPT THE REFORMATION, MARCH-APRIL 1536

The magistrates of Geneva already possessed Gaillard, Jussy and Peney. To these, they added Thiez in Faucigny, which was one of the dependencies of Geneva, the lands of the Chapter and of the Priory of Saint Victor, which are on this side of La Cluse, Céligny, the dependencies of Peney, Bellerive, and Gaillard. They received the fidelity oaths of the parishioners of these towns and provided them with castellans and judges on 21 February. They had the castles of Peney and Gaillard, which were a great nuisance, demolished. From the beginning, the Genevans exhorted these people to adopt the reformation such as they had in their city. Many who balked at this were induced by constraint. The priests of these lands were called before the Council on the following 3 April. The Council addressed them as it had previously addressed the priests of Geneva and they were exhorted by Farel in the presence of Furbity* who was still in prison and yet approved of the entire matter. Some agreed to the demands of the Council. Others pleaded for permission to live as their neighbors and asked for a period of one month in which to respond. They were granted the delay. Meanwhile, all masses and other papal superstitions were abolished. At the end of the month, they agreed to conform like the others. These newly reformed lands did not include those of Thiez. The King of France, beseeched by the Dame de Nemours, required in letters sent on 1 March that Geneva not change the religion of the people of Thiez who, for their part, did not wish to change either. Thus, the people of Geneva, without destroying their idols and attacking their priests, tried to convert them simply through exhortations, but with little luck.

A REFORMED ELEMENTARY SCHOOL IS ESTABLISHED
AT GENEVA, MAY 1536

At Geneva, from the time of the Papistry, there was an elementary school which until now was still not properly reformed. Thus, the people, preparing themselves to continue in the reformed religion, established a new elementary school in the Rive quarter. The new regent, Antoine Saunier, made a profession of the Gospel, and agreed that small children were also to be instructed in scripture. This was decreed on 21 May in the General Council. By unanimous oath with raised hands, the people swore to God that they detested the papal doctrine, masses and all else which appertained thereto. They affirmed that in the future they would live according to His Holy Gospel. In as much as many of the persons who left during the time of war now asked to be received again and promised complete obedience, the Council admitted many of them, but restricted their powers. Since that time, on 18 November 1537, it was ordained in the General Council that those who had been suspected of or indicted in the past troubles and those who had been restricted would never be admitted to office, nor would they have a voice in the General Council.

JOHN CALVIN ARRIVES AT GENEVA, JULY 1536

John Calvin from Noyon in Picardy was passing through Geneva. Farel begged and beseeched him to remain for the edification of the church. He

---

*Editor's Note: Guy Furbity, a Paris Dominican, was appointed Advent preacher at Geneva in 1532. He bitterly denounced the reformers and soon found himself in prison. In January and February 1534, he was worsted in a disputation with Geneva's Protestants. Finally, after two years of imprisonment he was allowed to return to France.

stayed and began to lecture on theology. Since that time, he has become very well known through the richness and grace by which God has built His church through him. The church may well bless the day he was born and Geneva the day he arrived here.

2

Jeanne de Jussie, *Calvinist Germs* or *the Beginning of Heresy in Geneva*

Born of a noble family whose lands lay within the territory controlled by Geneva, Jeanne de Jussie entered the city's Convent of the Poor Clares, also known as the Second Order of Saint Francis. During the crucial years preceding Calvin's arrival, she apparently served as the convent's official writer. Later, after the sisters moved from Geneva to Annecy, she became abbess. Her account, while obviously biased, has importance due to her participation in many of the events described. The work appears to have been largely written in 1535, shortly after her departure from Geneva. It was completed by 1546, but was not published until 1611, at Chambéry in France.

SOURCE: Jeanne de Jussie, *Le levain du calvinisme ou commencement de l'hérésie de Génève*, edited by Ad.-C. Grivel (Geneva: Fick, 1865), translation by Raymond A. Mentzer, Jr., pp. 35-36; 17-18; 70-72; 94; 99-100; 106-7; 116-18; 152-55; 203-8.

THE IMPACT OF THE PROTESTANT REFORMATION ON THE RELIGIOUS ORDERS AT GENEVA

At Geneva where heresy was implanted and held sway, no member of the Church remained unless he discarded his habit. Otherwise, they were pursued and expelled from their own land. And, they suffered greatly. You could easily call these times the era of the persecution of the holy Church. It is very true that the prelates and clergymen of these times did not properly maintain their vows and state. Rather, they dissolutely squandered the property of the Church and took women in lust and adultery. Nearly all of the people were infected with this abominable and detestable sinfulness. Thus, the sinfulness of the world abounded in all sorts of people who incited the ire of God to impose his divine punishment. This He did by means of these false and disloyal satellites of the Devil, masquerading in the form of human beings. The good monks and nuns were persecuted and they partook of the secret judgment of God along with the guilty. But, most assuredly, this was for their own salvation and the multiplication of merit with God.

Many good and devout monasteries were ruined and destroyed, but in spite of this, their residents were not perverted. Rather, they retired to the world, each where he could, in order to continue their holy vocation. Even at Berne, many Dominican nuns returned to their parents and served as chamber maids in order not to renounce their state. Others married. Within the Carthusian Order, the Augustinians, the monks of Saint Bernard, Saint Francis and Saint Dominic, and among all the orders of the world, there were perverted members, except for the nuns of Saint Clare of the reform *Beatae Collettae*. It happens that none have been perverted or inconstant, save a single one who entered religious life not through the good door of right intention, but through a feigned and evil hypocrisy.

THE BERNESE ARMY ENTERS GENEVA
WITH NINETEEN CANNON PIECES, 16 OCTOBER 1530

On Monday around noon, the army entered Geneva. They brought nineteen large artillery pieces, some of which they placed in the Saint Gervais quarter and the remainder in the Plainpalais quarter near a small church called the Oratoire. The soldiers of the Canton of Berne were lodged in the rue de la Rivière and the rue de la Corratterie as far as the Arve bridge. Six companies, all Lutherans, were lodged in the convent of Saint Dominic. The monks were forced to abandon the convent and retire to the city. The church remained closed and no harm was done, except that they burned and broke the statues which were outside and the beautiful ones which were within the convent in the area where the monks preached. Two hundred horses were kept in the cemetery and cloister and they left nothing to eat. A great quantity of men were lodged in the Augustinian convent of Notre Dame de Grace and one hundred and twenty in the convent of Saint Francis. As at the Dominican convent, all the provisions were consumed. Thirty-six horses were kept at the convent of Saint Clare. The soldiers were a heavy expense. They gave all the fodder to their horses, had provisions taken to their friends who were lodged in the city, and burned all of the supplies of wood. The poor sisters gave the soldiers all that they had in order to maintain them and to prevent them from going and stealing from the poor people.

THE LAST VISIT OF THE BISHOP, PIERRE de la BAUME, TO GENEVA, JULY 1533

After this homicide,* these accursed Lutherans did not cease to torment and molest the churches. They sought only to pillage, beat, massacre and kill, so much so that churchmen dared not show themselves unless they were well-armed beneath their long robes. Thus, that which Our Lord said to the Apostles in the twenty-second chapter of Saint Luke came to pass: He who has no sword, sell his coat and buy one.

If the Lords of the Church had not been courageous and magnanimous during these times, these ravaging wolves would have exterminated our holy Church. But God will not permit their accursed enterprise to have its effect.

On the first day of July, the Lord Bishop of Geneva (who had not been in the city for five years) came here to remedy the adversities. The Christians felt a great joy and consolation and the heretics a great contrition, because they knew he brought them no good, but meant to molest them as much as he could.

The day after his arrival, the general procession was commanded and proclaimed. It took place solemnly and with great devotion. Afterwards, the bell was rung to assemble the General Council and the Bourgeois and Citizens assembled before the Church of Saint Pierre. When all the people were assembled, the Lord Bishop and Prelate with his nobility and the Lord Syndics, the Bishop took his place and each of the others silently followed according to rank. The Lord Bailiff of Dole (on behalf of his Lord Master) addressed the people in the manner of a wise and eloquent man. When he finished, the Lord Bishop of Geneva began to speak with a fine, clear voice and in language intelligible to everyone. He first asked if they accepted him as their Prince and Lord. They answered yes. Then, as Prelate, for the discharge of his duty and the salvation of their souls, he exhorted and admonished them devoutly. He urged them to have the fear of God in observing His commandments and obeying as good Christians the holy Church, the bride of Jesus Christ. He also urged them to live together in peace as good citizens, friends and neighbors. He said these things in so humble and devout a fashion that everyone wept and there was not any quarrel or tumult, for which God be praised.

On the fifth day of July, ten of the leaders of the heresy were taken prisoner. Among them was Monsieur de Thoran, a gentleman allied to these men of Geneva. As soon as he was notified, the Very High Lord Philip of Savoy, Count of the Genevois, dispatched a garrison and confiscated all the lands and domains of de Thoran. The Very Excellent Lord the Vicomte confiscated that which adjoined his domain. Thus, the poor perverted individual was deprived of all his property. And, after he was released, he retired to Berne with his allies.

*Editor's Note: Jeanne de Jussie here refers to the killing of Werli, a canon of the Cathedral, in May 1533.

These heretics greatly persecuted the Lord Bishop of Geneva. Several times they tried to slay him and even came to his house at night to assail him. The Bishop, perceiving this danger and his inability to remedy it, left Geneva and retired to his residence of the Tour de May. As a result, all of the Christians were grieved and the prisoners were released.

A SECULAR PRIEST RENOUNCES THE PRIESTHOOD
IN ORDER TO MARRY, 1534

On the feast of Pentecost, Messire Louis Bernard, a secular priest who was a handsome man, an excellent cantor and one of the twelve chaplains of Saint Pierre, attended the sermon of the heretics. Afterwards, he cried out in a loud voice that he wished to join them. Within moments, he cast off his long robe and donned a Spanish cloak. Then, in great joy, all the members of this sect, men, women and children, welcomed him and paid tribute to him. After this, the preacher announced the marriage of Bernard and a young Lutheran widow. The following Tuesday, they were married. The Christians were greatly scandalized by this for he had benefices amounting to two hundred florins and more.

A DOMINICAN DISCARDS HIS HABIT,
MARRIES AND PREACHES IN THE LUTHERAN MANNER,
JULY 1534

On the last Sunday of July, after the bell was rung to assemble the people, a Dominican monk discarded the habit of his order before the multitude and straightaway ascended to the pulpit. Like someone in despair, he began to beg mercy of God and the world. He lamented, saying that in the past he had lived evilly and had greatly deceived the world by preaching pardons and praising the mass, the holy sacraments and the ceremonies of the Church. He now renounced them as vile and worthless objects. He then commenced to vilify the holy Church, the state of religious orders and virginity with words which cannot be written. After this, he preached a heretical sermon. And, following his sermon, he married a woman of ill repute, according to all accounts.

THE PROTESTANT BURIAL CEREMONY
FOR AN APOTHECARY, SEPTEMBER 1534

The following Friday, a Lutheran apothecary died suddenly. His wife was a good Christian and when she saw him close to death, she performed her duty of admonishing him to return to God and to confess. However, he would not listen to her. Thus, he asked and implored of her to have the accursed Farel come. She said that if he came, she would leave the house and would have nothing to do with such company. Thus, the apothecary died. In as much as he died in his error, his father who was a Christian had him cast from his house and carried to the cemetery of the Madeleine in order that his accomplices might do with him as they wished, because he himself would not recognize him as his son. His wife also took no more notice of him than of a dog. The heretics took him, buried him according to their custom and departed.

The small Christian children who had clearly seen how they had buried him said to one another: These people have not sprinkled holy water over their brother. Let us go and give him what he merits to refresh his soul. And, all together they went and pissed on his grave.

THE PREACHING OF FAREL AND VIRET AND THE RESULTING INSULTS TO THE SISTERS, APRIL 1535

In the month of April, the paltry preacher Guillaume Farel and Pierre Viret of Orbe took possession and residence at the convent of Saint Francis in the chamber of the Reverend Father Suffragan. Because they were near the convent of the Poor Sisters of Saint Clare, they made great trouble for them among their adherents, recommending this to their listeners from the pulpit. They said that the sisters were poor blind wanderers in the faith and that for their salvation they must be released from prison and everyone must stone them, because all of this is simply lewdness and hypocrisy. The sisters pretend that they preserve their virginity, something which God has never commanded because it is not possible to preserve it. And, they nourished these sanctimonious Franciscans with good partridges and fat capons in order to sleep with them at night. The Lords of the city must not suffer them, but should expel them from their convent and make all of them marry according to the commandment of God. On other occasions, they said that the sisters divided the city, that they prevented them from converting thy people, because they mocked all that they did, and that the city will never be united in faith until they are expelled from their convent. They said other wicked and dissolute things which one dares not write about the sisters and the monks, to such an extent that the heretics began to persecute the sisters by both words and works.

Because these accursed men occupied the galleries of the city to the right of the garden of the sisters and all day played with their harquebuses and sang shameful songs, the sisters could not enter their garden. They had only to see the sisters and they shouted to them in grossly shameful and injurious words. For this reason, the sisters dared not enter except in groups and with their faces covered. Finally, seeing that they would not respond and acknowledge them, the men began to throw stones in order to murder and wound them.

The stones were thrown so strongly that many of the sisters were hit and, if God had not wrought it, they would have broken their heads open. The sisters were obliged to close the door and to go into the garden for no more than a few necessities. They could not cultivate, plow, pick herbs or do any of the other necessary things. Thus, they experienced a great scarcity of food.

THE PROTESTANTS ENTER THE CONVENT OF
SAINT CLARE, 24 AUGUST 1535

On the feast of Saint Bartholomew the Apostle, great armed companies with all sorts of weapons came very peacefully and knocked at the great door of the convent. The poor monk inquired as to who they were and what they wanted. An accursed murderer feigned his words, pronouncing himself a friend of the order: Open for me without fear, for I am one of your friends and come for the consolation of the sisters.

With good intentions, the poor monk opened the door and immediately the entire multitude was inside. The poor monk remained paralyzed while they hurried through the convent to the rooms of the friars, breaking and destroying all that they found, statues, books, and breviaries. They did worse than they had done in any other church. Because the statues had been removed and hidden, they threatened to place the poor monk in manacles if he did not show them the statues. The poor friar, fearing them, opened the room where all were hidden. Like enraged wolves, they began to break these statues, especially a marvelously beautiful blessed crucifix and a statue of Our Lady, with large axes and hammers. They did not leave one statue intact.

Then, with a ladder, they mounted a large crucifix which was of marvelous beauty and pitiful to behold. Here they made a great effort and tumult with large axes, truncheons and all sorts of instruments. There were more than fifty men around it, but they could not damage it or take it down. As a result, they were greatly troubled.

The poor sisters, hearing this tumult, were saddened and filled with fear. They retired to the church and asked the aid and help of Our Lord. These iniquitous devils, after having vented their spite outside, went right to the *Tournoir* gate of the sisters. Pierre Vandelly and Baudichon, captain of this plague-ridden company, took to striking it with the large iron bars which they carried in order to break all the locks. With large axes, they demolished the *Tournoir* gate which was beautiful and strongly built of good walnut. The mother doorkeeper, seeing the fallen and scattered *Tournoir* gate, went to bar the door and propped her back against it to prevent opening it. However, one of them struck the door so strongly with his axe that it went through the door and he nearly put the axe into the back of the doorkeeper. However, God the Creator removed her miraculously and she left the gate-room with her companions. They closed the door of the room. It was double and strongly built. And, they closed another door which was after the first. All were strong and well-constructed. They then ran into the church and, all united together, the healthy and the ill, they looked at one another huddled in the middle of the choir. They were prostrate on the ground with their faces covered awaiting, in pitiful sorrow and incomparable sighs, corporal death or the peril of their souls. And, they were without hope or human consolation. Meanwhile, the iniquitous men had soon broken the *Tournoir* gate and the three doors and gained entry. They scattered throughout the convent in large troops. There were more than one hundred and fifty of them, all frantic to engage in evil. They did not neglect the statues or the devotional benches in the dormitory, infirmary, or any other place within the convent. Upon coming to the choir where the poor sisters were, they began to hack the beautiful statues, before their eyes, causing the chips to fly down and strike the sisters. Upon viewing this, the poor brave sisters, commencing with the Mother Vicar, began to cry ceaselessly for mercy, together and in a loud voice. The cry was so loud and frightful that it was heard for a great distance. The entire convent resounded with the violence in which these iniquitous men were engaged. They were very much astonished and also shouted in a loud voice against the sisters, saying: By the great devil, be quiet. But the Mother Vicar responded: We will cry to our blessed God until we have His help and grace. But you who perform diabolical works, by whose authority do you perform such violence? Are not the Lord Syndics and Governors here? We beg of them reason and justice and ask that they tell us who moved you to torment us unreasonably. Many were dumbfounded by this, but others like ravaging wolves did not cease to devour all which they found to be devotional. They continued to hack the beautiful walnut benches and chairs of the sisters. Nor did they leave intact the lectern and the book which was on it. I believe that never has there been such great insolence, vituperation and profligacy. And, never was there such pitiful crying and lamentations as that of the poor sisters. Many of them fainted with anxiety and lost the power to speak.

THE DEPARTURE OF THE SISTERS OF SAINT CLARE
FROM GENEVA, 30 AUGUST 1535

... the Mother Vicar went on her knees before the Syndics, saying: Lords, we have decided to leave in silence, without saying a word to anyone. Please give a strict command to everyone that none dare to speak to, touch or approach us, regardless of their status or position or their intention, in order to prevent the tumult which could result.

Certainly, Mother Vicar, answered the Syndic, you give very good counsel and it will be done accordingly. Have no doubts, for we will accompany you with the municipal guard which numbers about three hundred well-armed men. And, I myself am going to issue the prohibition. He then commanded upon pain of immediate decapitation with no allowance for mercy that no one say a word, either good or bad, at the departure of the Poor Sisters of Saint Clare. Upon hearing this, the good creatures nearly fainted with pity and sorrow. And, many respectable people secretly left the city, not to return again, in order to preserve their holy Faith. They said to one another: Alas! The city of Geneva today loses all of its good and all of its light. It will not be good to remain there. The Syndic returned and gave them permission to leave. He wished them to leave the convent by the *Tournoir* gate which the heretics had destroyed, but the sisters could not look upon the insolence which they had performed around the church to all the remembrances of God, of His Mother, and of the saints. Thus, Mother Vicar said: Lords, permit us to leave by the gate of the Convent. They agreed to this. When all were assembled, the door was opened. Many of the sisters nearly fainted with fear, but Mother Vicar took courage and said: My sisters, make the sign of the cross and keep Our Lord in your hearts. Have good faith and loyalty.

Then, she took her sister, Sister Catherine, who, carrying a small cane in her hand, was the most ill and was as weak as she was wondrous. She had Sister Cecile, the nurse, support her. Thus, the first sisters left with great courage. After them came Mother Abbess who was extremely debilitated by old age, sorrow, and illness. A strong sister supported her beneath her arms. Then she took Sister Jeanne de Jussie by the hand and gave her to Mother Doorkeeper, Sister Guillaume de Villette, saying: Take her Sister Guillaume. I place your niece in your hands. My Mother Abbess and I have protected her until now. Protect her well and keep her safe for us.

At these words, the poor Mother Doorkeeper took her closely by the arm and said: Mother Vicar, be assured that I will protect her as carefully as myself and will not abandon her in life or in death. Sister Collette was given to Sister Françoise, the strongest of the company. Sister Guillaume de la Frasse was given to her good aunt Sister Jeannette. Consequently, they went very religiously, orderly and quietly, two by two, holding hands, with their faces covered. This was very good, because, with an air of apparent indifference, they left amid a great crowd and tumult of people. It was a pitiful thing to watch and to hear the groans and sobs which were uttered.

It was an admirable, miraculous and dignified moment, long to be remembered for divine praise and greater certainty of the benevolence and mercifulness of God who never deserts those who serve Him with a true heart and who trust in His benevolence, because the accursed heretics were so greatly changed, illuminated and moved to pity that they no longer desired the damnation of the sisters. Thus, they became their escorts and protected them from the other heretical enemies.

In their departure, the poor sisters did not have their parents or any friendly creature or comfort except God alone and a poor monk named Friar Nicolas des Arnaux who was still so ill that he could not support himself. Nevertheless, he gathered the courage to accompany the sisters and to watch over whatever might happen to them. It was very pitiful to see them alone among the enemies of God and the holy Faith and among those who prior to this had everywhere procured their damnation. The Syndic, seeing many who had difficulty walking, had them led by strong men in order to aid and support them. They were flanked on the other side by the Syndic, the Lieutenant, Baptisard, and Pecollet who subtly watched over the sisters in order that no harm came to them, for he alone of all their company was secretly a good Christian. In front and on each side, there were three hundred well-armed archers, the guard of the Syndics. This was fortunate, because when the accursed children of the city, who had already been ordered to pillage and violate the sisters the following night, heard of their departure, they hastily assembled, some five hundred in number, and went to the rue Saint Antoine through which the sisters passed. They planned to pull away and detain the young sisters. Thus, they placed themselves in front of the sisters and one of them came up to the poor simple-hearted sister whom Mother Vicar was protecting in order that she did not separate from the group. He whispered in her ear: Sister Jacquemine, come here with me. I will treat you as my sister. Mother Vicar responded: Ha! Accursed boy, you are a liar. She cried: Lord Syndic, consider how badly you are obeyed. Move these young boys out of the way. With these words, she stopped firmly. The Syndic, seeing this band of accursed brats, was by the divine will greatly irritated. In a furious and horrible voice, he swore on the blood of Christ, saying: If there is a man who moves, he will be immediately decapitated without mercy on that very spot. He said to the archers: Noble companions, be fearless in the performance of your duty if there is need. Thus, by the divine will, they were scared and they moved away, withdrawing their fangs. From afar, they watched the sisters who continued walking, justifiably trembling with fear. When the sisters reached the Arve bridge which marked the end of the franchise of the city, everyone stopped. Some cried mockingly, as to Our Lord: Where is the great nobility to receive them? Where are the tents and canopies to protect them from the rain? Others derisively pretended to weep, saying: Alas Geneva, who will protect you? You are losing your light. Still others cried to God: The mice have left the nest and are going into the fields like poor strays. But the good people sobbed bitterly and even the Syndic, when he saw the departure, was moved to such pity that he sobbed loudly and wept bitterly as did his entire company. He took the sisters in order, put them on the bridge, took leave and said: Well, goodby dear ladies, certainly your departure displeases me. And, he said to himself like another Caiphas: Ah! Geneva, at this moment you lose all goodness and light. When all were on the bridge, he clapped his hands, saying: It is all concluded. There is no further remedy and no further discussion.

The sisters were on the bridge all alone, not knowing where to turn. No one from the city dared to cross, because the land beyond the bridge belonged to the Lord of Savoy and they did not doubt that he might have men waiting in ambush to massacre them. Nonetheless, observing that many of the poor elderly and sick sisters could not proceed, the magistrates gave permission to six or eight persons from the city to conduct the sisters across the bridge. They did this voluntarily, as much out of pity as to see who would help and guide the sisters.

3

The Reformation Ordinance of 1536

In the Spring of 1536, both the Small Council, which had responsibility for routine matters, and the Council of Two Hundred decided to adopt the Reformation. Guillaume Farel urged that the measure also be approved by the General Council, the assembly of all Genevan citizens which met for annual elections and when very important matters affecting the entire community were to be decided. Thus, on Sunday, 21 May 1536, the Small Council and the Two Hundred had the citizens assemble in the cathedral. By unanimous decision, the community voted to live by the Word of God and to establish a school for their children.

SOURCE: *Les sources du droit du canton de Genève,* published by Emile Rivoire and Victor van Berchem, II, 312-313 in *Les sources du droit suisse,* XXIIe partie (Aarau: Sauerländer, 1927-35), translation by Raymond A. Mentzer, Jr.

RESOLUTION TO LIVE ACCORDING
TO THE EVANGELICAL LAW

The General Council, 21 May 1536

The General Council in closed session

Pursuant to the resolution of the Small Council, the General Council was assembled by the sound of the bell and the trumpet as is customary. And by the motion of his Lordship Claude Savoye, first Syndic, the decree of the Small Council and of the Council of Two Hundred concerning the mode of living was proposed. And after this, by another motion, it was asked, that if there was anyone who could and would say something against the word and doctrine which is preached to us in this city, that he speak. The motion was, namely, if all wish to live according to the Gospel and the Word of God as has been preached and is preached to us since the abolition of the mass, without longing for or wishing any more masses, statues, idols or other papal abuses whatever they be. Upon which, without opposition and in agreement, it was generally decreed, concluded with the raising of hands in the air, and promised and vowed to God that: We wish to live in this holy evangelical law and Word of God, as it is announced to us, wishing to renounce all masses and other ceremonies and papal abuses, statues and idols, and all to which these things may pertain, to live in union and obedience to justice.

THE SCHOOLS

The General Council, 21 May 1536

At this session was also proposed the provision concerning the schools, upon which it was resolved by a unanimous vote that the city endeavor to have a learned man to effect this and that he be paid enough so that he may nourish himself and instruct the poor without asking any fees of them, and also, that everyone be required to send his children to the school and have them learn. And, all the students and teachers are required to reside in the great school where the rector and his assistant instructors, *bacheliers*, will be.

4

The Ecclesiastical Ordinances of 1541

When John Calvin returned to Geneva in 1541, after three years of exile in Strasbourg, he insisted upon a formal, written organization for his church. The city's magistrates agreed to his request and the famous Ecclesiastical Ordinances were prepared under Calvin's personal supervision. Although modified several times by the Genevan councils, they remained the basic statement of the city's ecclesiastical polity. The ordinances are, in essence, an explanation of the four orders of Calvin's church: pastors, doctors or teachers, elders, and deacons. While some portions have the appearance of being incomplete and hastily composed, the ordinances quickly became an important model for other Calvinist churches as the movement spread beyond its Genevan base.

SOURCE: *Registres de la Compagnie des Pasteurs et Professeurs de Genève, au temps de Calvin,* I, 1546-1553, edited by Jean-François Bergier (Geneva: Droz, 1964), pp. 1-3 and 6-8, translation by Raymond A. Mentzer, Jr. Also available in an English translation, *The Register of the Company of Pastors of Geneva in the Time of Calvin,* edited and translated by Philip E. Hughes (Grand Rapids, Mich.: Eerdmans, 1966), pp. 35-38 and 40-44.

*

In the name of the Almighty God, we the Syndics, the Small and Great Council, assembled with our people at the sound of the trumpet and the great bell, in accordance with our ancient customs, having considered that it is a thing worthy of commendation above all else that the doctrine of the holy Gospel of Our Lord be properly preserved in its purity and the Christian Church duly maintained, that the young be faithfully instructed for the future, and the hospital maintained in good order for the sustenance of the poor. This cannot be accomplished unless there is a certain rule and manner of living by which each estate understands the duty of its office. For this reason, it has seemed advisable to us that the spiritual government such as Our Lord has demonstrated and instituted by His Word be written down in good form that it may be established and observed among us. Thus, we have ordained and established in our city and territory the observation and maintenance of the ecclesiastical polity which follows, since we see that it is taken from the Gospel of Jesus Christ.

First, there are four orders of offices which Our Lord has instituted for the government of His Church, namely: the pastors, secondly, the doctors, then the elders, otherwise called those delegated by the Seigneury, and, fourthly, the deacons.

If, then, we wish to have the Church well ordered and maintain it in its entirety, we must observe this form of government.

CONCERNING THE DUTY OF THE PASTORS

With regard to the pastors, whom Scripture also sometimes calls supervisors, elders, and ministers, their office is to announce the Word of God for the purpose of instructing, admonishing, exhorting and reproving, both in public and in private, to administer the sacraments, and to exercise fraternal correction with the elders or delegates.

Now, lest there be confusion within the Church, none should enter into this office without a vocation, concerning which three things must be considered: first, the examination, which is the principal consideration; next, to whom it appertains to institute the ministers; and thirdly, what ceremony or mode of action is best followed in inducting them into the office.

CONCERNING THE EXAMINATION OF THE PASTORS

The examination consists of two parts, the first of which concerns doctrine, namely whether he who is to be ordained possesses a good and sound knowledge of Scripture, and then, whether he is competent and capable of communicating it to the people in an edifying manner.

Moreover, in order to avoid all danger that he who is to be received might hold some erroneous belief, it will be best for him to affirm his reception of and adherence to the doctrine approved by the Church. To determine whether he is fit to teach, it will be necessary to proceed by way of interrogations and by hearing him privately discuss the doctrine of the Lord.

The second part concerns his life, namely, whether he is of good morals and always conducts himself without reproach. The rule of procedure which will be observed is very amply demonstrated by Saint Paul.

TO WHOM IT APPERTAINS TO INSTITUTE THE PASTORS

First, the ministers elect he who is to be placed in the office, having made the choice known to the Seigneury. He is then presented to the Council. And, if he is found worthy, the Council shall receive and welcome him in a manner which it deems expedient, giving him its approval in order to present him to the people in the act of preaching, so that he is received by common consent of the company of the faithful. If he was found to be unworthy and shown to be such by legitimate proof, it shall be necessary to proceed to a new election to select another.

As for the manner of inducting him, since the ceremonies of former times have been transformed into numerous superstitions due to the infirmity of the times, it will be enough that one of the ministers make a declaration explaining the office to which the candidate is being ordained, and then, that prayers and orisons be offered so that the Lord grant him the grace to execute his office.

Following his election, he is to be sworn in by the Seigneury. There shall be a written form of the oath appropriate to that which is required of a minister, and the form employed is to be inserted.

Then, just as it is necessary to examine the ministers when one wishes to elect them, so also it is necessary to have proper discipline to maintain them in their duty.

ESTABLISHMENT OF A DAY OF THE WEEK
FOR ASSEMBLING

First, in order that all the ministers maintain doctrinal purity and concord among themselves, it will be expedient that they meet together on one particular day of the week for a conference on the Scriptures. No one shall be exempt without a legitimate excuse. If anyone is negligent with respect to this, he is to be admonished.

As for those who preach in the dependent villages of the Seigneury, our city's ministers should exhort them to attend whenever they are able. Absence for an entire month, however, is to be treated as gross negligence, except in the case of illness or other legitimate hindrance . . . .

CONCERNING THE SECOND ORDER
WHICH WE HAVE CALLED THE DOCTORS

The proper office of the doctors is to instruct the faithful in sound doctrine so that the purity of the Gospel is not corrupted either by ignorance or by erroneous belief. However, as things are arranged today, we understand by this title the aids and instruments for preserving the doctrine of God and for insuring that the Church is not desolated through a scarcity of pastors and ministers. Thus, to use a more intelligible word, we shall call it the order of the schools. The degree nearest to the ministry and most closely associated with the government of the Church is the lectureship in theology which rightly includes both the Old and New Testament.

THE ESTABLISHMENT OF A "COLLÈGE"

However, since it is possible to profit from such lessons only if first instructed in languages and the humanities, and since also there is need to raise up the seed for the future so that the Church is not left a desert to our children, a *collège* must be established in order to instruct them and to prepare them for the ministry as well as for the civil government.

First of all, a place, suitable for giving lessons as well as for housing the children and others who will wish to profit, must be assigned. There should be a learned and knowledgeable man in charge of both the house and the lectures and he should also be able to instruct. He should be engaged and hired on the condition that he have under his charge lecturers both in languages and in logic, if possible. And, there should be assistants, *bacheliers,* to teach the small children. All of this we wish and order to be accomplished.

All those who will be there are subject to ecclesiastical discipline like the ministers.

There is to be no other school in the city for the small children, except that the girls shall have their own separate school as has been the case in the past.

No one is to be appointed unless he has been approved by the ministers, after first having notified the Seigneury, and then in turn he is to be presented to the Council with their recommendation, as a safeguard against abuses. Moreover, the examination should be conducted in the presence of two members of the Small Council.

CONCERNING THE THIRD ORDER WHICH IS THAT OF THE ELDERS, WHO ARE SAID TO BE DELEGATED OR DEPUTIZED BY THE SEIGNEURY TO THE CONSISTORY

Their office is to watch over the life of each person, to admonish amicably those whom they see to be at fault and leading a disorderly life, and when necessary to report them to the Company, which will be authorized to administer fraternal correction and to do so in association with the others.

As this church is now organized, it will be desirable to elect two from the Small Council, four from the Council of Sixty, and six from the Council of Two Hundred. They should be men of virtuous lives, honest, without reproach and beyond all suspicion, above all God-fearing and of good spiritual prudence. And, they should be elected in such a manner that there will be some of them in each quarter of the city, so that their eyes will be everywhere; all of which we wish to be done.

CONCERNING THE MANNER OF THEIR ELECTION

In a similar way, we have determined that the manner of their election shall be as follows: the Small Council shall consider the nomination of the most suitable and competent men who can be found, and, in order to accomplish this, it shall summon the ministers for the purpose of consulting with them. Then, they shall present those whom they have considered to the Council of Two Hundred which will approve them. If, after being approved, they find them worthy, they shall take a special oath whose form shall be established as is that for the ministers. And, at the end of a year after their election by the Council, they will present themselves to the Seigneury so that it may consider whether to retain or replace them, although it would not be expedient to replace them frequently without cause if they are discharging their duties faithfully.

THE FOURTH ORDER OF ECCLESIASTICAL GOVERNMENT, NAMELY THE DEACONS

There were always two kinds of deacons in the early Church. Some were delegated to receive, dispense and preserve the property of the poor, daily alms as well as possessions, revenues, and pensions. Others were to care for and remember the sick and administer the food for the poor, a custom which we still retain at present. And, in order to avoid confusion, since we have both *procureurs* and *hospitalliers*, one of the four *procureurs* of the hospital shall be the receiver of all its property. And, he shall be sufficiently paid in order to better exercise his office.

THE "PROCUREURS" OF THE HOSPITAL

The number of four *procureurs* remains as it has been. One shall be in charge of the income as has been stated, in order that the provisions are dispensed on a more regular and punctual basis and that those who wish to contribute some charitable gift are better assured that the property will not be used other than according to their intention. And, if the revenue is insufficient or if an unusual necessity should arise, the Seigneury shall consider an adjustment according to the needs of the situation.

The election of both the *procureurs* and the *hospitalliers* shall be conducted as for the elders and the delegates to the Consistory. And, in electing them, the rule which Saint Paul sets down for deacons (I Timothy 3, Titus 1) shall be followed.

Concerning the office and authority of the *procureurs*, we confirm the articles which we have already prescribed for them, provided that in matters of urgency and where delay would be dangerous, especially when there is no great difficulty and no question of great expense, they should not be compelled to meet. Rather, one or two, in the absence of the others, may prescribe whatever will be reasonable.

CONCERNING THE HOSPITAL

It will be necessary to watch diligently that the communal hospital is well maintained. It is as much for the sick as for the elderly who cannot work, and, in addition, for widows, orphaned children and other poor persons. However, the latter are to be placed in a wing of the building apart and separate from the others.

The care of the poor who are dispersed throughout the city shall be realized there, according as the *procureurs* shall order it.

Beside the hospital for travellers which should be maintained, there should be some separate hospitality for those who are seen to be worthy of special charity. And for this purpose, there shall be a room designated for receiving those whom the *procureurs* shall recommend; and it shall be reserved for this use.

Besides all of this, there is the instruction that the families of the *hospitalliers* are managed honorably and according to God's commands, seeing that they have to govern a house dedicated to God.

The ministers and delegates or elders together with one of the Lord Syndics are, for their part, to take care to inquire whether there is any fault or deficiency of conduct, in order to beseech and admonish the Seigneury to correct it. And, for this purpose, every three months several of their company together with the *procureurs* shall visit and inspect the hospital to determine whether everything is well regulated.

It will also be necessary both for the poor of the hospital and for those of the city who do not have the means to help themselves, that there be a physician and a surgeon employed by the city. While practicing in the city, they shall be charged with the care of the hospital and the visitation of other poor persons.

As for the plague hospital, it is to be completely separate, especially in the event that this city is visited by this scourge of God.

Moreover, in order to prevent begging which is contrary to proper polity, it will be necessary for the Seigneury to appoint several of its officers and to station them at the exits of the churches to remove from these places those who might resist. And, if there are offenders or recalcitrant individuals, they are to bring them to one of the Lord Syndics. Similarly, at other times, the *dizainiers** are to watch that the prohibition against begging is properly observed.

*Editor's Note: The *dizainiers* were municipal officials in charge of the districts into which Geneva was divided.

5

François de Bonivard,
On the Ecclesiastical Polity of Geneva

The second son of a noble family of Savoy, François de Bonivard (1493-1570) was selected for an ecclesiastical career. In 1514, he succeeded his uncle as the prior of the Benedictine monastery of Saint Victor in Geneva. Shortly thereafter, he was ordained and appointed a canon of the city's cathedral. Bonivard soon became embroiled in Geneva's dispute with Savoy and in 1530 was captured and imprisoned by the Duke of Savoy. When finally released in 1536, he returned to a newly reformed Geneva. Faced with the loss of the revenues of Saint Victor and the refusal of the magistrates to provide adequate compensation, Bonivard retired to Lausanne. Then in 1543, Geneva asked him to write its official history and he returned there permanently. He was never an enthusiastic follower of Calvin and on more than one occasion was called before the Consistory for immoral behavior. His literary production was substantial. In addition to the commissioned *Chronicles of Geneva*, he composed a number of treatises on such diverse topics as the degrees of nobility, language, the origin of sin, the different types of Reformations, and true and false miracles. His *Opinion and Estimate of the Old and New Polity of Geneva*, from which the following selection is taken, is an essay of this type.

SOURCE: François de Bonivard, *Advis et devis de l'ancienne et nouvelle police de Gèneve* (Geneva; Fick, 1865), pp. 153-158, translation by Raymond A. Mentzer, Jr.

You have first seen the civil polity during the time of the troubles.* However, there still was no ecclesiastical polity for censuring morals, even though there were many respectable men who desired it and who endeavored to establish it in Geneva as it was in the other evangelical cities of the land of the [Swiss] Leagues. But certain muddled individuals, fearing correction, did

---

*Editor's Note: Described by Bonivard in the first part of this book.

not wish to consent to it, alleging in order to support their reasons that this would renew a papacy, giving such jurisdiction to the ministers as the Pope and the bishops formerly had. For these reasons, one could not set up the ecclesiastical authority and its Senate until after the death of Jean Philippe,** shepherd of the muddled individuals, because then the sheep were led astray. It was set up as follows: Of the four Syndics, one would always be Judge and Head of the Consistory with the assistance of certain laymen, some from the Small Council and others from the Council of Two Hundred, and the Preachers. They would be censors of morals before a case was referred to the temporal court for correction. Marital cases were handled in the same way. All was as in the court of the bishops previously. But in order that the ministers, notwithstanding their lay assistants, did not assume excessive authority, the aforementioned Consistorial Senate did not have the power to judge, with or without litigants. Thus, it could only admonish, if they were minor cases. It did not have the power to administer an oath. If there were important cases, they were referred to the Small Council for judgment on the following Monday, as the Consistory met on Thursday. They had jurisdiction to excommunicate, barring from Communion those who were obstinate in their sin. Whereas the papists, before receiving their sacrament, are compelled to confess their sins completely and orally to a priest, the members of the Consistory do not wait until one presents himself to them. They know each one has assigned to him by the public an area which is divided into various *dizaines*.*** They go, accompanied by the *dizainiers*, from house to house, asking all members of the household the reason of their faith. After this, if they sense that there is some fault, either in general or in particular, within the house, they admonish them to recognize their errors in order that they not receive the Sacrament unworthily. Such was the authority of the Consistory formerly; it recently received the authority to administer oaths.

The schools, for which provision has also been made within recent memory, are a part of the Church and spiritual assembly too. When the *Collège* of Lausanne was dissolved as the result of some difference that its faculty had with the magistrates of Berne, the majority of the Doctors withdrew to Geneva. Viewing this, the magistrates of Geneva, which without them already had many learned men, did not wish to receive the grace of God in vain. Rather, they set up a *collège* of very ample and magnificent appearance and very precious content. There are professors not only of the Holy Scriptures, but also of the literary languages and the liberal arts. Gold and silver are not spared to pay them such that they are content, notwithstanding the great charges which the magistrates have to fortify the city and provide other equipment to defend it in the event of war which they are always awaiting. In addition, to keep themselves always in the good grace of

**Editor's Note: Jean Philippe, a former magistrate of Geneva, was the leader of the "artichokes," a faction opposed to Guillaume Farel. In 1540, he was condemned and executed for having mortally wounded one of Farel's supporters.

***Editor's Note: Geneva was divided into *dizaines* for purposes of defense. The *dizainiers* were city officials in charge of these municipal districts.

God, their Sovereign Captain, they have endeavored and endeavor to clean and purge the city and its dependent jurisdiction of all filth and sordidness which they find displeasing to Him, as you will see by the edicts, laws and statutes which they have enacted and by their execution to the letter. Moreover, you must know that the magistrates of Geneva have not done as many others who have deprived the thief of his plunder, then have not rendered it to the robbed, but kept it for themselves. Knowing that the property of the Church appertains to such uses as we have heretofore mentioned, they have also applied it to the Ministers and Schools as we have stated above, which is for the service of truth. Next, it is applied to the service of charity, which is to nourish the poor, those unable to earn their living by the sweat of their brow as God commands; it also supports those who are strong and robust enough to nourish themselves but cannot feed their wives and children, because they have too great a number. Thus, aid is distributed to them in proportion to the burden which they have over and above that which they can support with their own hands. From the beginning of the abolition of papism, they took possession of the Convent of the Women of Saint Clare, chasing the sisters from it. Of it they made a hospital where are nourished not only the poor of the city, but those of all places from which their churches receive revenues. Transients have a free meal in the evening if they arrive here and breakfast the morning before they depart. The hospital has its own minister and its school-master and school-mistress for the boys and girls. The school-mistress teaches the girls to read and write and to sew, but instructs them principally in the knowledge of God, to love and fear Him. She has them make a declaration of their faith by question and answer, which is called the catechism. This is taught to the children from the moment they know how to speak in order to have them suckle the spiritual Christ with the corporal milk, so that there is no small child who does not render the reason of his faith as well as a Doctor of the Sorbonne renders his. Not only do the teachers of the hospital do this, but also the fathers and mothers of the entire city. When the boys have outgrown their childhood, they are placed in apprenticeship of the trade for which each of them is known to be suitable. The girls are also placed as maids here and there in order to earn their marriage dowry. And, if they cannot, the marriage dowry is provided from the revenue of the hospital. The hospital has its physician, its surgeon, and its apothecary. And, lest the *hospitallier* commit fraud, a Syndic and others, both from the Small Council and the Council of Two Hundred, are appointed as superintendents to whom he must render account. It is true that what remains of the property of the Church is employed for public uses, particularly for the fortification of the city and other defenses of war, which is only, after all, for the Church. Because, if the papal ecclesiastics wished to return to the thievery from which they were removed and they were not resisted, the poor would necessarily die of famine as previously. Thus the places where the affairs of piety govern have been delegated by good rules. There is the hospital where charity is exercised and close by the hospital, the *collège* where truth is taught.

Considering thus all the aforementioned things, do you know of any reason why Geneva ought not now call itself the true Church of God which has received and protected with all its power that which God first announced by His Prophets and later by His Son and the Apostles? Are they not other than formerly the Jews? I speak not of the papal Church, but still what primitive Church has been better reformed? And also, the Heavenly Father has certainly watched over Geneva, opposing all enterprises which have been raised against it, by means neither understood nor expected by men. Thus, as the pharaohs persecuted Him, so He had them plunge into the sea and drown. Let us persevere thus in His service and pray to Him that He give us assurance to persevere.

STEVEN OZMENT

Luther and the Late Middle Ages: The Formation of Reformation Thought

T HE SUCCESS OF THE REFORMATION in Germany was conditioned by a number of favorable external circumstances. There was the invention of the printing press, which made it possible to produce one-third of a million copies of Luther's tracts between 1517 and 1520. There was the consolidation of power by independence-minded German princes. There were the decades of economic grievances against Rome, which Luther brought together so effectively in his *Address to the Christian Nobility of the German Nation* (1520), and which the German estates itemized for the Emperor Charles V at the Diet of Worms in 1521. And there were the protracted wars with France and the relentless Western expansion of the Turks, which kept Charles preoccupied outside the Empire from 1521 to 1547 and unable to enforce his own edicts against the Lutherans.

The intellectual climate was no less receptive to change. Since the late thirteenth century the medieval church had been on the defensive not only against the emerging nation-states of Europe,

The following abbreviations are used in the footnotes to this essay:

WA = Martin Luther, Werke. Kritische Gesamtausgabe (Weimar, 1883ff).

WA Br = Martin Luther, Werke, Kritische Gesamtausgabe. Briefwechsel (Weimar, 1930ff).

WA Tr = Martin Luther, Werke. Kritische Gesamtausgabe. Tischreden (Weimar, 1912ff)

ARG = Archiv für Reformationsgeschichte

ZKG = Zeitschrift für Kirchengeschichte

but also against movements within her own scholastic and spiritual traditions. In the universities highly divisive conflicts between the followers of Thomas Aquinas and Duns Scotus (the *via antiqua*) and members of the school of William of Ockham (the *via moderna*) existed until the eve of the Reformation. (Jodocus Trutfetter, Luther's Ockhamist teacher in Erfurt, tried in vain for two years to promote the *via moderna* in Wittenberg before he was forced back to Erfurt in 1510 by the Wittenberg Thomist, Martin Mellerstadt.) The Great Schism (1378-1417) occasioned critical reflection on the nature of the church, culminating in the conciliar theory of ecclesiastical authority, the heavy artillery of reformers in the late Middle Ages. The late medieval heart was no less in ferment. From the mystical women's movements of the thirteenth century to the *Devotio moderna* of the fifteenth, lay piety burgeoned, and often with a fervor and idealism requiring papal warning.

In this period humanists opened the literary doors to the values and ideals of antiquity. It was in fact a young generation of humanists, fresh from combat with Cologne scholastics in the famous Reuchlin affair, that rushed to Luther's side when the ninety-five theses against indulgences became public. Civic and reform-minded humanists were Luther's first identifiable group of supporters. Although many humanists quickly backed away from Luther after his revolutionary intent became clear, humanist scholarship, satire, and eloquence greatly aided the inchoate reform—so much so that it has been argued that without humanism there would have been no Reformation.[1] When Luther and Philip Melanchthon revised the curriculum for the University of Wittenberg in the years 1518 to 1521, they did so with humanist *eloquentia* and practicality very much in mind.

But for all the intellectual conditions of the Reformation, none was more crucial to its success than the new Wittenberg theology. Luther, to be sure, was not the first to criticize Aristotle and indulgences; theological speculation and ecclesiastical malpractice had certainly been censured before. In this regard Luther himself found many "forerunners," as his often boundless praise of such diverse thinkers as Gregory of Rimini, Jan Hus, Jean Gerson, and Wessel Gansfort indicated. Still, after the external circumstances

---

[1] Bernd Moeller, "Der deutsche Humanismus und die Anfänge der Reformation," *ZKG* 70 (1959), pp. 46-61; 59. Cf. Lewis W. Spitz, "Humanism in the Reformation" in *Renaissance Studies in Honor of Hans Baron*, edited by Anthony Molho and J. A. Tedeschi (Dekalb: Northern Illinois University Press, 1971), pp. 634-62.

of the Reformation have been recited and forerunners enumerated, it remains the case that the Reformation owed its inception uniquely to the young "Augustine of Wittenberg," who so skillfully combined insight into the popular religious mind with mastery of the schoolmen. This is as true when one looks forward into the sixteenth century as it is when one looks back to the late Middle Ages. Although after 1525 the Reformation became as much a protest against Luther by divided Protestants as a protest against Rome by diverse Protestant groups, it was still from Luther that the Reformation received its constructive impulse and a program that could insure religious alternatives. As distinctive in origin and development as the reforms of Zwingli, Bucer, and Calvin were, they are not readily conceivable without the successful work of Luther.

It is customary to begin Luther's intellectual biography as a Reformer with the indulgence controversy of 1517. It was, as every schoolboy knows, Luther's protest of the sale of indulgences by the Dominican John Tetzel in the archbishopric of Mainz in that year that launched the Reformation movement. Some have argued that the ninety-five theses were in fact a rather mild protest, hardly the expression of a radically new theology that need have issued in the division of Christendom. Luther simply requested that the traditional teaching on indulgences be observed and the obvious malpractice of men like Tetzel stopped.[2] Had this petition fallen on open ears, it is argued, All Saints' Day might have remained a day of Catholic celebration only. This view goes on to stress Luther's insistence that he never intended to start a new church, only to reform the old. It was the intransigence of his superiors in the matter of indulgences that forced new, extreme countermeasures. It gave the spur to the formation of Reformation theology, with its fateful consequences. According to this interpretation, the Reformation began, as it were, accidentally, the result of a misunderstanding which might have been avoided by patience on Luther's part and a will to reform on the side of his superiors.

Over against this evaluation, it is important to bear in mind that Luther "posted" his theses against indulgences as one who had in his religious thinking, if not in his daily habits, broken

---

[2]Cf. Erwin Iserloh, *The Theses Were Not Posted* pp. 28-64; Jared Wicks, *Man Yearning for Grace* pp. 216-64; John M. Todd, *Reformation* (New York: Doubleday, 1971), pp. 144-57; and Ernest G. Schwiebert, "New Groups and Ideas at the University of Wittenberg," *ARG* 49 (1958), pp. 60-78.

decisively with late medieval theology. He had earlier (2 February 1517) criticized indulgences for creating false security and detracting from the sufficiency of Christ's redemption; "credere in Christum"—belief in Christ—was the surest "indulgence."[3] Luther was unquestionably sincere when he insisted that he was no revolutionary—no reformer at that time ever thought otherwise. And the ninety-five theses were certainly destined to have consequences Luther and his colleagues in Wittenberg did not foresee at the time of their issuance. It was a time for caution; Luther, for example, feared that the theses would be interpreted as a Saxon thrust at Brandenburg, inasmuch as Frederick the Wise, for political reasons, had at this time forbidden the St. Peter's indulgence, launched in rival Brandenburg, to be preached in Saxony. Still, despite his understandable hesitance in 1517 and the initially limited circulation of the ninety-five theses, the theses against indulgences were the first practical expression of a countervailing religious ideology. It is revealing that a scant six months after their issuance (9 May 1518), Luther could answer the criticism of his old teacher Jodocus Trutfetter with the words: "I believe absolutely that it is impossible to reform the church until, from the foundation up, canons, decretals, and scholastic theology, philosophy, and logic, as we now have them, are eradicated and other studies put in their place."[4]

Indulgences were a commentary not only on the pretensions of popes, but also on the genuine anxiety of the people.[5] Indulgences were not accidental to medieval theology. They were in fact a consistent expression of a common medieval belief that men could and indeed must, without detracting from God's grace and glory, contribute significantly, even decisively, to their salvation. Opposition to indulgences was just as logical a practical consequence of inchoate Reformation thought, which put aside the *necessity* as well as the possibility of man's contributing to his salvation. It is true that the ninety-five theses were the first halting steps of a new historical movement. But they were also the conclusion of a new assessment of man's nature and destiny. If, historically, they were a new beginning, ideologically, they were the end-product of a long period of thought. The Reformation was one of those rare

---

[3] "Omnis Scriptura sonare videtur unicum verbum de indulgentiis quod est credere in Christum." *WA* 4, p. 636.28-30.

[4] *WA Br* I, p. 170.

[5] R. W. Southern, *Western Society and the Church in the Middle Ages*, pp. 136-43.

happy instances for the historian where thought and deed seem to have combined perfectly—so much so that it may be argued that the Reformation began in 1517, not because each side understood the other too little, but because both sides understood the situation too well.

I

Formally defined, an indulgence is the remission of a temporal penalty imposed upon one for sins which have been forgiven only as far as guilt is concerned. Indulgences function within the sacrament of penance, in particular in regard to the last step of the sacrament, the "works of satisfaction." The sacrament of penance normally embraces four stages: attrition or contrition of the heart; confession to the priest; absolution by the priest; and the imposition on the penitent of works by which satisfaction for the transgression can be made. The first two steps, contrition and confession, overcome the subjective guilt one feels for the sins committed. And priestly absolution complements this subjective release by removing the objective guilt one bears in the eyes of God.

Although subjective and objective guilt are overcome, there remains a penalty for the transgression which must be borne if the injured parties are to receive full and just satisfaction. In priestly absolution the eternal penalty—that penalty God justly imposes for the sin committed—is transformed into a temporal penalty, a present punishment which can be borne in the performance of certain works prescribed by the priest. In the final stage of the sacrament the priest applies temporal penalties commensurate with the transgression; for example, prayers, fasting, good works, retreats, or pilgrimages. If these penalties are not worked off in this life, they must be worked off in purgatory.

It is at the point of the works of satisfaction that indulgences come into play. One can, by a monetary contribution (the good work of alms-giving), receive satisfaction which covers the penalties imposed by the priest. In the late Middle Ages such satisfactions or letters of indulgence were issued on the basis of a declared treasury of merit, an infinite reservoir of good works which the church controlled. This treasury was officially established by Pope Clement VI (1342-1352) in his bull *Unigenitus* (1343). Clement pointed out that Christ could have redeemed mankind with a single drop of blood, yet chose to do so with a "copious flood." That this superabundant effusion not be rendered idle and useless, it was given over to the church as a treasure to be dispensed at the discretion of the pope. Pope Sixtus IV (1471-1484) extended indulgences to purgatory in 1476.[6]

When John Tetzel preached the St. Peter's indulgence on the borders of Saxony, he took full advantage of the emotional potential of the extension of indulgences to loved ones in purgatory. With graphic detail he directed his audience to the voices of their wailing dead parents in purgatory, who pleaded for the release which a few alms could readily purchase.[7]

Tetzel, a veteran indulgence hawker in the employ of the papacy and the House of Fugger, was brought to Germany by Albrecht of Hohenzollern (1490-1545), the archbishop of Mainz. Albrecht also held sees in Magdeburg and Halberstadt. He paid handsomely for the papal dispensation to hold three ecclesiastical offices, as well as for the *pallium*, or the symbol of episcopal authority. To fund his investments Albrecht borrowed heavily from the House of Fugger, incurring a debt in excess of 26,000 ducats.[8] The papacy, the House of Fugger, and Albrecht himself had a large financial stake in the success of the St. Peter's indulgence in the dioceses controlled by Albrecht. The indulgence was in fact to be preached in his territories for a period of eight years, with half of the proceeds going to Rome and half to Albrecht and his creditors. Tetzel was hired because he was a professional. The abuses notwithstanding, it was a sterling example of the "ecclesio-commercial complex" of the late Middle Ages.

On or shortly before the day he posted his theses against indulgences, Luther sent a copy of the theses, together with a letter of explanation, to Archbishop Albrecht. The letter dealt with his grave concern about the effects of the indulgence on the people. Many, Luther pointed out, actually believed that the purchase of an indulgence assured salvation and even released souls from purgatory. He expressed shock that such "fables" had been associated with indulgences; they contradicted not only canon law, but also Holy Scripture which, Luther protested, commanded that the gospel, not indulgences, be preached. Ominously Luther signaled his "fear that something will happen soon" if the situation remained uncorrected.[9]

---

[6] Henricus Denzinger and Adolfus Schönmetzer, *Enchiridion symbolorum*, 32nd edition (Freiburg i.B., 1963), Nrs. 1025-1027; 1398.

[7] Hans J. Hillerbrand, *The Reformation*, pp. 41f.

[8] Iserloh, *op. cit.*, p. 19.

[9] Hillerbrand, *op. cit.*, pp. 50f.

II

The indulgence controversy of 1517 must of course remain a decisive event when one chronicles the Reformation. Although the nailing of ninety-five theses to the door of Castle Church in Wittenberg is very probably a legend created by Philip Melanchthon, it is clear that Luther and his fellow reformers were agreed that this date—All Saints' Day, 1517—should stand in history as the beginning of the Reformation. As central as this event was, however, it should not obscure the important formative years of Reformation thought. Luther's theses against indulgences were the first fruits of a young man's reflection on the Bible and critical dialogue with medieval theology over a period of at least eight years.

We are accustomed to think of the young Luther as a melancholy, often panic-stricken monk, excessively preoccupied with his own salvation. So conditioned are we by popular and polemical literature to accept this portrait that we tend to forget that he was a well-trained and highly disciplined theologian. On 19 October 1512, he received his Doctor's beret, and he never forgot the mandate it gave him. If he was, by his own confession, a monk's monk, he was even more, as his works and colleagues attest, a scholar's scholar. It was in fact not as a pious monk but as a learned theologian that Luther broke with Rome; the Reformation began with argument.

Rather than take a clue from those reports that exaggerate and even romanticize the ordeals of the young man Luther, a more accurate picture may be found in those recollections that describe the young scholastic Luther. One such recollection is the following. According to the recorder, Anton Lauterbach, Luther, in a cheerful mood, was conversing one evening with Nicholas von Amsdorf about "the works of that prior age when the most talented men were preoccupied with vain studies." Luther reminisced thus:

Those sophistical pursuits are completely behind us now. The men of our age would look upon them as barbarous. [Duns] Scotus, Bonaventure, Gabriel [Biel], and Thomas [Aquinas], having lived when the papacy was flourishing, were the most idle of men. With so much time on their hands, they naturally gave free rein to their fantasy. Gabriel wrote a book on the canon of the Mass. In my youth I considered it the best of books. When I read it my heart flowered. For me no authority on the Bible could match Gabriel. In fact, I still have his books, which I have annotated. Scotus wrote best on Book III of the *Sentences*. And Ockham, zealous for method, was the most ingenious of all. He was devoted to expanding and amplifying a topic endlessly. Thomas was the most loquacious because he had been seduced by metaphysics. But now God has wondrously led us away from all that. It is now over twenty years since he snatched me, still unknowing, away.[10]

Between 1509-10, when he wrote his commentary on Peter Lombard's *Sentences*, and the indulgence controversy of 1517, Luther covered an enormous amount of ground. He read deeply in Aristotle's *Physics*, *Metaphysics*, and *Ethics*. In addition to his sermons and letters, he wrote lectures on the Psalms (1513-15) and on Paul's letters to the Romans (1515-16) and to the Galatians (1516-17). Preparation for these lectures required extensive reading in medieval Biblical commentaries. Luther, further, annotated works by Augustine (1509-10), the *Psalterium Quincuplex* of Faber Stapulensis (1513), the sermons of Johannes Tauler (1515-16), and Gabriel Biel's *Exposition of the Canon of the Mass* and *Sentences* commentary (1517). He edited a portion of an anonymous mystical treatise, which he entitled the *German Theology* (1516). In 1518 he found and published the full manuscript of this work, calling it a precedent for the new "Wittenberg theology."

In addition, Luther was in daily contact with the written and oral traditions of his own Order of the Hermits of St. Augustine. In the library of his Order were volumes that protested the inordinate influence of Aristotle on theology. Echoes of the fourteenth-century works of the Augustinians Simon Fidati of Cascia and Hugolin of Orvieto have been noted in Luther's irreverent remarks on Aristotle in his maiden theological work, the commentary on Lombard's *Sentences*.[11] Luther was later to praise two members of his Order most highly: Gregory of Rimini and Johannes Staupitz. He looked on Gregory, who was perhaps the best Augustine scholar of the late Middle Ages, as the sole scholastic who was completely clean on the Pelagian* issue. And

---

[10] *Luthers Werke in Auswahl* VIII: *Tischreden*, edited by Otto Clemen (Berlin, 1950), Nr. 3722 (1538), pp. 149f.

[11] Adolar Zumkeller, "Die Augustinertheologen Simon Fidati von Cascia und Hugolin von Orvieto und Martin Luthers Kritik an Aristoteles," *ARG* 54 (1963), pp. 15-37.

Pelagianism is a Christian heresy which goes back to a fourth-century British monk, Pelagius. Pelagius felt the low moral state of his contemporaries was only encouraged by St. Augustine's doctrines of sin and predestination. Strongly critical of such teachings, Pelagius minimized the effects of sin on human nature and taught that men were free to initiate their own salvation. St. Augustine wrote at length against Pelagius and his followers. Luther saw himself in the role of Augustine against the "new Pelagians," the late medieval Ockhamists.

STUDY

to Staupitz, his immediate superior and confidant, he even gave credit for the Reformation itself.

As these facts and comments indicate, the young Luther was closely acquainted with the medieval theological traditions in their various exegetical, mystical, and scholastic forms. If Melanchthon can be believed, he was not only an authority on late medieval theology, but had even committed portions of Pierre d'Ailly and Gabriel Biel to memory.[12]   Luther did not enter the indulgence controversy as an innocent, but as a seasoned professional. In fact, his last work prior to the indulgence controversy was a broad attack on the whole of late medieval theology: the *Disputation Against Scholastic Theology* of 4 September 1517. This incisive work joined the classical medieval debates over the nature of religious justification and the extent of man's natural knowledge of God. Because of its proximity to the ninety-five theses, it provides an important gauge of Luther's thought on the eve of the indulgence controversy and a clue to just exactly what was involved in this controversy.

It was a traditional teaching of the medieval church, perhaps best formulated by Thomas Aquinas, that a man who freely performed good works in a state of grace cooperated in the attainment of his salvation. Religious life was organized around this premise. Day-to-day living was in this way taken up into the religious life; good works became a *sine qua non* of saving faith. He who did his moral best within a state of grace received salvation as his just due. In the technical language of the medieval theologian, faith formed by acts of charity (*fides caritate formata*) received eternal life as full or condign merit (*meritum de condigno*). Entrance into the state of grace, it was agreed, was God's exclusive and special gift, not man's achievement, and it was the indispensable foundation for man's moral cooperation. An "infusio gratiae" preceded every meritorious act. The steps to salvation can be summarized thus:

Aquinas

1	2	3
Gratuitous infusion of grace	Moral cooperation: doing the best one can with the aid of grace	Reward of eternal life as a just due

---

[12]Preface to volume II of the 1546 Wittenberg edition of Luther's Latin writings in *Martin Luther's 95 Theses with the Pertinent Documents from the History of the Reformation*, edited by Kurt Aland, p. 43.

In the Franciscan tradition, and especially among that group of theologians known as Ockhamists or late medieval nominalists, a significant adjustment was made in this traditional view. These men were keen on preserving human freedom, even from the salutary causality of a prevenient infusion of grace. If man loved God simply because God moved him to do so by a special internal grace, did he really love God freely? Was not free choice also a measure of a meritorious act? Ockhamists were impressed by the ethical resources of the natural man; God's natural gifts of reason and conscience had obviously not been eradicated by the Fall. Were there not historical examples of pagans who loved country and neighbor above self? Ockhamists were further impressed by Biblical injunctions that seemed clearly to say that it was man's duty to take the initiative for his salvation: "Turn to me and I will turn to you" (Zechariah 1:3); "Draw near to God, and he will draw near to you" (James 4:8); "If you seek me, you will find me" (Luke 11:9).

With such concerns in mind, Ockhamists asked: If God rewards good works done in a state of grace with eternal life as a just due, could He not also be expected to reward good works done in a state of nature with an infusion of grace as an appropriate due? Had God not in fact promised to do precisely that? Ockham and Biel answered these questions in the affirmative: in accordance with God's gracious goodness (*ex liberalitate Dei*), he who does his best in a state of nature will receive grace as a fitting reward (*meritum de congruo*). (See below, pp. 148f.) In summary form:

1	2	3	4
Moral effort: doing the best one can on the basis of natural moral ability	Infusion of grace as an appropriate reward	Moral coopera-tion: doing the best one can with the aid of grace	Reward of eternal life as a just due

Ockham and Biel did not consider this Pelagian; it was a part of the arrangement God himself had freely willed for man's salvation, God's very covenant. Absolutely considered, it was not human activity, either outside or within a state of grace, that determined man's salvation; it was rather God's willingness to value human effort so highly. Ockhamist theologians were convinced, however, that God meant for men to acquire grace as semi-merit within a state of nature and to earn salvation as full merit within a state of grace by doing their moral best. All the subtle and important qualifications notwithstanding, in this theology men could in fact initiate their salvation.[13]

It is this position that Luther assailed in the *Disputation Against Scholastic Theology*: man by nature lacks the freedom of will to do the good which Scotus, Ockham, d'Ailly, and Biel attribute to him. On this score, Luther felt he stood squarely with Augustine against the "new Pelagians" (see especially theses 5-8, 17-20, 28-30). (See below, pp. 151f.)

Luther's arguments in the *Disputation* culminated in a condemnation of Aristotle's *Ethics*: "The whole of Aristotle's *Ethics* is the worst enemy of grace" (thesis 41). He saw Aristotelian moral philosophy at the root of scholastic error. Specifically, he singled out Aristotle's definition of moral virtues as "acquired" virtues. For Aristotle, moral virtues, unlike natural virtues, must be gained by practice and effort; morally, one becomes virtuous by performing virtuous acts. Natural virtues, by contrast, precede their exercise. Men have the power of sight, a natural virtue, before they see; but they cannot "be" righteous until they have repeatedly done good works. According to Aristotle, men are naturally *equipped* to attain moral virtue; but they are not actually virtuous until they have learned to be so by habit.[14] Luther spied in this philosophical position the model for the arguments of the new Pelagians.

It has been argued that Luther at this time was opposed in principle to any theological use of Aristotle; the Bible alone sufficed for the theologian. Opposition to the new Pelagians was accordingly a consequence of opposition to scholastic theology generally. Hence it was not so much specific errors as Aristotelian categories and logic *per se* that he resisted, whether they be employed by Scotists, Ockhamists, or Thomists.[15]

Luther's opposition to Aristotle's infiltration of theology is indeed striking in 1517, especially in correspondence relating to the reform of the University of Wittenberg. This was an important concern he shared with the Erasmians. However, the *Disputation* of 1517 did not focus primarily on the inappropriateness of Aristotelian philosophy, but rather on the Pelagianism to which its theological application led: scholastic error disturbed Luther more

---

[13] Heiko A. Oberman, *The Harvest of Medieval Theology*, pp. 175ff.

[14] Aristotle, *Nichomachean Ethics* 1103a-1103b in *The Basic Works of Aristotle*, edited by Richard McKeon (New York, 1941), pp. 952f.

[15] Leif Grane, "Die Anfänge von Luthers Auseinandersetzung mit dem Thomismus," *Theologische Literaturzeitung* 95 (1970), pp. 242-248.

than scholastic method. As the later conflict with Erasmus confirmed for Luther, criticism of scholasticism did not necessarily ensure release from its errors. In defense of the freedom of the will the prince of the humanists embraced the very Ockhamist position earlier criticized by Luther.[16] Luther's retreat from scholastic theology was not humanist aversion to the inelegant and distracting; it was theological criticism of what he considered to be patently false, whether it was phrased in the categories of Aristotle or in those of the Bible and the Church Fathers.

The criticism of Aristotle at this point in the *Disputation* may also offer a clue to Luther's extension of his arguments to embrace "all scholastics"—not just the four mentioned by name. In the *Disputation* Luther was not conscious of attacking only one school of theology; in his mind he was opposing a position supported by the whole of scholastic theology, whether Scotist, Ockhamist, or Thomist. Did he really mean to attack the traditional as well as the peculiarly Scotist-Ockhamist version of the way to salvation? How could he have considered the former, which so carefully made God's grace paramount, Pelagian?

One possible explanation is the following. The Aristotelian pattern functioned for all scholastics, Thomists as well as Scotists and Ockhamists. Aristotle's definition of moral virtue was as applicable to the movement from a state of grace to eternal life as it was to the movement from a state of nature to a state of grace. In both instances whether in an initial or in a penultimate stage of the Christian's activity, moral effort was considered imperative and meritorious. By doing one's best in a state of nature one earned grace, according to Biel. By doing one's best in a state of grace one earned eternal life, according to all scholastics. The same pattern appeared on two different levels of the religious life. In the final analysis, earning by moral effort salvation as condign merit was only a higher form of earning by moral effort saving grace as semi-merit. To Luther in 1517, the former could very well have appeared to be only a more cautious "Pelagianism." For although good works were now done with the aid of grace, they still remained necessary for one's salvation.

Having said this, it must be added that Luther did appear to be primarily concerned with views peculiar to Ockhamists. Still, it is not necessarily to be inferred from this that he here erroneously identified the whole of scholastic theology with Ockhamism. Till

[16] John B. Payne, *Erasmus*, p. 267, n. 38.

the end of his life he associated "scholastic theology" with "Pelagianism" and the latter especially with the technical terms favored by Ockhamists ("doing the best that is in one" [*facere quod in se est*] and "congruent merit" [*meritum de congruo*]).[17] To the extent that his early writings already distinguish ethical activity and religious justification in principle—in anticipation of the position summarized so eloquently in the treatise *On the Freedom of a Christian* (1520)—the Thomist position squares as well with his definition of scholastic theology as does that of the Ockhamists. They are two sides of the same coin.

Although Ockhamists seem so boldly Pelagian, such was not, as Luther must also have known, the sum total of their teaching. If they glorified the will of man, they also exalted the will of God. For they left little doubt that, when all things were considered, salvation hinged not on man's activity but on God's willingness to accept and value human effort so highly. If this was Pelagianism, it was so by God's express design. It has in fact been argued that Ockhamists inconsistently juxtaposed an Aristotelian concept of man with an Augustinian concept of God.[18] This dual heritage of Ockhamism should be borne in mind when we see Luther force an Augustinian consistency on the issue in the *Disputation*. Luther could very well have found the remedy, as well as the disease, in his patient.

The *Disputation Against Scholastic Theology* scored illicit theological speculation as well as Pelagianism. To Luther, the schoolmen understood the relationship between reason and revelation no better than they understood that between man's will and salvation. He opposed in particular the efforts of Pierre d'Ailly and Robert Holcot to construct a higher "logic of faith" (thesis 46).

D'Ailly and Holcot, although Ockhamists in philosophical outlook, were far from being skeptics and fideists. To be sure, they believed that reason was powerless to penetrate beyond God's revelation. But, once given this revelation, reason could set about analysing it. Among scholastics it was especially the Ockhamists who delighted in speculation on the conditions of revelation, surmising what might have been had God in eternity decided to pursue alternative systems of salvation. Ockham could imagine for example, God's redemption of men by incarnation in a donkey

[17]Cf. *WA* II, p. 401 and *Dokumente zu Luthers Entwicklung (bis 1519)*, edited by Otto Scheel (Tübingen, 1929), Nr. 488, p. 162.

[18]Leif Grane, *Contra Gabrielem: Luthers Auseinandersetzung mit Gabriel Biel in der Disputatio contra Scholasticam Theologiam 1517* (Gyldendal, 1962), p. 217.

rather than in human flesh. Had he so wished, God might even have made hatred rather than love of himself the condition of salvation. Behind such fanciful speculations on what might have been was a desire to demonstrate the reasonableness of what in fact was. Speculation on the absolute power of God was intended to show not only the contingency but also the appropriateness of the system God finally ordained. Despite the infinite possibilities open to him in eternity, God chose in fact to save men through a church, priests, sacraments, infused grace, and good works—all things considered, a fair and sensible arrangement.

It was clear to d'Ailly and Holcot that natural logic was only marginally successful when applied to the articles of faith. Syllogistic or Aristotelian logic—All men are mortal/Socrates is a man/Socrates is mortal—when strictly applied, was no tool for the data of revelation. One could not properly demonstrate in Aristotelian syllogisms that three are one and one is three. D'Ailly and Holcot were nonetheless convinced that reason could be very helpful in clarifying articles of faith, and Aristotelian logic was the model of rationality. One may not be able to demonstrate the truth of the trinity but one could make the trinity an object of systematic rational inquiry and employ logical rules that made sense to faith. The probable arguments of reason were of value; rationality was no enemy of revelation. It has been argued that, in this way, Ockhamists actually maintained the *harmony* of reason and faith.[19]

Luther clearly would have none of this: "In vain does one transcend natural logic to construct a logic of faith" (thesis 46). He saw here only an effort to manipulate revelation with reason, to conform the thoughts of God to the thoughts of men, just as the new Pelagians had also tried to manipulate God's grace with free will and man's natural moral ability. Here, as was also the case in Luther's attack on the new Pelagianism, Aristotle was singled out as being at the root of an effort to rationalize faith out of existence. Hence the (in)famous snort: "The whole of Aristotle is to theology as darkness to light" (thesis 50).

In its context, this statement was a rejection neither of reason nor of Aristotle *per se*; it was rather a plea to keep syllogisms, even of a higher order, and inordinate speculation on the conditions of

---

[19] Bengt Hägglund, *Theologie und Philosophie bei Luther und in der occamistischen Tradition* (Lund, 1955), p. 86. Cf. H. A. Oberman, "Facientibus Quod in se est Deus non Denegat Gratiam: Robert Holcot O.P. and the Beginnings of Luther's Theology" in *The Reformation in Medieval Perspective*, edited by S. E. Ozment, pp. 128-129.

revelation out of the sphere of faith. Where logic applied, Luther argued, one dealt with knowledge and not with faith (thesis 49). As he later put it: the articles of faith are "not against dialectical truth [Aristotelian logic], but rather outside, under, above, below, around, and beyond it (*non quidem contra, sed extra, intra, supra, infra, citra, ultra omnem veritatem dialecticam*)."[20]

Luther's infamous thesis 50 was in truth as much a defense as it was a rejection of Aristotle and philosophy. The latter were censured not *per se*, but because of a theological application which, to Luther's mind, distorted the limits of reason as much as it presumed on the boundaries of revelation. Here Luther may have been more consistently Ockhamist than were d'Ailly and Holcot. The latter in fact appear to be closer to Anselm of Canterbury and Thomas Aquinas on this particular point than to the stricter Ockhamist view. Indeed, the proximity of their arguments to the Thomist definition of theology as a rational science with its own axioms and logic may be another clue to Luther's extension of the *Disputation* to embrace "all scholastics." For all scholastics truly desired a theology which was a rational science on the model of Aristotelian philosophy. Ockhamists no more than Thomists were ready to surrender the medieval ideal of faith seeking understanding (*fides quaerens intellectum*) for the "sheer faith" (*sola fides*) of the Reformation. By contrast, Luther's almost brutal constriction of reason's sphere of competence in theological matters accords with a very strict Aristotelian definition of *scientia*.

When Luther later praised Ockham as his master, it was always in terms of his dialectical skill—as a philosopher—rather than for his theology, which, as we have seen, he considered Pelagian. "Ockham, my teacher, was the greatest of the dialecticians, but he was not skilled in preaching (*sed gratiam non habuit loquendi*)."[21] "Ockham alone understood dialectic, that it involves defining and distinguishing words, but he was no preacher (*non potuit eloqui*)."[22] "Ockham was the most prudent and the most learned [of scholastics], but rhetoric was not among his skills (*sed defuit ei rhetorica*)."[23] It was not from Ockham, the "doctor who is more than subtle," or from any of the scholastic doctors, but from the *ecclesiastici et Biblia*—the Church Fathers and the Bible—that

[20] *WA* 9/32, p. 4.34. cited by Hägglund, *op. cit.*, p. 53.
[21] *WA Tr* II, Nr. 2544a (1532) in Scheel, *op. cit.*, Nr. 223, p. 87.
[22] *WA Tr* I, Nr. 193 (1532) in Scheel, *op. cit.*, Nr. 220, p. 86.
[23] *WA Tr* I, Nr. 338 (1532) in Scheel, *op. cit.*, Nr. 239, p. 94.

Luther learned the "divine arts." Still, he may have learned from Ockham's example, as well as from St. Paul, that in the matter of reason and revelation good fences made good neighbors. For on this issue, as on that of grace and free will, there are resources in the Ockhamist tradition itself to oppose the Ockhamists.

III

Behind Luther's criticism of indulgences lay a break with what to him was a general Pelagian tendency in medieval theology. The ninety-five theses against indulgences did not come out of the blue but were preceded by the *Disputation Against Scholastic Theology*. What lay behind the latter? The assault on the alleged Pelagianism of scholastic theology in the *Disputation* of 1517 also did not arise in a vacuum. It resulted from still more basic departures from fundamental axioms of medieval theology which began to emerge during the course of Luther's lectures on the Psalms and on Romans (1513-16). These shifts can be summarized as Luther's rejection of the common medieval conviction that "likeness" is the *sine qua non* for union with God.

Medieval theology generally was convinced that likeness (*similitudo, conformitas*) was the indispensable condition of saving knowledge and relationship. If man is to be one with God he must be "like" God. Only like can truly know like, only the pure can embrace and be embraced by the pure. This was the underlying rationale of monastic practices: through rigorous physical and intellectual exercises to replace one's own (false) self with a God-like self. It was the precondition of mystical union: "Our becoming like God (*similitudo*)," writes the mystical theologian, Jean Gerson, "is the cause of our union with him."[24] And it was the *raison d'être* of the sacramental system of the church: infused grace qualitatively conforms human to divine being. As indicated by the superiority of the monastic virtues, the distinctions between cleric and layman, and the sacramental rituals, the human and temporal were considered to be secondary to the divine and spiritual. The final goal of monk, mystic, and pilgrim alike was conformity so complete that only God was an object of consciousness, a point where likeness might give way even to identity. Medieval theology was devoted to the proposition that God became man so that men could become God.

---

[24] Jean Gerson, *De Mystica theologia speculativa*, edited by André Combes (Lugano, 1958), *cons.* 41, p. 111.

For the medieval theologian the central religious concept was accordingly *caritas*—love—and not faith. The way of salvation was summarized by the scholastic formula "fides caritate formata," faith formed by love. Saving faith was faith formed by sacramentally infused and ethically active love, a love which transformed the nature of the person, expressed itself in good works, and received eternal life as condign merit. *deserved*

Faith alone, by contrast, was not considered a uniting force. It was an initial intellectual assent to the data of revelation made by one who was still far from pure and godly. *Sola fides,* all agreed, was a *fides informis*, even a *fides mortua*—an unformed, dead faith which even demons could have. Such faith left man on the fringe of the religious life, very much at a distance from God. Love, not faith, was the religious glue.[25] Love was the tie that bound the persons of the trinity, the soul with God, and man with his neighbor. In medieval theology, the Holy Spirit, the reciprocal love of Father and Son, was "uncreated love"; sacramental grace was "created love"; and meritorious works were "acts of love." Because it was the principle of likeness, love was the principle of union.

This same reasoning underlay descriptions of human nature and the efficacy of the sacraments. It was commonly assumed that an inextinguishable spark of goodness existed in man's reason and will (the *synteresis rationis et voluntatis*) a natural point at which every man, even if he did not consciously choose to be so, was conformed to God. Here was a residue of man's prefallen and even precreated purity—now experienced as pangs of conscience and an irrepressible desire for truth and goodness. It was a permanent reminder of man's eternal origin, his original unity with God.

Sacramental grace was described as a "gratia gratum faciens"—a grace which truly "graced" man, purifying the soul and subjecting it to God. Like the *synteresis*, grace was an agent that "likened" man to God in being and in act. In Thomistic terminology, it was an accidental form of the soul, a habit of godly living, the elevation and perfection of human nature. It can be said that medieval theology was firm in the conviction that opposites do not attract.

Young theologian Luther encountered the principle of likeness in exaggerated anthropological form in the sermons of the German mystical theologian John Tauler, a disciple of Meister Eckhart. Luther read closely and annotated these sermons in 1515-16.

[25] S. E. Ozment, "Homo Viator: Luther and Late Medieval Theology" in *The Reformation in Medieval Perspective*, pp. 142-154.

According to Tauler, man was "threefold": a natural man, who lived according to his five senses; a rational man, who acted according to reason and will; and a spiritual man, whom Tauler described in terms of a "pure and simple substance of the soul." The spiritual man lived from the depths of his heart, in accordance with a special mystical structure, the "ground of the soul."

The first time Luther saw this scheme, he referred the reader to the mystical theology of Gerson. Gerson, he pointed out, says the same as Tauler, only he defines the spiritual man with the term "synteresis." The second time Luther confronted Tauler's view of man, however, he set forth his own scheme, which agreed with Tauler save at the point of the spiritual man. Here Luther appealed neither to the "ground of the soul" nor to a "synteresis," but simply wrote: "the spiritual man is one who lives by faith." Religious man is defined by "sheer" and "naked" faith, Luther concluded, not by a special religious structure or agent within his soul that makes him like God.

Even taken alone this substitution of faith would be significant. It reflects in fact a still larger development of the same motif in this early period, especially in Luther's searching lectures on the Psalms. The young Luther was repeatedly impressed by the way the Psalmist was forced to rely only on God's word and promise. He saw connections between the Old Testament faithful and contemporary men of faith, between the synagogue and the church.[26] Both had all their goods in words and promises; each had as much as he believed. As in the marginal comments on Tauler, so in the lectures on the Psalms: faith and hope emerged as the peculiar defining characteristics of the spiritual man and true Christian.

When he read the Psalms, Luther was especially struck by the way union with God was accompanied by the awareness of distance from God; to be "conformed" with God meant to "agree" with God's judgment of all men as sinful. According to the Psalmist, Luther argued, that man was most beautiful to God who confessed his utter dissimilarity from God. "It is not he who considers himself the most lowly of men but he who sees himself as even the most vile who is most beautiful to God." In this sense, "unlikeness" was the unitive principle; confession of sin justified both God (in His words) and man. The young Luther was quite carried away by this correlation and devoted the bulk of his

---

[26] James S. Preus, *From Shadow to Promise*, pp. 212ff.

commentary on Psalm 50 to it, replete with a highly imaginative diagram of the matter. (See below, p. 134.) Men who remained sinful in themselves could still be one with God!

There are, to be sure, parallel themes in medieval spirituality, and one must not too hastily read the mature Reformer into the young doctor of Scripture.[27] Still, the young Luther gave the traditional themes a distinctive, forward-looking twist. The conformity that conditioned salvation was executed by faith and hope, not by love.[28] The key ingredient in this faith was the ability of the believer to accept God's judgment of him as sinful—unlike and opposed to God. The religiously righteous man was one who believed that God was truthful when He pronounced men sinful and nonetheless pledged their salvation.

Already in Luther's first lectures on the Psalms, the religious problem emerged as one of trust and belief and not one of individual moral transformation. Or, put another way, the "transformation" now at issue was from a state of doubt and uncertainty to a state of trust and belief in words and promises which lacked immediate verification. The basic question became not whether one was inwardly and outwardly righteous, but whether God was truthful in his judgment of human nature and destiny, whether, despite all evidence to the contrary, life was meaningful. The heart of the matter was not whether man, in himself, was "like" God, but whether God would keep his promise to save those who were always, in themselves, unworthy. It was not so much an individual question of personal salvation as it was an objective assessment of the nature of man and God.

What did this have to do with the *Disputation Against Scholastic Theology* and the ninety-five theses against indulgences? I would submit that the break with the *synteresis* anthropology and the *caritas* soteriology of the Middle Ages in this early period was the foundation of the decisive events of 1517. Luther had earlier accepted the *synteresis* anthropology uncritically, although never in an extravagant form; for him, it was a traditional antidote to Manichaeism.* He in fact preached a sermon on it in December

---

[27] Cf. Wicks, *op. cit.*

[28] Cf. Reinhard Schwarz, *Fides, Spes und Caritas beim jungen Luther* (Berlin, 1962).

Manichaeism is a Christian heresy which goes back to the teaching of a Persian, Mani, the author of a syncretistic dualist religion. Mani taught that the created world was a sphere of total darkness, an evil prison from which man's eternal spirit must be progressively liberated. By contrast, it is orthodox Christian teaching that the material world, although sinful and fallen, was still created good. The doctrine of the spark of the soul (*synteresis*) points to the persistence of this created goodness even in fallen man.

1514. (See below, pp. 136 ff.) By the time of his lectures on Romans, however, he considered this anthropological concept to be the root of Pelagianism and traced the "monstrosities" of what he called the "pig-theologians" (ostensibly the Ockhamists) to it. (See below, p. 147.) On the eve of the *Disputation Against Scholastic Theology*, he censured Biel's "foolish assumptions" about the power of man's will and reason as the very foundation of his errors about man's salvation. (See below, pp. 149f.) The "new Pelagians" erred in their assessment of human activity because they erred in their evaluation of man's natural abilities. They thought man could do God-like works because they believed he was really God-like. Luther's constriction of the *synteresis* concept was theologically the first step in his rejection of the Pelagianism of Ockhamist theology. The same faith that replaced the *synteresis* in the marginals on Tauler also supplanted good works in subsequent writings against scholastic theology: in nature and in act, the spiritual man lived by "faith alone." Human nature and activity were "secularized." After 1516, the *facere quod in se est* was mentioned only critically and the term *synteresis* passed out of Luther's theological vocabulary. Whereas medieval theology was devoted to the proposition that God became man so that men could become God, Reformation theology would insist that God became man so that men would remain men.

From his Biblical studies and theological investigations the young Luther concluded that to be righteous in faith and hope meant to base salvation on a promise, to trust in a word, and not to look for religious import in oneself, one's good deeds, or one's ecclesiastical purchases. That was the theological matrix out of which theses against indulgences were issued and without which the Reformation, at least in the form we know it today, would not have occurred.

The new theology had great appeal to men of all stations. It offered a realistic assessment of the human condition, confirming the experiences of sixteenth century social engineers as well as those of the man on the street.[29] But more significantly, it let men get on with day-to-day living, confident about the ultimate matters. Simple faith in Christ settled once and for all the problems of sin, death, and the Devil. Preoccupation with one's motives and final destiny was not only unnecessary, it was even

---

[29] Cf. Gerald Strauss, "Protestant Dogma and City Government: The Case of Nuremberg," *Past and Present* 36 (1967), pp. 38-58, and Bernd Moeller, *Reichsstadt und Reformation* (Gütersloh, 1962).

irreligious, a certain sign of a lack of trust in God's word. In the bondage of the will lay a new freedom; with the removal of the possibility of earning one's salvation came also the denial of the necessity of doing so. The Reformation answered medieval man's religious crisis by making life less religious than it had been. But if this was a new freedom it was also a new responsibility. Now one must be a responsible citizen, a servant to his neighbor, not in order to insure salvation, but simply because one was "frei aus Glauben," free to do so by the security of his faith.

FOR FURTHER READING

Aland, Kurt, ed. *Martin Luther's 95 Theses with the Pertinent Documents from the History of the Reformation.* St. Louis: Concordia, 1967.

Ebeling, Gerhard. *Luther: An Introduction to His Thought.* Philadelphia: Fortress, 1970.

Hillerbrand, Hans J. *The Reformation: A Narrative History Related by Contemporary Observers and Participants.* New York: Harper, 1964.

Iserloh, Erwin. *The Theses Were Not Posted: Luther Between Reform and Reformation.* Boston: Beacon Press, 1968.

Oberman, Heiko A. *The Harvest of Medieval Theology*, rev. ed. Grand Rapids, Mich.: Eerdmans, 1968.

Ozment, Steven E., ed. *The Reformation in Medieval Perspective.* Chicago: Quadrangle, 1971.

Ozment, Steven E. *Mysticism and Dissent: Religious Ideology and Social Protest in the 16th Century.* New Haven: Yale University Press, 1973.

Payne, John B. *Erasmus: His Theology of the Sacraments.* Richmond, Va.: John Knox, 1970.

Preus, James S. *From Shadow to Promise: Old Testament Interpretation from Augustine to Young Luther.* Cambridge, Mass.: Harvard University Press, 1969.

Southern, R.W. *Western Society and the Church in the Middle Ages.* Harmondsworth, Middlesex: Penguin Books, 1970.

Trinkaus, Charles. *In Our Image and Likeness: Humanity and Divinity in Italian Humanist Thought.* 2 vols. Chicago: University of Chicago Press, 1970.

Trinkaus, Charles, and Oberman, H. A., eds. *The Pursuit of Holiness in the Late Middle Ages and Renaissance.* Leiden: Brill, 1974.

Wicks, Jared. *Man Yearning for Grace: Luther's Early Spiritual Teaching.* Washington, D.C.: Corpus, 1968.

THE ESSAYIST'S SOURCES

I. The Changing Assessment of Human Nature

1

The Scholia to Psalm 50(51):6
(Spring, 1514)

The first selection in this section, Luther's exposition of Psalm 50(51):6,* shows the young Luther at his most imaginative and, over against the medieval exegetical tradition, innovative. The exegesis of this one verse occupies the bulk of the scholia—a most inordinate preoccupation in comparison with previous interpretations of this psalm. It is a revealing commentary that the words, "Against you only have I sinned," struck such a responsive chord in the young Luther.

In his interlinear gloss on this verse, which was part of the preparation for the scholia, Luther associated the confession of sin with original rather than with actual sin. In the medieval sacrament of penance original sin was considered to have been removed by baptism; hence, confession of sin always involved sins consciously committed. A medieval theologian would have been puzzled by Luther's modification of the content of traditional theological vocabulary. Luther's novelty on this point, however, is indicative less of egregious misunderstanding than of a very profound belief in human sinfulness.

Parallels with Ockhamism are to be noted both in Luther's appeal to God's covenant and in the strong tendency to make confession of sin not only logically prior to religious justification but also a condition for it. On the other hand, Luther describes the just man as one who considers himself "always sinful"; simultaneity, rather than a cause-effect sequence, seems in the end to characterize the relation between confession and justification. Luther is also struck by the way union with God goes

---

*All Biblical references are to the *Vulgate* as quoted by Luther. The *Revised Standard Version* psalm number, where different, is shown in parentheses.

together with distance from God. The man who confesses, "Against you only have I sinned," is actually conformed to God's word and one with God.

The student of the later Luther will see here forward-looking thoughts, surely in transition from the *synteresis* anthropology and *caritas* soteriology of medieval theology, and pointing to the distinctive Lutheran doctrines of salvation by faith alone (*sola fides*) and description of the faithful as simultaneously righteous and sinful (*simul iustus et peccator*). Still, the new is very much in the mold of the old at this point in Luther's development.

SOURCE: *Dictata super Psalterium, Martin Luther, Werke. Kritische Gesamtausgabe* (Weimar, 1883ff.), Vol. III, pp. 287-92.

This psalm is the most popular and surely the most difficult to interpret, especially in verse 6 ["Against you only have I sinned and done evil in your sight; so that you may be justified in your words and prevail when you are judged"], where we find almost as many different expositions as expositors. Therefore, we want to follow the [interpretation of the] Apostle [Paul], who proves in Romans 3[:4] that every man is a liar and sinner, while God alone is true and righteous. This refers of course to those who have not yet been justified and united with God. Therefore, the Apostle says: "Let God be true and every man a liar, as it is written: 'So that you may be justified in your words and overcome when you are judged.'" And he adds what some consider to be a corollary: "But if our iniquity commends the righteousness of God [what shall we say?]" This would seem to follow from verse 6: "Against you have I sinned . . . so that you may be justified"—as if God could be righteous only if we first sinned! But let us pursue the matter with the following propositions:

1. All men are in sins and do in fact sin before God, that is, they are truly sinners.

2. God has made this manifest through the prophets and finally proved it through the passion of Christ; for God made Christ suffer and die because of the sins of men.

3. God is not justified in himself, but in his words and in us.

4. We become sinners when we acknowledge ourselves to be such, for such we are before God.

From these propositions it follows that he who is not a sinner (i.e., does not confess his sin) obviously wants to condemn God in his words, which declare us sinners. And he further denies that Christ died for the sins [of men]. Hence, he judges God and tries to make him a liar. But he will not be successful, for God has prevailed. The Jews tried this [unsuccessfully], and there are those who still do so today.

There are many statements in the gospel and by the Apostle which seem to induce us to sin, when, in truth, the intent is only that we confess and acknowledge ourselves to be sinners. The psalmist says: "Against you only have I sinned," thereby making God righteous and truthful in his words which declared us sinners. And so God prevails [in his words] over those who had falsely judged him [by denying they were sinners].

When he says, "Against you only have I sinned," the justifications possible through the law are excluded. His meaning is: "I do not confess sins against the sacred rites of the law, for such are external sins and can be taken away by the law. Rather I confess those sins which no sacrifices, washings, or rites of the law can remove. Therefore, I have sinned against you only, because the sins I confess are true sins, not the shadows of sin. For [as verse 8 says] 'Behold, you have loved truth.'" Hence the preceding verse [5: "For I know my iniquity and my sin is always accusing me"] expresses the nature of the sin the psalmist knows, viz. sin which is not figurative or capable of removal through the blood of goats. So to confess one's sins is to justify God and let him prevail. This still today offends the Jews, who want to remove sins by animal sacrifices, thinking they have only figurative sins. Hence, these are opposites:

To deny and refuse to confess ⟷ To justify God
        that one is sinful
To justify oneself before God ⟷ To glorify God

God is justified only by one who accuses, damns, and judges himself. "The righteous man first accuses himself" [Prov. 18:17]; he pronounces damnation and judgment upon himself. Hence, he justifies God and lets him overcome and prevail. Conversely, the man who is impious and prideful first excuses and defends himself; he justifies himself and becomes his own savior. That is why he says he needs no God to save him. He sits in judgment on God's words and concludes that God is unrighteous, a liar, and a fraud. But God, not he, will conquer and prevail.

If, by this point, one still does not understand that no man is righteous before God, that God alone is justified, the psalm states the matter more sharply: "Behold, I was conceived in iniquities" [50:7]. Hence, it is true that I am a sinner and have sinned so that God alone may be glorified in righteousness; for we are all sinners. Indeed, it is true. Therefore, because we are unrighteous and unworthy before God, whatever we are able to do is nothing in his presence. Indeed, even the faith and grace by which we are today made righteous would have no justifying power had God not made a covenant. Precisely for this reason are we saved: because God has made a testament and covenant with us to the effect that "whosoever believes and is baptised will be saved" [Mark 16:16]. In this covenant, God is true and faithful and keeps his promise. Therefore, it is true that we are always sinful before God so that, obviously, he may be the one who justifies in the covenant and testament which he has contracted with us. That is why the Hebrew text reads literally: "Against you only have I sinned; therefore, you will justify in your word," i.e., covenant. Hence, he who sins not and confesses no sin is not justified by God in his covenant: for "he who does not believe, etc." [Mark 16:16]; for that reason God cannot [justify] him.

The psalmist says "against you [God] only" in order to exclude those legal sins from which one could be cleansed through the law (as e.g. touching the dead, bodily pollutions, and the like). Such sins pertain to the law and are against Moses rather than God. When the psalmist here says, "I have sinned," he obviously means true and spiritual sin, like that described in Psalm 18 [19:13]: "Cleanse me from my secret sins." This is the "judgment" which "loves the honor of the king" [Psalm 98(99):4] and loves the Lord: to accuse and judge oneself. When this happens God is justified in his words. As Psalm 144 [145:17] says: "The Lord is righteous in his words," namely, in those words which declare all men sinners.

The psalmist goes on to say: "that you [God] may be justified." Such happens in those men who judge rather than justify themselves; God is thereby declared just, and they in turn are justified by him. But he says, "that you may be justified," rather than, "that you may be made truthful," because he speaks here directly against the Jews, who, as Romans 3 makes clear, were not, or at least should not have been, unaware that all men are sinful. But, having believed that they could justify themselves by their own righteous works, they made God unrighteous. As if God deals unjustly with them when he denies that they can justify themselves! To the gentiles, however, he is true and just.

"So that you [God] may overcome," namely, in evil and incredulous men who judge God when they should be judging themselves. Instead of saying, "Against you have I sinned," such men maintain that they have not sinned. And so they necessarily condemn God by justifying themselves. It is of such men that Proverbs 30[:20] speaks when it refers to that "race of men who wipe their mouths and say, 'We have done no wrong.' " These two things necessarily go together, He who justifies himself condemns God, who, throughout the Scriptures and especially in Psalm 13 [14:3], as the Apostle points out [Rom. 3:10], declares him to be a sinner. And, conversely, he who judges and confesses his sin, justifies and renders God truthful, for he says the very same thing about himself that God does. Hence, he is conformed to God, and he is true and just like the God with whom he agrees. He is one with God because they say the same thing. God says what is true and just, and he says what is true and just. Therefore, he, with God, is true and just.

The others, however, fight with God for the truth. God calls them impious, and they in turn deny it. Either they or God must be lying, for both judge and condemn the other. But it is not possible for God to lie. Hence, the psalmist: "that you (God) may overcome when you are judged," namely "in your words," for God is not judged and justified in himself.

From this the difference between judgment and justification is clear:

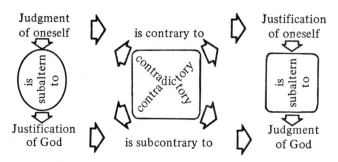

To these let us now apply the logical rules which govern opposed propositions.

1. Everyone who accuses himself justifies God, but the contrary, everyone who justifies God judges himself, is not true; for one who is impious can glorify God, as demonic persons do.

2. Everyone who justifies himself condemns God, but the contrary, everyone who condemns God justifies himself, is not true; for the damned judge God, and still they do not justify themselves.

3. No one who justifies himself justifies God; but the contrary is certainly true: anyone who justifies God justifies himself.

All of this is said in the preceding psalm [49(50):23]: "He who makes praise his sacrifice will honor me, etc." And Job [15:15; 25:5] says: "Even the heavens are unclean in his presence"; "Before him the stars are impure and the moon pale," i.e. the saints are not saintly in his presence. Hence Isaiah 40[:17]: "Before him all nations are regarded as nothing, empty and hollow." Saints confess themselves to be the most unclean of men, saying, "Against you only have I sinned . . . so that you may be justified." That is why one brilliant star [the Apostle Paul] said: "Jesus Christ came to save sinners, and I am foremost among them" [I Tim. 1:15]. Behold how that star, which shone with such brightness among men, is impure before God. This is where that saying originated: "Marvelous is God in his saints" [Ps. 67(68):36]. For it is true: He who is most beautiful to God is the basest of men in his own eyes and, vice versa, he who is most unsightly to himself is most beautiful to God. He who is most pleased with himself is most vile to God. And why? Because God says, "He who makes confession his sacrifice will honor me" [Ps. 49(50):23]. There is no ornament or vestment of the church more excellent than the garb of confession; nothing is more fitting to the church. Hence, the psalmist: "Confession and beauty are in his sight" [Ps. 95(96):6]. "You are clothed in confession and beauty" [Ps. 103(104):1]. "His work is confession and majesty" [Ps. 110(111):3]. Hence Psalm 44 [45:11] says: "Listen my daughter, behold and lend your ear: be humble and the king will desire your beauty."

It is not he who considers himself the most lowly of men but he who sees himself as even the most foul and vile who is most beautiful to God. For he would never see his own deformity were he not illuminated deep within by a holy light. Because he has such light within he is beautiful; and the more clearly it shines, the more beautiful he is. And yet the more clearly it shines the more surely does he also see his deformity and unworthiness. So it is true: he who finds himself most unsightly is most beautiful to God, and he who is most beautiful in his own eyes is most unsightly to God; for he lacks the light to see himself as he truly is. So the holy Virgin says: "He has regarded the lowliness of his handmaiden" [Luke 1:48].

This is the marrow of Scripture, the kernel of heavenly grain, more dear than the glories of riches. "Your law is better to me than a thousand pieces of gold and silver" [Ps. 118(119):72]. Had I the option, I would not trade such understanding for all the world's riches. "Sweeter than honey and the honeycomb" [Ps. 18(19):11] are those words of God.

And so it happens that even the saints do not glory in their own powers; they rejoice in them only by referring them to him who gave them. To be prideful because one wears another's coat is as foolish as taking pride in one's own poverty. Yet those who justify themselves when they are in fact impious do the latter, while the righteous who boast of their virtue and seek public acclaim do the former. The righteous may certainly rejoice in their powers, but only as I said above [by referring them to their source].

Sin is always to be feared, and we are always to accuse and judge ourselves before God. For "if we judge ourselves, we will certainly not be judged" by the Lord [1 Cor. 11:31]. God will not judge the same person twice. He is not able to condemn a man who has already been judged by himself and, consequently, by the words of God. God cannot deny himself. He it was who first judged this man to be a sinner, and now the man he judged does the same. God cannot, therefore, take a stand against one who so judges himself. Otherwise, he would oppose himself by rejecting one who is conformed with him in judgment. Hence, it is necessary that God acknowledge and approve his own judgment in one [who judges himself].

It is, therefore, clear that this psalm, properly understood, is not about David; it is spoken prophetically in the person of the church, that is, David, given the historical occasion mentioned in the title, speaks as if he were a part of the church. The particular historical occasion of the psalm was Nathan's rebuke. Reproached by the prophet, David immediately acknowledged and confessed his sin, saying, "I have sinned" [2 Sam. 12:13], and he made this confession most powerfully in the psalm: "For I know my iniquity" [vs. 3]. David understood that to accuse himself was to justify God and, in turn, himself. Not so Saul, who, when rebuked by Samuel, protested: "Truly I have obeyed the voice of God" [1 Sam. 15:20]. Saul spoke as the figure of the synagogue. Like him, the synagogue turned its back when reproached and preferred the dead letter to the life-giving spirit.

If you want an example of this matter, look to Christ upon the cross. One thief judges, condemns, and curses him, while the other thief judges himself and justifies Christ, saying: "We [are] indeed justly [executed] (which is to confess, 'Against you only have I sinned'), but this man has done no wrong (which is to say, 'That you may be justified')" [Luke 23:41]. Even if Christ is now judged rather than justified, God will still overcome and be justified by men, even against their will. For those who do not now choose to respond to God's mercy and goodness, accuse themselves, and justify God will finally be forced to do so as captives of his power and wrath after death and at the last judgment.

An understanding of this matter is useful not only for this verse and psalm, but for all the psalms which tell us to praise God and be mindful of his righteousness and glory. For God cannot be praised, justified, and glorified unless we simultaneously and previously curse, accuse, and confound ourselves. When we are confused and accuse ourselves, God is praised and his righteousness is remembered.

2

Sermon Preached on the Feast of Saint Stephen (26 December 1514)

The following selection deals more directly with the doctrine of the *synteresis voluntatis et rationis*, that spark of will and reason thought to remain in every man after the Fall as a natural witness to truth and goodness. In classical medieval anthropology, this innate spark designated man's highest intellective and affective powers. The concept, whose ancestry can be traced to Stoicism, was very important in late medieval scholastic and mystical theology. Ockhamists employed it as a base for the ethical activity necessary to place one in a state of grace. For the mystical theologian, it was the medium for God's birth in the soul.

Luther's Sermon on the Feast of Saint Stephen elaborates the traditional concept. The *synteresis* is presented as a natural endowment without which man would be a "Sodom"; it is a foothold for man's rehabilitation, for the resuscitation of human nature by grace. Yet, according to Luther, this innate desire for God and salvation can also guide man to his damnation. For while it directs every man to the goal of salvation and pleasing God, it does not show him the true means to this end, which, according to Luther, is faith in Jesus Christ. The wisdom of the flesh, following the *synteresis*, can erect a contrary means of salvation. The *synteresis* attests man's natural goodness and ability to choose the good, but, Luther insists, it does not guarantee that he will choose the "right good."

Despite his positive conclusions about the *synteresis*, there remains in this sermon a very uneasy tension between the "alien, covering" righteousness of Christ and man's innate *synteresis*. In one sense they are allies; in another, however, deadly enemies. Even the best in man can lead him to hell.

SOURCE: *Martin Luther, Werke. Kritische Gesamtausgabe* (Weimar, 1883ff), Vol. I, pp. 30-37.

"Behold I send you prophets, wise men, and scribes" [Matt. 23:34]. Why does Jesus not say that he is sending men who are just and good, or otherwise distinguished in will and virtue? Why does he send only those who excel in words and wisdom? Because he here signifies three kinds of men who have received instruction from God, corresponding to the three traditional ways in which God teaches. Some are inspired directly by God, taught without a human teacher by divine inspiration and revelation. These are the prophets. According to 2 Peter 1 [:20-21], they are the saintly men who have spoken under the inspiration of the Holy Spirit, for no prophecy has ever come forth from the mind of man. Secondly, there are those who are taught by God indirectly by the words of men. God educates all men in righteousness by human ministry. Here we find the wise men, who are described in Psalm 36 [37:20] . . . and [Psalm 49:4]. Finally, there are those who are taught neither by the ministry of men nor directly by God alone, but rather by poring over Scripture. Reading and meditating, they work their way into the knowledge of truth and become expert interpreters of Scripture and authors of books. And these are the scribes.

Here we see that the word is threefold: known or mental, spoken or vocal, and read or written. Accordingly, there are three kinds of men equipped to teach about God: prophets, who receive their teaching through the heart; wise men, who are taught by ear; and scribes, who grasp their message with the eye. Instruction which occurs directly in the mind is more alive than that which comes by word of mouth, and the latter is more immediate than learning through a written account. For the letter is a dead voice, and the spoken word, although a living letter, is still dead thought. What occurs directly in the mind, however, is written by the very finger of God and gives life to both word and letter. What is spoken moves more than what is only written, and what is thought is more moving still than what is only heard.

God writes in hearts and makes prophets, while man marks on the ears and in books with words and letters.

God sends these three rather than those who are "righteous" in order to show that all who resist him do so because of the unruly wisdom of the flesh. All men truly desire God and believe they obey him with a good will. But they are not in line with Scripture; they have not humbled their minds. That is why they will seek and embrace one who is just, devout, and mild, but repudiate one who is true, sure, and wise.

The whole conflict [in religion] is over means to the end. All agree about the end itself, that is, all want to be saved and please God, but they disagree over the way to do it. The prideful have always opposed the righteousness of God, regarding the wisdom which he sends as foolishness and rejecting his truth as a lie. In fact, they persecuted and killed those who told them the truth.

Whenever I preach about Christ, our "hen," the following statement is thrown back at me as false: "The Lord wants to be our hen and gather us together in salvation, but we are unwilling" [Matt. 23:37]. I am challenged here because I deny that we can save ourselves by our own righteousness and insist that we must rather take refuge under the wings of this "hen," so that we may receive from his fullness what is only very small in ourselves. So Malachi 4[:2]: "The sun of righteousness will arise for those who fear my name, and salvation will be found under his wings." And Psalm 90 [91:4]: "he will cover you with his pinions, and you will find hope under his wings." And Psalm 62 [63:8-9]: "I will hope in the shadow of your wings; your right hand upholds me." Otherwise, the "vultures," those most cruel of evil spirits, will tear to pieces one who tries to walk secure in his own righteousness.

Look at how our Lord stretched out his wings on the cross so that he might protect us. But now men not only turn away from these wings to their own good works, but even refuse to listen to the voice of the "hen." They refuse to hear that the things they count as righteousness are sins and that they stand in need of the "hen." And, what is still worse, they themselves become vultures and try to pull away those "chicks" who do hope in the mercy of the "hen" and persecute them. Having severed their trust in Christ and clothed them improperly with trust in their own righteousness, they more surely devour these "chicks." Those who fight most strongly against grace are those who insist most forcefully upon it. Among the Jews, those who were truly intent on being just were persecuted in the name of righteousness by those who defined righteousness to suit their own fancy. Likewise, these men now dream up their own views of grace.

But let it stand unshaken; it is fitting that it be this way. When the prophets, wise men, and scribes are sent to those who are just, holy, and devout, they are not received but rather killed. But send them among the unrighteous, among sinners, publicans, and whores, and they are embraced, for these people are hungry and desire to be taught, while the others are sated and filled to excess.

FIRST DOCTRINE

God wants all men to be saved and desires no man's damnation. It is only because of the wisdom of the flesh that the wisdom of God must say, "I was willing, but you refused." It is strange that contradiction and discord should exist between God's will and ours [since we both want salvation]. But that such conflict does exist is evident not only from 1 Timothy 2[:4], but also from everyone's experience. 1 Timothy tells us that God wants all men to be saved and understand the truth. In Ezekiel 18[:23] the Lord protests, "Do I will the death of the unrighteous?" Psalm 29 [30:6] points out that wrath lies in God's displeasure but life in his will. We learn in the Book of Wisdom [1:13-14] that God did not create death and does not rejoice when the unrighteous perish; rather, he is a God who would heal the nations of the world. And whenever we are asked if we want to be saved, do we not say without hesitation that we do, and when asked if we want to be damned, do we not just so quickly insist that we do not?

Still, it is not surprising that, while God and man agree that all should be saved, the one still says to the other: "I was willing but you refused." For there is a spark (*synteresis*) built permanently into man's will, which desires to be saved, to live a good and blessed life, and which recoils at the thought of damnation. Likewise an inextinguishable spark is present in man's reason and cries out for the highest things—for what is true, right, and just. This spark of will and reason is the conservation, the remains or residue [of man's prefallen state], the highest part of a vitiated nature now lost in corruption. It is like a tinderbox, a seed, the matrix of a nature which is to be resuscitated and restored by grace. As Isaiah [43:3] says: "A bruised reed he will not break, and a dimly burning wick he will not extinguish." God will restore and strengthen the reed and cause the wick to blaze up and take fire. According to Isaiah [1:9], if God had not left a remnant, we would have become like Sodom. Morally interpreted, this means that had God not conserved the *synteresis* and remains of [prefallen] nature, everything would have been lost. In Job [14:7-9] we read: "For there is hope for a tree, if it be cut down, that it will sprout again, and that its shoots will not cease. Though its root grow old in the earth, and its stump die in the ground, yet at the scent of water it will bud and put forth branches like a young plant."

So nature can be resuscitated if we do not, like the unrighteous, resist grace and put an obstacle in its path. Supported by [the impulse of] their *synteresis*, the unrighteous still follow their own will and wisdom and do not want to be restored, since they think themselves already whole. We see that that part of the will [the *synteresis*] is firmly rooted, so that even in the damned the only cause of the whole infernal penalty is their refusing him [sc. Christ, God's means] and, with intense vehemence, willing a contrary [way to] salvation.

St. Augustine says that sorrow is to oppose and suffer unwillingly what happens to you. Joy, by contrast, is to agree with and choose the things that one must bear. Sorrow will be the lot of the unrighteous in eternity, for they will try to flee damnation, and yet find themselves surrounded by it on all sides. The first Psalm [vss. 4-5] describes the future state of the wicked as being like dust in the wind, always agitated and running from frightful terror, yet not escaping terrible misery. The righteous, however, stand firm in God amidst the running waters (i.e., in the torrent of worldly pleasures) [Ps. 1:3].

COROLLARY

Is it not ironic that sinners are punished by their very will for salvation and fear of damnation, that is, by that very will in which they are conformed to God who wills salvation for all and damnation for no man? That this is true is evident from Proverbs 1[:6] ... Psalm 1[:6] ... and 108 [109:7] ... and the Book of Wisdom [5:15] ... That good will, as I have said, is indelibly impressed into man by God; indeed, man will be severely punished by it when [in hell] he is unable to refuse his punishment and yet equally unable not to will peace and salvation.

The second part of the conclusion [that God and man differ over the true way to salvation] is demonstrated by the fact that the wisdom of the flesh so destroys the will conformed to God that it no longer chooses what it ought and what God would have it choose in order to be saved. Rather it now wills what seems to itself, or what man himself deems to be, joy and salvation. Here God and man disagree not over the end but over the way to it. Matthew 5[:25] tells us to agree with our adversary while we are going along with him, as if to say: "The wisdom of God and the wisdom of the flesh tend toward the same end, but they are not in agreement on the way to it." When two workers are doing the same job and pursue it by different approaches, contrary means, and opposite plans, one of the two will necessarily err and only one will proceed correctly. If two builders set out to construct a house and one correctly and with skill prepared and formed the wood for a house while the other, disagreeing with him and boasting of a better plan, arranged the lumber in a way fitting for a bridge or a fence, we would have to conclude that the latter was really not a builder, but simply destructive. And what would we think of a tailor who, having set out to make a coat, became intoxicated by his own design, went his own way, and ended up making a boot? Horace speaks to the point: "If, with the turning of the [potter's] wheel, the wine bottle begins to appear, why does the water-pot depart?" And again: "If mountains desire to give birth, a funny little mouse will be born."

So all agree about life's goal, the righteous and the perverse, the learned and the ignorant, alike. But since they hold discordant views about the way to it, they unintentionally deceive one another. Hence, the righteous can say to the unrighteous: "We were willing, but you were not." And the unrighteous can reply: "We were willing as you, but we were not able [to grasp salvation]." Why? Because their own wisdom shut them off from it. The one sought salvation in his own honor, the other in his riches, another in his wisdom, and still another in his righteousness. By so turning to their own understanding, to the wisdom of the flesh and their own counsel, they turned away from God. God wills that man reach the goal of salvation through the humility of the cross and the confession of sin. But they look to the counsel of the unrighteous, about which Psalm 1[:1] warns. The generation of the righteous, on the other hand, will be blessed. They have a good and true heart and pursue salvation with the right counsel; the unrighteous, by contrast, also seek remission of their sins and desire God and salvation, but they do so without understanding.

Scripture desires nothing so much as to humiliate and extinguish the wisdom of the flesh. When that is done, man can hear the voice of God directing him along the true way to the goal which he wants all men to reach, but which none can attain by himself. So Psalm 95[:7-10]: "If you hear his voice today, do not harden your heart," adding that the unrighteous always err in the heart, as if to say: "although they are zealous and have a good will, they are misdirected." Psalm 111 [112:4] has it that the light of a good heart rises out of darkness, and in Psalm 96 [97:11] we read that light rises before the righteous, that is, before one who believes the word and counsel of God and has rejected his own. Hence, a good heart is joyous. Psalm 32 [33:1] urges the righteous to rejoice in the Lord, to believe the counsels of God. Praise befits the righteous. Here [Psalm 33:10] it is also written that the Lord disperses the counsels of the nations, reproves the plans of the peoples and the advice of princes. In the whole of the 119th Psalm, in practically every verse, the law, mandate, word, speech, judgment, righteousness, and justifications [of God], that is, the true God-given way to the end which all desire, is set forth. It is not necessary for us to pray that we choose what is good; rather must we pray that we choose the *right* and *true* good.

That is why, in this gospel text [Matt. 23:34], the Lord does not promise to send those who are righteous, good, and pious, but rather prophets, wise men, and scribes, for they are leaders and guides, true counsellors. God is careful to send a sure cure for the wisdom of the flesh and human counsel, and through the right means. The wisdom of the flesh, popularly known as "sensuality," is in one's own counsel and emerges when reason pronounces what seems to it to be right and good. But reason should rather ask God to send his Spirit so that it might learn not the things that only seem to be right and good but those that truly are. Hence, the Word took flesh and the wisdom of God became hidden and emptied [in Christ] so that this miserable wisdom of ours, which is so full of vanity, error, and sin, might be hidden and emptied.

SECOND DOCTRINE

All the blood of the righteous will be upon one who refuses to obey the counsels of Christ and turns to his own. For even though he kills no man, he still allies himself with that generation of murderers. Christ says that he who is not with him is against him and that those who agree with the murderous works of their fathers, even though they themselves kill not, are also murderers. For he who does not turn away from the generation that killed the prophets agrees by his (in)action with it, just as one who lives with thieves and cut-throats shows his approval. And as he will share their punishment, so has he also shared their crime, even though he himself has done no harmful act. Just as today [on the feast of St. Stephen] Paul stoned Stephen with the hands of the Jews, as he himself confesses in Acts [6:10], so the blood of Christ and his saints is imputed to all evil men because they share the destiny of the generation of those who killed them. O horrible word! O fleshly wisdom zealously to be fled! What else does one love who loves his own understanding, the wisdom of the flesh and his own counsel, than the very weapons by which Christ and his saints were murdered? What but the madness and love of one's own wisdom and counsel killed Christ? What if you did not kill the son of a prince, but still delighted in the arms and weapons, plots and schemes, which did kill him? And what if you continued to keep and use those arms and weapons which the prince, having cursed and ordered destroyed, forbade as a capital offense? Would not the prince justly damn you for disobedience, supposing either that you had done or were planning to do similar deeds?

So it will happen to all who love their own counsel. For such love the instruments which killed Christ and the righteous, the very instruments which every friend of God should utterly despise. When you hold in your very hand the weapons by which they were killed, it is useless to argue that you had no part in their deaths. If you say that you handle these weapons only because they are beautiful and you like their feel, God replies: "But these are the weapons which killed my son!" Although you may not have known that before, now that you see that these weapons are a cruel and bloody witness to the death of Christ, be horrified at their sight, just as a son recoils from the weapons which have killed his father and brother. One should, in revulsion, make every effort to escape this bloody "dragon" and his gory weapons of madness, pride, and anger and, with pious haste, flee to the knowledge of humility. Solomon warns us of this generation which entices to sin and rushes to shed blood [Prov. 1:10, 16]. Also Romans 3[:15] ... Acts [2:40] ... and Psalms 11 [12:8].

COROLLARY

Whenever we sense that our own understanding is setting our opinion in place of God's, we should, with groaning, detest ourselves and bewail our misery. It is horrible for a Christian to find in himself that deadly spear by which Christ was pierced, and to war against the Lord for whom he ought rather fight to the death. So we always find reason in ourselves for great sorrow and cause for the most humble confession. We perceive in ourselves those same bloody shafts with which that generation of murderers killed the righteous. And if such perception does not make us suffer and groan, then rightly will all the shed blood of the righteous be placed upon us.

THIRD DOCTRINE

Although God has imposed upon us the impossible, which we lack the power to do, still no one can draw from this an excuse. Indeed, he who looks for an excuse will be still more severely accused. The first point is clear because God wants to save us by invisible things to which the wisdom of the flesh cannot even reach, much less grasp. Further, the wisdom of the flesh is carnal and cannot fulfil the law which is spiritual. Hence, Paul in Romans 8[:6-7] says that the wisdom of the flesh is death because it does not and cannot subject itself to God. Carnal men cannot fulfil the law. Christ alone fulfils what we cannot until we are set free from the wisdom of the flesh. According to the apostle Paul [Romans 8:3] the law cannot set us free because it is weakened by the flesh; our own carnal wisdom makes the law impossible for us.

Christ, however, imparts his own fulfillment of the law to us when he presents himself as our "hen," allowing us to hide under his wings, and, in his fulfillment of the law, to meet the requirements laid upon us. O sweet hen! O blessed brood of this hen!

Secondly, it is obvious that the impossible has been imposed upon us so that we might be driven to grace and turned away from the wisdom of the flesh. It is through the law, which demands the impossible, that knowledge of sin comes [Rom. 3:20]. Knowing that no counsel or act of our own removes our sinful desire, and that such desire stands in contradiction with the commandment of the law, we experience the absolutely invincible nature of our sin. What then remains for us to do but to seek elsewhere assistance that can conquer what we cannot? And therein lies the point of our text: "So often have I wanted to gather you in as a hen gathers her chicks, but you were not willing" [Mat. 23:37]. See how grace is offered even to those who don't seek it!

He who excuses himself obviously incurs still greater guilt. For, having been admonished by the law, he not only fails to seek grace, but he even refuses it, reproaching the spirit of grace and defiling the blood that has been shed for him. Truly he defiles grace who finds his own counsel sufficient, neither believing nor wanting to hear that he is obligated to a law he cannot fulfil. Truly, his house is a desolate abode [Matt. 23:38]. But let us, like simple "chicks," pray with St. Stephen . . . and with those who rejoice and hope in the protection of God's wings [Ps. 36:8, 91:4]. Romans [8:3-4] tells us that God sent his son in the likeness of sinful flesh to damn sin and make it possible that the righteousness of the law could appear in us.

When we hear it said that man's will is conformed to God's will, we should understand that spark (*synteresis*), or highest part of man's will, which by nature chooses what is good. The will as a whole, however, fails to love what is good, just as reason fails to grasp what is right and true. Just as the spark of reason is conformed to the wisdom of God even though the whole of reason is completely contrary to it, so the spark of the will is conformed to the will of God, even though the whole will is not. The invisible and hidden things of God are no more understood by man's reason than they are loved by his will, although, because of the spark, reason and will have the inclination and ability to know and love them. Still, reason as a whole remains blind and the will weak. Inwardly and outwardly reason knows only the shadows of invisible things, only visible appearances which can be adapted to them. And the same is true for the will, which cannot reach the point of loving the invisible things of God above what are only their likenesses. By invisible things I mean only those things which are in God; and by visible things I understand what is not God himself—like wisdom, virtues, and the gifts of grace. Although the latter are not sensual, carnal, or corporeal, they are still things apparent to man and presently known by him. It is especially in these that heretics and the prideful lose themselves, thinking that they love God when they tenaciously cling to these things. They puff up in anger and self-defense when they are reprehended for this, parading zeal for God which lacks knowledge. The command to love God above all things is directed not to the "gifts" of God, but exclusively to the invisible things which do not enter into the reason of man, nor are seen with his eyes or heard with his ears.

However much heretics and the prideful may understand, or however well they may live, they are still rightly said to live according to the wisdom of the flesh, and much more so than those who know only corporeal goods. For they are servants who live without fear and pride themselves in the most refined ways. The precept, "love the Lord your God," is quite clearly directed against both love for and meditation upon visible things.

It was to illumine reason that the Word, the very wisdom of the Father, assumed flesh, and it was to heal the will that the Spirit was sent. The former illumines reason and the latter enlivens the will so that man may understand and love the invisible things that transcend him. He is already predisposed to understand and love these things through the spark of reason and will, but because reason is impeded and the will weak, he neither understands nor loves them. Therefore, we should always groan and pray.

Take the example of a sick man and his medicine. A sick man retains a spark of health, which physicians call the powers of nature. Although these natural powers cannot restore his health, they predispose him to health. And were this residue not present, his illness would have to be given up as incurable. He should not consider himself well, however, just because he is able to take various medicines. He is not cured until he no longer needs his medicine and has regained his appetite for solid food. It is just as foolish for hypocrites to presume themselves whole and righteous after they have received the virtues and graces of God as it is for a sick man to presume himself well and dismiss his physician after he has taken some medicine. His medicine is not health itself but only a remedy which leads to it. Likewise, the works and gifts of righteousness are not salvation itself but aids to salvation and righteousness. God alone is salvation, and while he should be sought in all these things, one ought not think to have found him in them. Neither the sick nor the righteous should be without fear, even though the one is able to take medicine and the other to perform good works. For both still face the possibility of perdition.

3

Marginal Comments on
Johannes Tauler's Sermons (1515-16)

In the two final selections the enmity between Christ's righteousness and the *synteresis* has enlarged to the breaking point. When he comes upon the *synteresis* in the sermons of Tauler, Luther simply replaces it with "faith"—a striking revision. In the series of statements on the *synteresis* from the *Lectures on Romans,* (Selection 4) he considers exaggerated views about the powers of the *synteresis* to underlie the Pelagianism of what he calls the "pig-theologians." He finally denies altogether a general knowledge and desire for good in human nature.

SOURCE: *Martin Luther, Werke. Kritische Gesamtausgabe* (Weimar, 1883ff), Vol. IX, pp. 99.36ff; 103.38ff. For Tauler, see Ferdinand Vetter, *Die Predigten Taulers* (Berlin, 1910), pp. 21.9ff; 248.22ff.

Tauler: There are three things within man. The first is the physical sense or sensuality, which clings to flesh and blood. The second is reason. And the third is a pure and simple substance of the soul.

Luther: The three here are sensuality, reason, and the mind or that highest part of the mind which is called the [intellective] *synteresis*, the spark [of the mind]. On this matter see Gerson's *On Mystical*

Theology. As there are three intellective powers of the soul, so there are also three [parallel] affective powers: sensual desire or appetite, intellectual desire, and the [affective] *synteresis*, the spark [of the will].

Tauler: Although he is one man, man exists as if he were three. The first is the outward, animal, sensual man; the second, the rational man with his powers of reason; and the third man is the heart, the highest part of the soul. All these make one man.

Luther: There is a sensual man who uses the senses, a rational man who employs reason, and spiritual man who looks to faith. The Apostle calls the first carnal, the second filled with life, and the third spiritual. Worldly men know only the first, philosophers and heretics reach the second, but only true Christians attain the third.

Not so!

4

The *Lectures on Romans* (1515-16)

SOURCE: *Martin Luther, Werke. Kritische Gesamtausgabe* (Weimar, 1883ff), Vol. LVI, pp. 177.11ff (Scholia to Romans 1:19-20); pp. 236.31ff (Scholia to Romans 3:10); pp. 275. 17ff (Scholia to Romans 4:7); pp. 355.28ff (Scholia to Romans 8:3).

The Gentiles knew that it is characteristic of divine nature or of God to be powerful, invisible, righteous, immortal, and good. Therefore, they knew the invisible things of God and his eternal power and divinity. This they knew through the theological *synteresis*, which forms the major premise of the practical syllogism. This *synteresis* is in every man and cannot be obscured. In the minor premise of the syllogism, however, they erred, because they concluded that Jupiter or some idol like him was God. Here the error began and fostered idolatry, as each tried to subject God to his own desire.

. . . .

That statement of Seneca is full of pride and every sin: "Should I know that men would not see it and the gods would overlook it, still I would not sin." Now in the first place, it is impossible for man to have such a will from himself, for he is always inclined toward evil and only through the grace of God can he be moved to do good. Therefore, he who presumes that he can do so much does not yet know himself. Certainly he can choose and do some good things with that frame of mind, but hardly all. For we are not so completely inclined toward evil that a portion does not still remain which is directed to good, as the presence of the *synteresis* makes clear. But even if he says that he would not sin although the gods would overlook it and men would not see it, I wonder if he would be so bold as to say that he would not sin if he knew that neither the gods nor men would care if he did. If he so dares, then he is as arrogant as he is bold. For he would not avoid prideful self-satisfaction. Man is simply not able to seek anything except what is his own and to love himself above all things. That is the sum of all his faults. Even in their good and virtuous deeds such men seek themselves.

. . . .

It is sheer delusion when it is said that man, by his own powers, can love God above all things and perform the works of the law according to the substance of the act, although not according to the intention of the Lawgiver. (The latter is denied because man is said to be not yet in a state of grace.) O fools, O pig-theologians! . . . All these monstrosities came from the fact that these theologians did not know either what sin or its remission were. For they reduced sin and righteousness to a certain small motion of the soul. Because the will had that *synteresis,* they believed that, although feebly, it was "inclined to good." And they dreamed that this little motion to God (which the soul is by nature able to make) was an act of loving God above all things! But just look at this man who is completely filled with sinful desires—and they are not obstructed by that tiny motion to good! The law commands him to empty himself so that he may be turned completely to God. Isaiah 41[:23] chides them: "Do good or evil—if you can!"

. . . .

It is said that human nature knows and wills good in a general and universal sense, but errs and refuses what is good in particular cases. It would be better to say the reverse: human nature knows and wills good in particular cases, but in a universal sense neither knows nor wills what is good. Human nature knows only its own good or what is good, honorable, and useful for itself, not what is such before God and with other men. Therefore, it is more in regard to particular good, indeed it is only in regard to that good which serves the individual, that human nature knows and wills what is good. And this agrees with the teaching of Scripture, which describes man as turned in upon himself, so that in both corporeal and spiritual goods, in all things, he seeks only himself. This condition is natural; it is a natural fault and evil. Therefore, man does not find help in his natural powers, but must seek it from another and more powerful source, which is not in himself.

II. Against the Pelagianism and Speculation of the Scholastics

5

Gabriel Biel:
On Doing the Best That Is In One

The following selections deal with the Pelagian errors of scholastic theology as Luther perceived and criticized them primarily in the theology of the Ockhamists. In the first selection, Gabriel Biel, quoting Alexander of Hales at length, presents a concise definition of what it means for man to earn grace by doing the best that is in him.

SOURCE: *Canonis Missae Expositio*, ed. H. A. Oberman and W. J. Courtenay, Vol. II (Mainz, 1965), Lect. LIX P, p. 443.

You ask what it means for a man to do what is in him. Alexander of Hales answers as follows. "If we want to know what it means for one to do what is in him, let us first note that every man by nature possesses right reason. This uprightness of reason consists of a natural understanding of what is good. It is given to every man by the Creator, and by it every soul can know its origin, God, in accordance with the words of the psalm: 'Know that the Lord is God, he it is who has made us and not we ourselves' [Ps. 99(100):3]. Every soul knows that it has not always existed; it is aware that it has been created. It knows that it had a beginning and that whatever it may have it has received from its Origin and not from itself. It knows further that it should seek the good from its Creator, that all men should beg what they still lack from their

Origin. If a man acts in accordance with this innate knowledge and directs his will to him whom he knows to be his praiseworthy Creator, then he does what is in him. This is generally what it means for any man to do what is in him. The infidel in mortal sin, however, needs more light, for his faith is unformed, lacking charity. But this unformed faith can still make two things clear to him: divine justice which damns those who are false and divine mercy which saves the righteous. Knowledge of the former creates fear, and knowledge of the latter hope. To fear God's justice and hope in his mercy is to do what is in one." So Alexander. From this we can now say that he does what is in him who, illumined by the light of natural reason or of faith, or of both, knows the baseness of sin, and, having resolved to depart from it, desires the divine aid [i.e. grace] by which he can cleanse himself and cling to God his maker. To the one who does this God necessarily grants grace—but by a necessity based on the immutability of his decisions, not on external coercion, as Alexander also declares.

6

Marginal Comments on Gabriel Biel's *Collectorium* and *Canonis Missae Expositio* (1517)

This selection contains Luther's criticism of Biel's teaching as set forth in his marginal comments on Biel's *Sentences* commentary and *Exposition of the Canon of the Mass.*

SOURCE: *Luthers Randbemerkungen zu Gabriel Biels Collectorium in quattuor libros sententiarum und zu dessen Sacri canonis missae expositio Lyon 1514*, ed. H. Degering, *Festgabe der Kommission zur Herausgabe der Werke Martin Luthers zur Feier des 450. Geburtstages Luthers* (Weimar, 1933), p. 14.23-24; p. 16.1-17.

Biel: During his pilgrimage on earth, man's will is able by its nature to love God above all things. The proof is this. The will can naturally conform to every dictate of right reason. To love God is such a dictate. Therefore, the will can naturally conform to this dictate and consequently love God above all things.

Luther: And consequently the will is not infirm and in need of God's grace. All these statements proceed from the foolish assumption that the will is free to move as it chooses in either a good or an evil direction, when, in truth, it is inclined only to evil. If it does manage to oppose its proneness to evil, it is only because it is externally coerced, and this can hardly be called an act of love.

Biel: It is proved [that man can naturally dispose himself for grace] ; for according to God's ordained law grace is given to one who does what is in him. When one has sufficiently prepared himself for the reception of grace, God infuses grace in accordance with the words of the prophet Zechariah [1:3], "Turn to me and I will turn to you," and of James [4:8], "Draw near to God and he will draw near to you," namely, by grace. And in Luke 11[:9] we read: "Seek and you will find, knock and it will be opened." And in Jeremiah 29[:13]: "If you seek me with your whole heart, you will find me." And Psalm 21[:27]: "The hearts of those who seek God are alive."

Luther: He talks as if these words mean that it is within our power, grace excluded, to seek and turn to God, when it is' written in Psalm 13[:2] that man does not understand or seek God. None of these passages support his point.

7

The *Disputation Against Scholastic Theology* (September 1517)

In this selection Luther's key theses against scholastic Pelagianism and speculation in the *Disputation Against Scholastic Theology* are brought together.

SOURCE: *Martin Luther, Werke. Kritische Gesamtausgabe* (Weimar, 1883ff), Vol. I, pp. 224-26.

I. Against the Pelagianism of the Scholastics:

    a)   5. It is false to say, "man is free to move in either a good or an evil direction," since he is not free but captive. This against common opinion.

          6. It is false to say, "man's will can by nature conform to a right dictate [of reason]." This against [Duns] Scotus and Gabriel [Biel].

          7. Without the grace of God the will necessarily chooses what is evil and perverse.

          8. But it does not therefore follow that the will is essentially evil, i.e., evil in its very nature, as the Manichaeans maintain.

          9. Still, the will is naturally and unavoidably evil and corrupt.

    b) 17. It is not true that "man by nature wants God to be God." By nature he rather wants himself to be God.

        18. For man "to love God above all things by nature"—that is a fabrication, a sheer fiction. This against almost everyone.

        19. Nor are we helped here by citing Scotus' example of the brave citizen who loves his country more than himself.

        20. An act of friendship [between man and God] comes not by nature, but by prevenient grace. This against Gabriel [Biel].

    c) 28. According to St. Augustine, to appeal to the following authorities is simply to repeat the Pelagians, if these passages are interpreted to mean that nature makes the first move and grace the second: "Turn to me and I will turn to you" [Zech. 1:3]; "Draw near to God, and he will draw near to you" [James 4:8]; "If you seek me you will find me" [Luke 11:9]; and the like.

29. The highest and surest preparation and the singular disposition for grace is the eternal election and predestination of God.
30. And on the part of man nothing precedes grace except a disinclination toward it, nay, rebellion against it.

d)   40. We do not "become righteous by doing righteous deeds"; rather, having been made righteous, we do righteous deeds. This against the philosophers.
41. The whole of Aristotle's *Ethics* is the worst enemy of grace. This against the scholastics.

II.   Against Scholastic Speculation:

43. It is an error to say: "Without Aristotle no one can become a theologian." This against common opinion.
44. Indeed, no one can become a theologian who does not put Aristotle aside.
45. To say, "A theologian who is not a logician is a monstrous heretic," is itself monstrous and heretical. This against common opinion.
46. In vain does one transcend natural logic to construct a logic of faith, using terms which stand for but do not fully correspond to the reality of which they speak. This against recent dialecticians [Pierre d'Ailly and Robert Holcot].
47. No syllogistic form is valid in divine matters. This against the cardinal [Pierre d'Ailly].
48. But it does not therefore follow that the truth of the doctrine of the trinity is hostile to syllogistic logic. This against the dialecticians and the cardinal.
49. If syllogistic logic can be applied to divine matters, then the trinity will no longer be an article of faith, but rather a part of our knowledge.
50. In sum, the whole of Aristotle is to theology as darkness to light.

LEWIS W. SPITZ

Humanism and the Reformation

THE INTENSE SCHOLARLY DEBATE over historical periodization and the concept of the Renaissance, the "most intractable child of historiography," has resulted in a better understanding of the true nature of the Renaissance and of its relation to the Middle Ages which preceded it. The relation of the Renaissance to the age of the Reformation which followed it, however, has received less careful scrutiny and is less well understood than the importance of the question warrants.

The discussion of this problem has progressed very little beyond the level of the classic exchange between the great German scholars Wilhelm Dilthey and Ernst Troeltsch in the early decades of the twentieth century. Dilthey, the intellectual historian, held the Renaissance and the Reformation to be cultural and religious expressions respectively of a generally progressive and forward looking development in western civilization. They were the twin sources and common cradle of modernity. Troeltsch, the sociologist of religion, on the other hand, held that while the Renaissance was generically related to the Enlightenment and modern tendencies, the Reformation constituted a revival of otherworldly religiosity and was bound by interior lines to the medieval world view, a throwback in that respect to the earlier centuries. The Reformation proved to be the stronger movement, for it was rooted in deep veins of popular religious belief and was institutionally formative and sociologically more productive than was the aristocratic and elitist Renaissance. The Renaissance, according to Troeltsch, went underground and emerged again in the eighteenth century Enlightenment. Troeltsch, however, at least conceded that the Reformation, in both its Protestant and Catholic expressions, was not entirely negative in its effect upon Renaissance culture or destructive of humanist values. For humanist culture was absorbed by the upper classes and was gradually diffused throughout society during the course of the sixteenth century. The nature of this humanist culture requires closer examination if we are to achieve clarity as to the relation of humanism and the Reformation.

The term "humanism" has been used by the historians to describe various intellectual phenomena in modern times. A German pedagogue, F. J. Niethammer, first used the word in 1808 for a philosophy of education which emphasized the importance of the Greek and Roman classics in the school curriculum. The term was also used in the early nineteenth century for the program of Wilhelm von Humboldt and other idealists, who made reason and experience the sole criteria of truth. This variety of humanism was loosely associated with the humanitarian and rationalistic values of the Enlightenment. In the twentieth century humanism has often been militantly anthropocentric or man-centered, and sometimes anti-religious or even atheistic, assuming many different forms such as existential humanism, communist "progressive" humanism, or merely gentle humanitarianism. The historian must clear his mind of these modern connotations in order to grasp the phenomenon in its Renaissance and Reformation context.

It is impossible for the historian to reduce to a simple definition or formula such a protean phenomenon as Renaissance humanism, for it included a great diversity of emphases and underwent constant change throughout a span of more than three centuries. The noted scholar Paul Joachimsen proposed a simple and fairly concrete definition of humanism as "an intellectual movement, primarily literary and philological, which was rooted in the love and desire for the rebirth of classical antiquity." Humanism was not mere antiquarianism, an interest in classical culture for its own sake. Rather, it was a special way of looking at antiquity and of relating it to the present. Classical culture not only provided the humanists with certain forms for artistic and literary expression, but also with new norms for judging and directing thought and action. The humanist believed that the liberal arts, the *humaniora*, were the studies best designed to perfect and to ornament man.

They embraced especially grammar, rhetoric, poetry, history, and moral philosophy. They all held rhetoric in high regard and frequently cited Cicero's definition from his *On Oratory*: "For eloquence is nothing else than wisdom speaking copiously." Wisdom must be applied to life in the most direct and effective way. Wisdom must be so brought home to the hearer that he is both intellectually convinced and emotionally moved to action. The humanists thought of the power of speech as a singular characteristic of man and had great faith in the power of the spoken and written word. Professionally the humanists were teachers of the *ars dictaminis*, the epistolary techniques and skills useful for a city secretary, a chancellor, or church official, and as such they stood in the medieval tradition of the *dictatores*. But they stressed rhetoric and classicism more intensely and the pursuit of eloquence was engaged in by many humanists of other stations in life who were neither teachers nor city secretaries.

In a way there could be a genuine rebirth or Renaissance in all aspects of culture including art only in the Italian homeland. Italy gave birth to the foremost humanists of the Renaissance, to the literary humanists Petrarch, Boccaccio, Poggio, and Filelfo, the civic humanists Salutati and Bruni, the great educators Vergerio, Vittorino da Feltre, Guarino da Verona, philosophers such as Pico, Ficino, and Pomponazzi, and one of the keenest critical minds of all times, Lorenzo Valla. In northern and western Europe, which had once been outlying provinces of the Roman empire or had even lain beyond its frontiers, there developed not so much a genuine rebirth of classical culture during the fourteenth and fifteenth centuries as a gradual development of a humanist literary culture and some artistic adaptation to Italian Renaissance style. One can more appropriately speak of northern humanism than of a northern Renaissance.

During the fifteenth and the sixteenth centuries there was an accelerated two-way traffic of men and ideas between Italy and the North. Italian humanists travelled beyond the Alps as ecclesiastical legates, diplomatic emissaries, or business representatives and served northern bishops, princes, and cities as secretaries. Northerners, in turn, increasingly sojourned in Italy as students of law, medicine, and the liberal arts. As urban culture developed in the wooded North, the atmosphere became less feudal and Gothic, more congenial for the development of a humanist culture. Princes and courts, prince-bishops, and city councils began to emulate Italian practices. The orators and philosopher-poets (*vates*) promoted the liberal arts (*studia humanitatis*) in the universities, competing with the scholastic dialecticians for endowed chairs. As humanist culture began to take hold, enthusiasm for classical culture mounted until humanism developed as a major cultural force in the northern lands.

In each of the major countries in the North one can distinguish three generations of humanists, showing how this intellectual movement began, developed, and finally encountered the Reformation. A pioneering generation expended much of its energy in acquiring the classical languages and wrestling with the normative religious and cultural issues raised by the new learning. A second generation achieved a high degree of mastery of the classics and produced original creations of their own. A third and younger generation set out to put their new learning and ideals into action in order to reform the ills in the church and society which their predecessors had merely criticized. In England such pioneers in classical studies as Grocyn and Linacre were overshadowed by the great humanists Thomas More, John Colet, and Erasmus. They were in turn superseded by such young activists as Thomas Starkey and Richard Morison, expeditors of Tudor statecraft, the latter strongly influenced theologically by Luther, or John Tyndale, Richard Mulcaster, Roger Ascham and others, who led the way in theological and educational reform. In France such early leaders as Fichet, Standonck, and Gaguin were dwarfed by intellectual giants such as Guillaume Budé and Lefèvre d'Etaples. Then young humanists such as Nicholas Cop, Olivetan, and John Calvin were caught up in the evangelical cause and played a key role in the Reformation.

Humanism came earlier to the Germanies because of their geographical proximity to Italy and the many ecclesiastical, political, and educational contacts with Italy, also thanks to an extended period of peace during the many decades while France and England were embroiled in the Hundred Years War. By the mid-fifteenth century some half-scholastic humanists and "migratory poets" had appeared on the scene as harbingers of a new spring. The real "father of German humanism," however, Rudolph Agricola, flourished in the second half of the century as the "Petrarch of the North." He was followed during the last decade of that century and the first two decades of the sixteenth century by such prominent humanists as Celtis, the arch-humanist, Pirckheimer, Wimpheling, Peutinger, Reuchlin, Mutian, and the ubiquitous Erasmus. The younger or third generation of human-

ists, Ulrich von Hutten, Eobanus Hessus, Philip Melanchthon,
impatient for changes, with Luther made the Reformation. Without the humanists there would have been no Reformation, at least
not the kind of Reformation that actually occurred.

Most of the prominent leaders in the Reformation movement
passed through a humanist phase into the evangelical reform.
Melanchthon, Oecolampadius, Bucer, and Vadian were such
humanist-reformers. A larger number of the left-wing or radical
reformers, too, had a more respectable humanist education than
was formerly fully appreciated, for example, Balthasar Hubmaier,
the anabaptist, Sebastian Franck, the spiritualist, Servetus, or
Castellio, the evangelical rationalists. A whole army of less well-
known younger men were Christian humanists in their formative
years and became local leaders in the Reformation movement.
Hubmaier once observed that nearly all the learned were Lutherans.

During the course of the decade following the year 1510 a
subtle change took place in the world of humanism. The younger
humanists were seeking ways of applying their philosophy to life
and of effecting the changes necessary for realizing their ethical
ideals. In the key cities of the Empire humanist sodalities reinforced their common interest in change. When in 1517 Luther
electrified the German nation with his Ninety-Five Theses, the
humanist sodalities became the chief agents for their publication
and distribution within a fortnight throughout the land. By 1520
Luther was the most widely read author in Germany, rating in
popularity even ahead of the militant young humanist Ulrich von
Hutten. Without the comprehensive and nearly universal support
of the humanists, Luther's reform may well not have succeeded at
all. At the outset most of the older humanists, including Erasmus,
wished him well. They believed that Luther (or Eleutherius, the
free man or liberator, as he styled himself) was one of theirs who
would battle for culture and purified religion against the superstitious monks, the barbarous scholastics, and the tyrannous Roman
popes. The young humanists greeted Luther with wild enthusiasm
as the man who would destroy Aristotle, vindicate Reuchlin, and
renovate theology. They appreciated especially Luther's rejection
of life-denying scholasticism and his rediscovery and glorification
of the Holy Scriptures as the fountain of wisdom. They did not
fully appreciate the fact that Luther did not oppose the scholastics
as a rhetorician because of their barbarous dialectical style but
because of their theology of self-glory. Nor did they adequately

grasp the truth that Luther exalted the Holy Scriptures as the sole authority not because it was an ancient source, but because it was the sole carrier of the Word of God, the message of God's full, free, and final forgiveness of the believer's sin thanks to the vicarious suffering and death of Christ, the Son of God.

The year 1520 saw a dividing of the spirits, for Luther's publication of his treatise *On the Babylonian Captivity of the Church*, in which he criticized the sacramental-sacerdotal system and reduced the number of sacraments from seven to a dominical three, opened the eyes of the older humanists to the radical nature of his theology and many of them turned away. They found that in their innermost convictions they were Catholic and wished to remain loyal to the unity and catholicity of the old Church. Mutian, the canon at Gotha, who had taught and inspired so many of the young humanists at the University of Erfurt while Luther was a student there, was shocked at the iconoclasm and violence of some of the protesters, the rockthrowers who even broke some of his windows. But that very treatise of Luther's served as a great stimulus to many of the younger humanists who became fervent evangelicals. Almost all of Luther's followers were young, although not all of the young became his followers. After Luther's stand at Worms in 1521 he became a hero for the younger generation. When Luther nailed his theses to the church door in Wittenberg he was thirty-four years old. Nearly all of his early followers were only thirty years old or younger, many of them humanists turned evangelicals. Nearly all of Luther's major opponents were older, scholastics or humanists, and many of them fifty years old or older, a good number over seventy. There was an obvious generation gap between Luther's most ardent followers and his most distinguished opponents. This, then, is how the humanists related to the Reformation. Equally important for our problem is how the reformers related to humanism.

One of the intriguing and surprising facts about the Reformation is that despite the reformers' subjective principle of authority, Protestantism did not atomize into thousands or countless separate groups of Christians, each asserting its own right to private or individual interpretation of the Scriptures and insisting literally upon the priesthood of every believer. In reality the radicals comprised fewer than one percent of all Protestants and the overwhelming majority of the people remained within the Lutheran, Calvinist, Swiss Reformed, or Anglican communions. The position taken by the magisterial reformers was therefore of crucial importance for the survival and the vitality of humanism.

Luther's attitude was one neither of an unreserved affirmation of secular culture nor of an absolute rejection. Luther gave enthusiastic support to humanist culture in its sphere, and through the years developed an ever-increasing interest in humanist learning, but he sharply rebuffed the encroachments of humanist philosophy into the domain of theology where God's Word and not human letters reigns supreme. Luther owed much to the humanists, to their criticisms of abuses in the church as well as to their cultural reform program. At the University of Erfurt he had enjoyed some contacts with such humanists as Crotus Rubeanus. When he entered the monastery he took along a copy of Virgil and of Plautus. He was a gifted linguist and learned Greek and Hebrew in addition to his Latin. He used the best critical texts available, turning to Erasmus's Greek New Testament (1516) midway through his own commentary on *Romans*. He expressed regret in later years that he had in school and the university been forced to concentrate on dialectics for so many years without an opportunity to study history, poetry, and other humanist disciplines. Through the years, especially during the last decade and a half of his life when the pressure of events had eased up somewhat, under the influence and guidance of Melanchthon, he cultivated his interest in history and other humanist disciplines. He praised the renaissance of the humane letters as a John the Baptist heralding the advent of the evangelical renewal. "Learning, wisdom, and writers should rule the world," he exclaimed, "and should God ever in his wrath take away all learned men from the world, what else would the people who are left be except beasts!"

Even though Luther offered a historical justification and a theological rationale for the aesthetic-literary secular culture of humanism, his own preoccupation was so exclusively theological that he cannot properly be considered a humanist. He was a professor of theology, not of rhetoric. Nor was he a Christian humanist like Erasmus, for his evangelical message with its stress upon sin and grace drew upon greater depths of the Christian faith than did the program of the humanists for religious enlightenment. Luther did not merely advocate the imitation of Christ as the archetype of humanity at its best. Rather, his message was one of the boundless love and mercy of God, the forgiveness of sin which he offers to all men no matter how abject their condition, and the reconciliation of all men to himself through Christ. Theology is not a synthesis of learning and revelation, justification is not a supplementing of nature with grace, nor is salvation a reward for good works together with faith and love. For Luther all worldly culture was a great but conditional good, for its benefits extended to this life only. The gospel, however, was an unqualified good, for it brought benefits not only in this life but also in the eternal life to come.

The second man of the Reformation, the Frenchman John Calvin, was in every way a worthy successor to Luther. On the question of humanism and theology his resolution was virtually the same as Luther's, even though in his personal background he was more thoroughly educated in the humanist disciplines and untrained in scholastic theology compared with the older man. Calvin learned his grammar as a boy living with a noble family. When only fourteen he went to Paris where he studied at the Collège de la Marche with Mathurin Cordier, one of the best Latin teachers of the time. Calvin transferred to the Collège de Montaigu, which was more scholastic and ecclesiastical in nature, and there took the elementary arts course. Calvin seemed destined to take orders in the church, but at that point his father had a falling out with the canons of Noyons and came to favor a law career for John. Even while he was studying law at Orléans, however, Calvin was caught up with the humanistic study of the classics. He studied Roman law with Alciati and learned to read the New Testament in Greek and began the study of Hebrew. In 1532 he published his first book, a Latin commentary on Seneca's *De clementia*. As a self-conscious young humanist, Calvin presented a copy to Erasmus, the prince of the humanists. Less than two years later Calvin fled Paris as a convinced evangelical. He never lost his affection for Cicero, Quintilian, and Plato, but from then on he was dedicated almost exclusively to preaching Christ from the very fountains themselves, the Scriptures.

The third man of the Reformation, the Swiss Ulrich Zwingli, likewise evolved from a learned humanist into an ecclesiastical reformer of major importance. He learned his first letters in Wesen, then at ten moved to Basel, where he studied Latin, dialectics, and music for three years. He continued his studies for two years in Bern under Heinrich Wölflin, a great enthusiast for humanist educational ideals, who instilled in him a keen love of music and the classics. He next attended the University of Vienna, where the liveliest spirit was Conrad Celtis, the German arch-humanist, who taught the classics, directed humanist plays, and served as head of the college of poets and mathematicians. As a loyal Swiss Zwingli returned to Basel where he came under the influence of Thomas Wyttenbach, a reform-minded Erasmian who was opposed to scholasticism and monasticism and urged the study of the New Testament and the patristic writings. As a priest at Glarus Zwingli studied Greek and Hebrew, collected a library of 350 volumes on a wide range of subjects, especially the classics, and came to be known to his friends as "the Cicero of our age." He corresponded with Erasmus and made a pilgrimage to see him in Basel. Zwingli's initial reform experience was more as an Erasmian in criticizing abuses, driving back to the sources, and stressing spirit over letter. Even his teaching of the extreme form of double predestination seems to have originated more from his reading of St. Paul's epistle than from any existential experience of his own. But his close brush with death in the bubonic plague which struck Zurich in 1519, during his first year as preacher in the great minster, and his fervent study of the Scriptures developed in him a very serious mood and inspired him with greater evangelical fervor. It has been contended that he carried over into his theology more evidence of his humanist conceptions than did the other two leading reformers.

Many of the other leading reformers moved from humanism into the evangelical cause, such as Vadian at St. Gallen, Bucer at Strassburg, and Oecolampadius at Basel. In England, too, many reformers and makers of Tudor policy had enjoyed a humanist education designed to prepare them for service to the church and to the commonwealth.

The crucial question was whether the reformers with their powerful theological emphasis and single-minded devotion to the evangelical cause would find a proper and an important place for humanist disciplines in their total program of action. A positive response and happy outcome, which in retrospect may seem to have been predictable, could by no means be taken for granted. Had the revolutionary Muentzer instead of Luther, the less cultured Amsdorf instead of Melanchthon, the fiery Farel instead of Calvin taken over the leadership of the Reformation movement, it might well have spiralled off into an anti-intellectual or anti-humanist direction. There were, after all, anti-intellectual sects and individual cultural atavists who were ready to jettison secular culture along with the world itself. A successful peasant or proletarian revolt might have brutalized culture and destroyed the hard-won and painfully acquired refinements of centuries. Religious wars might have developed much earlier, before the consolidation of the movement or the cultural transition from the Renaissance to the Reformation had been effected. Moreover, the magisterial reformers themselves could have become so preoccupied with purely religious matters that they might well have felt little concern and devoted less energy to the humane studies or liberal arts. That the magisterial reformers assumed a positive stance toward humanist culture as of great value in this life was a factor of tremendous importance for all subsequent western history. The cultivation of humanist learning was for them, like other mundane vocations a *negotium cum deo*, an activity carried on as a co-worker with God. Humanist learning and higher culture remained for these university men a "sphere of faith's works."

It proved to be an equally momentous development that the next generation of young reformers took up the torch of humanist learning, preserved, cultivated, and transmitted it to the centuries which followed. Though some spontaneity and verve was gradually lost and creativity came to be partially smothered by pedantry, the cultural inheritance of the Renaissance was preserved for men in modern times. The attitudes of these younger reformers toward the humanities constitute our special problem. The most satisfactory resolution of this problem is to follow the advice of the English historian James Froude, "To look wherever we can through the eyes of contemporaries, from whom the future was concealed."

The pivotal figure for humanism in the Lutheran Reformation was Philipp Melanchthon, Luther's lieutenant, who came to be known as the *Praeceptor Germaniae*. When he arrived at the University of Wittenberg in 1518 as a brilliant young humanist of twenty-one, he delivered an inaugural lecture "On Improving the Studies of Youth" which was a clarion call to a humanist program. He berated the scholastics, depicted the centuries preceding as the dark ages, called for a revival of the "letters of culture reborn," and spoke out for the entire humanist curriculum, rhetoric first of all, Greek and Hebrew, history, philosophy and science. Luther himself took the initiative, working closely with Melanchthon, in achieving the humanistic reform of the university curriculum at Wittenberg. He hoped that students would enter upon their studies with the theological faculty with a different set of mental habits than had been the case when the arts curriculum was so heavily loaded with dialectics. Melanchthon's many orations, treatises, prefaces, and editions during the following decades promoted the *studia humanitatis* and validated humanist learning for the Protestant world.

Melanchthon became the commanding figure in an aggressive

army of penmen who promoted the cause of humanist learning in
the age of the Reformation. At the University of Leipzig Peter
Mosellanus, who had been Melanchthon's rival for the appointment at Wittenberg, delivered a forceful *Oration Concerning the
Knowledge of Various Languages Which Must Be Esteemed.* He
inspired Andreas Althamer, who became, in turn, a leading
reformer in Brandenburg-Anspach. At the Leipzig debate between
Dr. Eck and Luther and Carlstadt in 1519, Mosellanus delivered
the preliminary oration on *The Right Method of Disputing.*
Leipzig subsequently turned Lutheran and a school of evangelical
humanists who had studied with Mosellanus developed, men such
as J. Lonicerus and Arnold Burenius. Another "Melanchthonian"
humanist, Joachim Camerarius (1500-1574), became one of the
leading classical scholars of the century. He studied at Leipzig,
Erfurt, and Wittenberg, and then taught history and Greek at the
Nuremberg gymnasium for several years. He helped Melanchthon
to formulate the Augsburg Confession of 1530, reorganized the
University of Tübingen in 1535 and the University of Leipzig,
where he devoted the remainder of his life to classical scholarship,
in 1541. He wrote more than one hundred and fifty works, and
translated many major Greek authors like Homer, Theocritus,
Sophocles, Lucian, Demosthenes, into Latin. In a score of orations
he praised classical learning, which, when combined with evangelical faith, he believed made possible the fullest development of
man's humanity.

A very similar cultural development took place in reformed
Switzerland where Zwingli had set the tone. In Geneva Calvin
founded the Academy which later became the University of
Geneva. On the festive occasion Theodore Beza, the professor of
Greek, delivered an *Address at the Solemn Opening of the Academy
in Geneva*, in which he praised the good arts and learned
disciplines. John Calvin himself made the closing remarks at the
ceremony. Calvin's own Latin teacher, Mathurin Cordier, who had
followed him into exile from France, lived out his days in Geneva
as a model of the evangelical humanist educator. Representative of
those Calvinist educators who carried the Geneva ideal to France,
Scotland, England, and other areas of Calvinist penetration was
Claude Baduel, who taught for many years as a humanist professor
at Nîmes. He had been a student of Melanchthon at Wittenberg
and a friend of the great Strassburg educator Johannes Sturm. His
two great passions were beautiful language and evangelical theology in harmony with the new learning.

The reformers followed the lead of the humanists in emphasizing the great value of education, the classics, rhetoric, poetry, history, and religion. With the possible exception of our own day, never in history was so much published on educational theory and practice as in the Renaissance and Reformation era. The reformers moved beyond the elitism of the Renaissance in pressing for universal compulsory education in order to achieve literacy for boys and girls alike. The idea of the universal priesthood of all believers implied that all who had the wit should at least be sufficiently educated to read the Scriptures. The reformers developed a system of secondary school education in the classical gymnasium or lycée which would prepare students for more advanced work in the university. Formerly boys were often merely twelve, thirteen, or fourteen years old when they were trundled off to the universities. Moreover, the reformers stressed the lofty role of teaching as a divine vocation, second only to the office of preaching. Luther's educational treatises are widely known, such as his *Sermon on the Duty of Sending Children to School* and his *Letter to the Mayors and Aldermen of the Cities of Germany in Behalf of Christian Schools*. We have noted the critical importance of Melanchthon for Protestant education. A typical statement was his *Oration in Praise of a New School*, which he delivered at the opening of the gymnasium or classical secondary school at Nuremberg in 1526, a school which survived the bombing of the second World War and is still in operation today. Johannes Sturm wrote a sizable shelf of books on the nobility of classical letters and his program for Christian humanist education. David Chytraeus published in Wittenberg (1564) an ambitious work on the art of teaching and the right ordering of studies in the individual arts. In England Richard Mulcaster's *Positions* presented the enlightened views of a seasoned sixteenth-century schoolmaster. The prominent English educator and tutor of Queen Elizabeth, Roger Ascham, preached what he practiced as an educator.

The Protestant educators stressed the great value of grammar and rhetoric. The many volumes published on the structure of classical and vernacular vocabulary, figures of speech, rules of syntax, and the art of languages provide ample evidence of the importance which they attached to grammar for exegetical study, homiletical or expository communication. A working knowledge of Greek and Hebrew which was a rarity in the *Quattrocento* became almost a commonplace during the course of the sixteenth and seventeenth centuries. Moreover, the Protestant stress upon preaching and the spoken word of the Gospel coincided harmoniously with the humanist appreciation of rhetoric. They, too, saw man as a "living creature" having the power of speech. They also could appreciate the special power of rhetoric in moving men to action, not merely in convincing them intellectually by syllogisms or other devices of dialectics. Once again, Melanchthon's *Encomium on Eloquence* was one of the finest among many Protestant treatises in praise of rhetoric. Melanchthon wrote a volume on rhetoric himself and his *Loci Communes*, or commonplaces, applied the topical approach of rhetoric to theology. Cicero served as the model of the orator for the reformers as he had been for the humanists. Similarly many of the Lutheran, Calvinist, and Anglican *literati* such as Eobanus Hessus, Jacobus Micyllus, Clement Marot, Georg Major, Michael Neander, or Johannes Secundus Everardus in the Netherlands contributed to poetic culture and hymnody.

The reformers took history very seriously. In part they were thereby following in the footsteps of the humanists who saw a pragmatic purpose in history as moral philosophy teaching by example. If their history was less overtly patriotic than that of many Italians with their fierce city-state loyalties or of the northern humanists with their cultural nationalism, they added a serious religious dimension to the study of history. History was important polemically as a weapon in ecclesiastical controversy. Beyond that, history, like nature, provided evidence of God's having acted. The history of salvation ran like a golden thread through the intricate universal history. Luther not only wrote prefaces to the histories and editions of Galeatius Capella, Lazarus Spengler, Georg Spalatin, Robert Barnes and the like, but he compiled for his own use a chronological outline of world history. Melanchthon composed his famous *Preface to Cuspinian's Chronicle* (1541) which gave expression to the ideas most characteristic of the Reformation view of history. He himself wrote the largest part of *Carion's Chronicle*. Johann Sleidan was the author of the very excellent *Commentaries on the Condition of Religion and the Republic Under Charles V* (1555). Flacius Illyricus set the pattern for a more polemical tradition of historiography with his massive *Catalogue of the Witnesses of Truth* (1556) and the *Magdeburg Centuries* (13 vols., 1559-1574), in which he rewrote ecclesiastical history from a Protestant point of view. The reformers also developed patristic studies further than the humanists, even Erasmus, had brought them. Although the Scriptures remained for them the source and norm (*norma normans*) of doctrine, the fathers were key witnesses to the original and true (*primum et verum*) understanding of doctrine.

The Reformation was at its very heart so much a religious movement and Luther's interests were so predominantly theological as to raise the key question whether secular culture could be related to religious faith in such a way as to maintain an authenticity of its own without capitulating entirely to otherworldly interests. The Reformation determined the destiny of humanism, but humanism helped to define the nature and direction of the Reformation. The reformers basically accepted the stoic-Ciceronian anthropology common to many humanists, which predicated a dualistic compound of body and soul, reason and will, higher and lower impulses. Their disagreement was not with the humanist anthropology as such. They had a high regard for "natural man," whose reason is the loftiest creation of God. Luther expressed a preference for Plato over Aristotle in philosophy, whereas Melanchthon inclined more toward Aristotle, and in due course helped to enthrone the Stagirite in the universities once again. The reformers were inclined to be more realistic about man's finitude, moral flaws, wilfulness, and general limitations than were the humanists, at least in those exalted orations on the dignity of man. "Sweaty realists," Aldous Huxley has called them. But the real test for man, the reformers held, is how he measures up when standing *coram deo*, in the immediate presence of the holy God. Before God man is nothing in terms of his own righteousness, for he is in every way a debtor to God, totally dependent upon God's grace and mercy. All worldly culture, therefore, is merely a relative good, lofty and glorious though its achievements may be. The reformers struggled to relate religion and culture, theology and philosophy in a satisfactory way. Melanchthon himself made a forceful statement on the place of philosophy in religion and learning. A variety of syntheses evolved during subsequent decades, among them a return of Aristotle to theology, despite Luther's efforts to differentiate the respective realms of faith and culture.

The Renaissance and Reformation, then, did not constitute the clear and evident division of European culture into its classic and Christian components. Renaissance humanist learning was not only widespread during the Reformation horizontally on a European scale, but it lived on vertically through the centuries into modern times. This reading of a major problem in European intellectual history depends upon the study of a vast number of addresses, letters, treatises and books by those reformers who carried on in the evangelical movement a sound tradition of Christian humanism. A small sample of these historical documents follows, with Philipp Melanchthon serving as the star witness.

FOR FURTHER READING

Breen, Quirinus. *Christianity and Humanism: Studies in the History of Ideas.* Grand Rapids, Mich.: Eerdmans, 1968.

Forell, George W., and others. *Luther and Culture.* Martin Luther Lectures, vol. 4, Decorah, Iowa: Luther College Press, 1960.

Gerrish, Brian, ed. *Reformers in Profile.* Philadelphia: Fortress, 1967.

Gerrish, Brian. *Grace and Reason: A Study in the Theology of Martin Luther.* New York: Oxford University Press, 1962.

Harbison, E. Harris. *The Christian Scholar in the Age of the Reformation.* New York: Scribner, 1956.

Holl, Karl. *The Cultural Significance of the Reformation.* New York: Meridian Books, 1959.

Moeller, Bernd. *Imperial Cities and the Reformation. Three Essays.* Philadelphia: Fortress, 1972.

Pauck, Wilhelm. *The Heritage of the Reformation.* Boston: Beacon Press, 1950.

Schwoebel, Robert. *Renaissance Men and Ideas.* New York: St. Martin's Press, 1971.

Spitz, Lewis W. *The Reformation—Basic Interpretations.* Lexington, Mass.: Heath, 1972.

Spitz, Lewis W. *The Renaissance and Reformation Movements.* 2 vols. Chicago: Rand McNally, 1972.

THE ESSAYIST'S SOURCES

1

On Improving the Studies of Youth

Philipp Melanchthon came to the University of Wittenberg as a young professor in the year 1518. In his inaugural lecture he called for a reform of university education away from scholastic

philosophy in favor of humanistic studies, especially the classics
and rhetoric, as well as the Scriptures. He described the medieval
period as the "dark ages" preceding the Renaissance of culture.

SOURCE: Philipp Melanchthon, *De corrigendis adolescentiae
studiis*. Robert Stupperich, ed., *Melanchthons Werke in Auswahl,
III, Humanistische Schriften* (Gütersloh: Verlaghaus Gerd Mohn,
1961), 29-42, translated by Lewis W. Spitz, Sr.

I may indeed seem impudent and wholly forgetful of myself in this
assembly, as one, magnificent lord rector and distinguished deans of the
academy, who will speak even though otherwise both my natural disposition
and a contemplative kind of studies would call me away from this kind of
stage and this praiseworthy assembly as it were, of orators. Particularly the
difficulty of the subject that I shall undertake could only frighten me away, if
the love of proper studies as well as the considerations of my official duties
did not incite me to desire that good letters and renascent Muses should be
commended as fully as possible to all of you. For I have taken it upon myself
to defend their cause against those who have everywhere arrogated to
themselves the titles and rewards of teachers in the schools, barbarians with
barbarous artifices, that is by force and fraud, and still restrain the people
with crafty inventions. With more than Thracian fabrication, they call back
the German youth as from the middle of the course, who only a few years
back ventured here and there to enter the happy contest of letters, now
already quite a number. They say that the study of renascent letters is more
difficult than useful; Greek is taken up by some lazy loafers and acquired for
ostentation; Hebrew is of doubtful value; that meanwhile letters of genuine
culture perish; philosophy is being deserted, and so on with further wrang-
lings. With such a herd of contentious ignoramuses, who cannot see that even
for Hercules more than one Theseus is needed?

What is more, I may be pronounced brash rather than equal to the task
assumed. Granted, however, that I should remain silent, that I can scarcely
carry out this charge without jeopardizing modesty, may I perish for it, if I
have ever before sold short any part of the humanities. For I burn with love
for the right, and, young men, inasmuch as I desire that your studies should be
vigorously supported, it is possible that I may speak some things more freely
than they wish. But since either reason (for so I view it) or some other factor
impels me hereto, I desire to have you, illustrious men, share this opportunity with me, for through your industry, counsels, and labors it is coming
to pass that far and wide letters are being cleansed of rust and squalor, and
are, it is hoped, everywhere about to regain their native splendor.

Therefore I am pleased briefly to remind the youth of our illustrious academy how relevant it is to the high rank of your glorious institution, what the rationale of the renascent studies is, what it is of theirs and what of those that our barbaric ancestors brought from the Scots to Gaul, from the Gauls to Germany, so that having recognized the order and structure of each kind, you yourselves can judge whether they can be embraced with greater reward or with less peril. And my entire address has the single purpose of raising your hope for elegant literature (I am speaking of Greek and Latin). For I know that very many, if not deterred, are certainly frightened already at the very outset by the newness of the occasion. It was preferable, however, to take the theme of the address and, as it were, the thread from the very fountains of studies and from the learned precepts of all ages; but these things belong to another scene. For the present purpose I shall describe barbarous studies with a few sincere words and I shall present the auspices under which Latin is to be learned and Greek to be undertaken. Meanwhile, I pray, hear from the speaker benignly what either my singular zeal for you or the dignity of letters itself will do for you. . . .

The studies for youth that they call preparatory exercises—grammar, dialectic, rhetoric—must be learned to the point where, instructed to speak and to discern, you shall not strive towards the high summits of these studies without a purpose. Greek letters should be added to Latin, so that reading the philosophers, theologians, historians, orators, poets, wherever you turn, you may gain the very substance, not the shadow of things, as Ixion intending to embrace Juno fell upon a cloud. This provision for the journey as it were having been prepared, approach philosophy, as Plato says, by shortcuts and with ease. For I am fully of the opinion, that whoever desires to undertake anything distinguished, either in the sacred cults or in the affairs of state, will achieve but very little, unless he has previously exercised his mind prudently and sufficiently with humane disciplines, for that is what I call philosophy. I would not, however, have anyone trifle with philosophizing, for thereby you will eventually forget also the general sense. But of the best select the best and those that pertain to the knowledge of nature as well as to the formation of character. Here, above all, the erudition of the Greeks, which comprises the universal knowledge of nature, is necessary, so that you can discuss behavior fitly and fully. The most valuable are Aristotle's *Ethics*, Plato's *Laws*, the Poets, and certainly also those that are the best and can be read for the purpose of educating the minds. For the Greeks Homer is the fountain of all disciplines, Vergil and Horace for the Latins.

For this purpose history is altogether indispensable, and to it alone, if I should be so bold, I would, by Hercules, not have been unwilling to yield whatever praises the whole world of the arts deserves. It says more fully and better than Chrysippus and Crantor what is noble, what shameful, what useful, what not. No part of life, neither public nor private, can remain unaffected by it. Both public as well as personal concerns are indebted to it. And I do not know if our world would suffer less harm without the sun, its soul as it were, than without history, the principle of all civil activities. Our forebears have often insisted unanimously that the Muses were born from memory. Hence, lest I am mistaken, it is shown that every kind of art flows from history.

With the name "philosophy" I therefore include the science of nature, the principles and examples of behavior. Whoever has been properly imbued with these has secured for himself the way to the summit. The attorney at law will have the source for preparing an oration rich in content and forceful; the statesman the source from which he may acquire formulas for the peaceful, the good, the just. . . .

For this very reason I said that the church, deprived of the use of letters, had somewhere corrupted true and genuine piety with human traditions. After the comments of men began to please us, we, overcome by the love of our works, partook Baal-peor for manna; we began to be humans and not christs [Num. 25:3-5; Deut. 4:3; Joshua 22:17]. In saying these things I wish to be understood as I think. But I fully think nothing else than what is approved by the decrees of the church for the Evangelical truth, and I shall hold to what the Hebrews say: "His faithfulness is a shield and buckler" [Ps. 91:4]. Do you not now see clearly how important the renascent studies are, how much they conduce to the cultivating of good minds? Who would not be saddened by the former age, which, deserted by such a bright light of studies, fell into the darkness of Orcus and I know not what dregs of letters? Who would not be moved by the dreadful calamity of our time which has been robbed even of the old authors of our own countries, because afterwards these would also have gained the desired profit from the good, if those had not perished.

There remains then, young men, for you to hear, that although it is this way and the things that are excellent are hard, nevertheless diligence overcomes difficulty, so that I hope you will obtain the good at far lower cost than the bad. . . . Therefore take hold of sound studies and turn over in your mind what the poet says: He has half done who has begun. Dare to know, cultivate the ancient Latins, embrace Greek, without which Latin cannot be rightly pursued. These will nourish the talent for the use of all letters more gently and will render it more elegant whatever its origin. The past few years there have come to light men who should serve you both as example and stimulus, for in silence I seem to see that Germany at various places is blossoming again and is growing mild both in ethics and in ordinary human affection, and once brutal with barbarous disciplines, is, as it were, being tamed; I do not know what monstrosity it has been accustomed to breathe out. Accordingly then you will arrange your work not only for your own good and to pass it on to the coming generations, but altogether for the immortal glory of, according to common consent, the best prince, who holds nothing more dear than the cultivation of good letters. Likewise, as for me, I shall do everything possible not to appear to fail either the will of the most pious prince, most noble hearers, or your studies. And this, most noble heads of the Saxon academy, I promise and vow upon my honor; it will be your responsibility to guard and conserve benignly and dutifully my youth, consecrated to good letters, imbued with the best of arts, and, in conclusion, commended sedulously to your trust. I have spoken.

2

The Oration of Philipp Melanchthon *In Praise of a New School*, Delivered at Nuremberg in an Assembly of Very Learned Men and nearly the Entire Senate (1526)

In the spring of 1526 the city council of Nuremberg opened a humanistic gymnasium or secondary school for the liberal arts. For this festive occasion they naturally invited Philipp Melanchthon, whom they had very much wanted as the first rector and professor of rhetoric, to deliver the main address. On May 26 he delivered *The Oration in Praise of a New School* in St. Aegidien's Church.

SOURCE: Philipp Melanchthon, *In laudem novae scholae*, 1526. Robert Stupperich, ed., *Melanchthons Werke in Auswahl*, III, *Humanistische Schriften* (Gütersloh: Verlagshaus Gerd Mohn, 1961), 63-69, translated by Lewis W. Spitz, Sr.

May all good fortune and happiness be yours and your children's and the entire state's. Most illustrious men, as you desired, these men whom you called here in behalf of the state to teach honorable discipline have opened a school of letters, and they wished to announce this publicly to you with my address. For in accordance with the practice of the stage that the prologue speaks of the poet's purpose or the theme of the drama before the performance, so they have asked me, for the sake of the friendship that I have shared with them for a very long time, to serve as the prologue of the drama to be performed by them. And it was not proper for me to refuse their wish, although it was an impudence to do something that makes me appear as though I about snatched away from the most eloquent speakers the most important parts in speaking. But it was necessary to oblige these very friendly people, even at some peril on my part, and the parts had to be taken up that I did not of my own accord take for myself, but which they imposed on me by virtue of their personal right.

But since this occasion demands that we adorn your resolution that you made regarding the establishment of the school, I wish that this cause were treated by some more eloquent orators, who could speak in accord with its merit and could match the greatness of the matter with their speech. For I am afraid in my lack of eloquence that by want of talent I shall diminish your praises of extraordinary and nearly divine wisdom. For surely, because you have perceived that the power and usefulness of letters, unknown to the public and far removed from the view of the multitude, must be preserved and have decided that they must be kept from destruction, particularly at this time when we are in danger everywhere, this is indeed a certain kind of divine wisdom. For what else brings greater benefits to the whole human race than letters? No art, no work, not, by Hercules, the very fruits born of the earth, not, finally, this sun, which many have believed is the author of life, is as necessary as the knowledge of letters. For since neither the state nor an assembly of people can be gathered and governed without laws and courts of justice and without religious institutions, the human race will rove around like wild beasts if these have perished, from which good laws have come forth, good morals and gentleness have been born, and by which religion has been propagated and endures to our memory. If anyone has too little faith in my speech, let him consider the morals and the kind of life of the nations that have not known letters, as they report regarding the Scythians. These, in the first place, have no states established by laws, no courts of justice, right is whatever those have done who are strongest either by force or factions, no commerce with neighboring markets, no exchange of things. The only protection against famine is to rob many people. There is also a rumor that they feed on the flesh of strangers, but at home there is not only no discipline, but also those affections that nature generally generates in men's hearts, conjugal faithfulness, love of offspring, love of neighbors and servants, have been extinguished by barbaric morals. There is no knowledge of educating children, without which no good men can be produced, no admiration of virtue, no comprehension of the honest, no friendships formed by honorable favors, no sense of humanity, finally no right opinions regarding religion and the will of God toward mortals. So in kind are other barbarians, some more, others less savage, living a kind of cyclopian life. For the morals of these peoples must degenerate into barbarity of this kind, if they are not excited and shaped by letters to virtue, to humanity, to piety. You have done something admirably and wisely, when you bring to your city honorable disciplines, nourishers of all virtues, and strive to protect and preserve them with power. Furthermore, in these hard times above all things your counsel is deserving of praise, since there is danger that letters will suffer shipwreck in this dangerous turmoil in public affairs. For due to some error of the masses the schools are being deserted. For certain stupid demagogues detract from letters, a large part fearing for their stomach take recourse in gainful arts, after hope has been lost of living on the income of priests, which they believed to be the only rewards for their labor. For how few admire virtue so much that they reckon it ought to be cultivated gratis. Inasmuch as the matter of letters is in this crisis, it has behooved all kings and princes of the states to render aid to the endangered disciplines. But our rulers are in part so dull that they do not understand the worth of letters, in part so evil that they believe it to be advantageous to their despotic rule that all laws, religion, and civil discipline be abolished together. What shall I say of the bishops, whom our rulers desired to be at the head of both sacred affairs and of the studies of letters? Nor were the colleges of priests at one time otherwise than the schools, and most ample grants were established for the colleges so that there might be more than enough leisure and support for the learners. Nor does it seem altogether unfortunate that at one time other letters as well as sacred were treated by this class of men. Now we nowhere see more hostile foes of the good arts than in those associations of priests. Therefore in a time of need it entered your mind hospitably to welcome letters, exiled from their abodes, and to bring them, as it were, back home. It should not be unpleasant to add this embellishment to the other ornaments of your city, which even before flourished so with riches, structures, geniuses of artisans, that it could justly be compared with any one of the cities most highly praised by the ancients. Nor did any other city in Germany heretofore have more learned citizens, who, because they applied the knowledge of the finest arts to the governing of the state, brought it about that this one excelled by far all other cities of Germany. But since you have now established here an abode for honorable disciplines, it is unbelievable how great an accession has been made to that accumulation of your praises. For if you continue to excite the desires of men to learning, you will most gloriously merit the supreme thanks of the fatherland and of those outside. When under your leadership youth has been rightly instructed, it will serve as an aid to the fatherland, for no bulwarks or walls are stronger monuments than citizens endowed with erudition, prudence, and other virtues. The Spartan said that walls must be of iron not of stone. But I judge it to be defended not so much with weapons as with prudence, moderation, and piety. Then this benefaction of yours will extend to the rest of Germany, which till now (only may God favor the enterprise!), seemed inclined not to trouble itself about improving and educating youth, and it will judge those primarily able to regulate public affairs who have been instructed and habituated to virtue in this city as in a school. The name of this city is carried with the highest praise by visitors to those outside and by your benefaction you will retain the devoted hearts of men—good opinions which, unless I am mistaken, will delight you more than any imperial powers.

But although this city can vie by virtue of a great number of endowments even with Marseilles and certain other ancient cities, nevertheless I now wish rather to present to you examples of those cities that flourish in our times. Shortly before these times the city of Florence contributed the greatest benefit to all of Europe, when it first asked the teachers of Greek letters, expelled from their fatherland, to sojourn with it. It not only aided them with its hospitality, but also restored to them their studies, after it rewarded them with very ample stipends to teach. In the rest of Italy no one looked with respect on the teachers of the arts who fled from Greece, and we would have lost Greek letters together with Greece, if Florence had not rescued these most learned men from calamity, because but for the Florentines the Latin language would have been totally corrupted, vitiated and spoiled so by barbarity, and no vestiges of the Greek language would exist anymore, and with it the monuments of our religion would have collapsed, nor would anyone have understood the titles of the sacred books with the loss of Greek. For in Rome those exiles miserably suffered hunger, since the wealth of the pontiff had to be spent principally either on those who suffered great damage or on those who aided religion with the use of letters.

Theodore Gaza, good God, how great a man! They say that when he offered the books of Aristotle and Theophrastus translated into Latin and exhibited a codex sumptuously illuminated, the pontiff asked for how much he had embellished the book and paid nothing above those costs, gave no reward to the author for the labors he had expended in translating this very difficult work. Moreover, as an example, it was suitable that richer rewards should be given even for a book not so useful as that was. But the usefulness of the work did not move the pontiff to remit a richer reward equal to its worth. But after honorable arts began to revive through the benefaction of the Florentines, much usefulness has been gained from them for all peoples; everywhere the talents of many have been stirred up to the study of the best subjects. For the emulation of the Greeks stimulated also the Latins to restore their native language, which had almost totally gone to ruin. Public laws have been emended in the cities, finally religion, which previously lay buried and suppressed by the drama of the monks, has been cleansed. For this reason, though the opinions of men vary, I, nevertheless, think thus: good men discern the power and nature of religion more rightly and have at this time surer consolations of conscience than those were which the monks offered a short time ago. There is therefore no doubt that Florence, which, as it were, rescued letters from shipwreck, brought them to port, and preserved them, is very clearly deserving of all nations.

According to the example of that city you are protecting good arts in these miserable times, when bishops resort to arms instead of letters and other princes regard this concern unworthy of them, Germany is everywhere in tumult and calls to arms, and as the old verse says: "Wisdom is banished from the midst, the business is transacted by force." This obstructs these studies the most. For if laws are silent among arms, as Cicero rightly says, how much more dumb are these our arts, born and nourished in leisure. If God does not sustain and give to those who control affairs a mind to restore the interests in letters, all good arts are threatened with ruin in these disturbances. But you do not abstain from urging the most honorable and sacred purpose. For no honorable service can be offered more pleasing to God or more useful to your citizenry.

Furthermore, since envy very often pursues things rightly done, I do not doubt that you will have to contend with the wicked judgments of some. But a brave man must contemn envy of things rightly done. You will, perchance, have to contend with other difficulties as well, which, it seems, will obstruct your counsels in promoting the school, and these, too, you will overcome if you keep in mind that in this matter you are doing God's will. For unless you preserve letters, religion and good laws cannot endure. Besides, God demands that you instruct your children to virtue and religion. But not only is he impious toward the gods above, but plainly conceals the mind of a beast with a human form, who makes no effort rightly to instruct his children. This distinction nature has made between man and beast, that beasts discard the care of offspring when it has grown up, [but] on man it has enjoined [the duty] to nourish those procreated by him not only in earliest childhood, but, much more, to form their morals in accord with probity, when they have grown up.

Therefore above all things in a well-constituted state, schools are necessary where youth, which is the seed-plot of the state, will be educated. For if anyone thinks that genuine virtue can be acquired without teaching, he is very much deceived. Nor is anyone capable of governing the state without the knowledge of those letters with which every principle of ruling states is maintained. If you ponder these things, you will suffer yourselves to be frightened away neither by envy nor by any other difficulties, so that you do not invite your citizens to learning. As far as your teachers are concerned, I can give you this promise that their erudition is equal to the task they undertake and that there will be the greatest faithfulness in the performance of their office. I pray Christ to favor the beginnings of this most serious work and to prosper your counsels and the studies of the learners. I have spoken.

3

Beza's Address at the Solemn Opening of the Academy in Geneva

The year 1559 saw the opening of the Geneva Academy, Calvin's leading educational institution, which is today known as the

University of Geneva. The college offered a humanistic curriculum, including Latin, Greek, and Hebrew, in addition to philosophy and theology. The Venerable Company of Pastors nominated to the Little Council for approval as rector of the Academy Theodore Beza, professor of Greek, and later Calvin's successor as head of the movement. Beza delivered the main address at the opening of the Academy in June.

SOURCE: Theodore Beza, *Oratio Bezae in solenni actu inaurationis academiae Genevensis*, in *Ioannis Calvini Opera Quae Supersunt Omnia, Guilielmus Baum et alii*, eds., XVII (Brunswick: C.A. Schwetschke et Filium, 1877), cols. 542-546, translated by Lewis W. Spitz, Sr.

I surely . . . highly esteemed and distinguished gentlemen, sincerely wished (and this would not have been difficult at all) that the heavy burden of presiding over this school had been committed to someone more capable. But since your authority has indeed imposed this necessity on me, I shall, notwithstanding, relying in the first place on the grace of God and next also on your prayers, endeavor to support it with all my strength. Now inasmuch as I observe that this scholarly assembly is looking forward to some [statement] from me, and all of us have met here in order to hear the rules with which the highly esteemed Senate of this state has resolved to establish and maintain this academy, I shall recall a few facts regarding the very institution of schools itself. But I shall use plain and simple speech because here, too, the saying applies, "simple is the word of truth." And in order that no one should look down on these scholarly assemblages for the reason that in them outward splendor either does not shine forth at all or only faintly and thus regard them not so useful or not very necessary, I shall briefly show their great age, dignity and excellence. For another occasion will be given us to speak of the rules themselves. For truly if anyone believes that these assemblages have come into existence by change or did not aforetime begin for just and necessary reasons, he errs greatly. For though men are born in possession of reason and intelligence and so great a superiority of talent shines forth in some that they seem not so much to have learned something as to conceive it, Aristotle's opinion is nevertheless very true (which common sense itself and the constant experience of all ages confirms), that people are born neither learned nor polished and also much less experienced in the things of which knowledge is required for passing this life agreeably, but regarding this matter are born merely apt and able to perceive them. But what is the difference between a person who is altogether unpolished and unlearned and beasts devoid of reason? That least experienced judge of human affairs clearly bears witness that there is nothing more unjust than an inexperienced person, and that accordingly no more pernicious monster exists on earth than when every disorder is perceived under the pretence of injustice. Hence men must acquire learning and experience by some method that nature itself has not given them, and one must cultivate and perfect also the very best talent like fertile soil with a good education and diligence. For the saying is most surely true, "those who have learned letters see doubly." But though the brevity of human life has for a long time been such that no one person, however endowed with excellent talent, however much diligence he may apply, can observe so many things, not to mention those (as we naturally lean from work to pleasure) who are occupied with some other matters rather than with those with which one ought to be spending his whole life. For these reasons it was necessary for certain eminent talents to be raised up by God (for to whom else shall we give credit for receiving this favor, so clearly divine?). Yes, I say for certain eminent talents to be raised up by God who should surely excel by a certain divine virtue, partly in finding out some of the best things by thinking, partly in observing, and in being distributed in a certain order, that is, reduced to art. In saying this I am thinking of those who first brought to light the good arts and disciplines which are known by the general name "philosophy." For what purpose, however, are the disciplines, if there are no teachers and pupils? But our scholarly republic consists of these as parts. And since this is the case, it follows, as I proposed, that scholastic assemblages doubtless began neither by accident nor out of nothing, nor only a few centuries back, but have always been customary among ancient people by virtue of a certain divine favor, and in them, it is evident, both logs and wild and coarse beasts were through some most fortunate metamorphosis transformed into men of reason and intelligence. But come! these facts we shall, then, also prove with plain and clear examples. Passing over that pair of columns, one of brick, the other of stone, erected by Sethus (as Josephus says) and which the same writer relates of Abraham (for they are, so it seems to me at least, to be numbered among Jewish fables, and I am in the habit of numbering Josephus not only among the profane but also among the ridiculous and inept writers), I believe that from the beginning the houses of the patriarchs were schools of true and solid learning, in which the image of God, though destroyed in men by sin but restored through their faith, also with the extraordinary help of God, who supplied them with all surpassing gifts, should so shine, that whoever went there should return much more cultured and polished. We know for a certainty that Moses is commended for that fame because he thoroughly understood all the wisdom of the Egyptians. It is, however, established that the studies of true philosophy were brought from Egypt to Greece. Likewise the learning of Solomon and Daniel in every kind of good arts is reported, which some undeservedly (as I at least believe) call profane, since whether you look at God the Best and Greatest, their author, or at their proper use, nothing shall appear in them that is not sacred and right. It is also probable that there were as many schools as there were companies of prophets, in which that celestial wisdom eminently excelled that exceeds all human understanding; nevertheless, according to the custom of the time and as fully as the circumstance would bear, those studies flourished of which the knowledge accrued to the study of religion as a certain increment. But that among the gentile nations and particularly among the Greeks, though also this benefaction of God like all the others was miserably profaned, nevertheless that in such great darkness the light of truth remained somewhat unextinguished, that human society was preserved by them, that the gentiles from whom the Lord resolved in His time to gather the church for Himself did not completely extinguish themselves—all this we owe, next to God, only to those very ancient academies. But when the barbarity from the North flooded the entire West, the Lord again raised up heroic talents, for instance Charles the Great and some other Caesars as founders of the academies through which Europe flourishes today. When, therefore, the highly esteemed Senate of this city (whose lights we discern with our own eyes right in this assemblage) had most wisely weighed these reasons, these examples and other numerous arguments of the greatest weight, it could do no better than to add to the other ornaments of this city (which are both very many and very great) also the ornament of an academy. And inasmuch as it clearly saw that all assemblages first meet and are maintained with certain rules, it took pains to propose these, than which, at least for the present, none could have been proposed either more sacred or better or more suitable for securing the foundations of the academy. But another occasion, I hope, will be given to speak on the virtue of the distinguished Senate and the excellence of the laws themselves.

I shall now direct myself totally to you students and plead with you that you may not be regarded as having yourselves neglected your own advantage. The saying of Plato is well known: Knowledge that is devoid of righteousness must be called shrewdness rather than knowledge. Accordingly also the spiritually blind philosophers have observed that all good arts are relevant to the life that is to be achieved from virtue. And truly, for us to disregard this and even not to evince it with the very fact would have been too shameful. For it is small wonder that those have erred from the goal who have embraced superstition for righteousness (with which we, as it were, return to God the things that are God's), nothingness for true virtues, certain imitations of virtues and (what the poets have invented regarding their Ixion), seemingly empty clouds. But what pretext can you invent like that for whom it will be granted to suck successively almost with the very milk both solid piety and true erudition? If only (what I trust all will do voluntarily) you will have adapted your studies to the norm and the pattern of those rules. But in order that you may achieve this, it has first of all been placed under the protection of God the Greatest and Best (and that this has been prepared and set forth for you, as a great many other things, so also this day declares abundantly), then also in your diligence, and that neither the wisdom, will, liberality of the highly esteemed Senate nor the erudition, zeal [and] industry of the most learned teachers will be wanting you, you have yourselves personally observed and will hereafter, as I hope, experience even better. For this reason there remains to be urged that you do not show yourselves unworthy of so great a blessing of God the Best and Greatest through faithlessness or any negligence. Yes indeed, as you gathered at this place not in the least as once very many of the Greeks did to see their gymnastic plays and to observe their vain endeavors, but rather, imbued with the knowledge of true religion and of all good arts, to be able to magnify the glory of God and to be an ornament to the fatherland and also for an aid to yourselves, you shall remember ever and again that you must render an account of this sacred service to the Supreme Ruler. Surely (what God may avert and certainly, I trust, will avert) you will ensure for yourselves everlasting shame if, as all things are offered to you over abundantly and freely, you yourselves neglect your own advantages, you yourselves (I say) shall be seen to have conspired in your own ruin.

4

Concerning the College and University of Nîmes

[handwritten annotations: (2nd ed.) — Has a Roman Style bldg. which is the model for the Richmond Capitol.]

The Calvinists founded new universities in Leiden, Edinburgh, Groningen, Amsterdam, Utrecht, Franeker, Montauban, Saumur, Sedan, and Nîmes. At Nîmes the humanist professor Claude Baduel (1491-1561), a student of Melanchthon and a friend of the great Strassburg educator Johannes Sturm, delivered an address on the founding of the College and University of Nîmes, reflecting evangelical humanistic concerns.

SOURCE: Claude Baduel, *De Collegio et Universitate Nemausensi* (Lyons: apud Seb. Gryphium, 1540), translated by Theodore Casteel.

The most Christian king [Francis I] authorized last year [1539] the foundation of a college and university in the city of Nîmes, and he has granted to this establishment all of the privileges in effect in those localities where the liberal arts and letters are taught. Good are the motives which led the Sovereign to confer this benefit on our city: the principle is the fitness of

the place to become the seat of studies in Narbonne, a fitness recognized by
the most competent men. This creation has been greeted with satisfaction,
not only by the inhabitants of Nîmes who requested and obtained this favor,
but also by the other cities of the region which are delighted by this royal
kindness and are disposed to profit from it. And this sentiment is natural. For
if the school founded at Nîmes is organized as was agreed, it will assure to the
whole province the greatest and most noble advantages; it will revive the style
of letters, which formerly flourished in all our cities, especially in Marseilles,
and which declined; it will enlighten and improve the spirit of our citizens, a
spirit gifted with much vigor and flexibility, and which has lacked nothing to
the present day except the knowledge and the elegance of letters; it will free
the families of the great sacrifice required to educate their sons in distant
places, and of the anxieties which they suffer over the perils which are
encountered in the midst of so many vices and pleasures. Furthermore, the
thought of all of these benefits has everywhere provoked an unbelievable
desire to carry the enterprise to a good end: The magistrates pledge the
support of their authority, the bishops, a generous part of the wealth of the
Church. Finally, masters have been summoned who lack neither the knowledge for the instruction of youth, nor the virtue to form its character, nor
the kindness to encourage its progress, and they have been awarded an
honorable salary.

There has not been until now any care for the order in which it is
appropriate to teach letters and it has been completely mixed up and
confused. These vicious customs are going to be banished from the new
school where a method will be followed which is more in conformity with the
practices of the ancients, more appropriate to the diverse stages of the child's
development and to the nature of the materials which he should study, more
conformed, in a word, to our intention of reestablishing the purity of Latin
and eloquence. The school will be divided into various classes, according to
the age and development of the students. One will be the instruction of early
childhood, another that of adolescence, and each of the two will have its
beginnings, its progressive advancement, and its end. One does not know
Latin, according to the accurate remark already made in antiquity, until first
of all one can speak it and write it with clarity and accuracy, then with
elegance, and finally adapting it to the subject treated. These are three
different studies, corresponding to different ages; and it is necessary to begin
with that which conforms to the aptitudes of the young children that which
teaches to speak and write in Latin with accuracy and clarity. When more
powers are acquired with age, and this first instruction is accomplished, one
passes on to the other two stages whose purpose is to speak and write with
elegance to adapt to the subject treated.

In conformity with this division of the qualities of discourse and with the
diversity of ages and aptitudes which they suppose, eight classes are
established in which the studies of childhood are divided. Arriving at the
school at around five or six years of age, the student is kept there until age
fifteen, going through one stage each year; and as soon as he has finished the

series of classes and received in each of them that portion of instruction which is appropriate to him, he leaves there in order to go on to more liberal and difficult studies. From ages fifteen to twenty, he follows public lessons and is initiated into the advanced sciences and the arts. Until then submitted to the discipline of masters, he can neither pass to a higher class without having satisfied the regent of the preceding class, nor leave the division of classical studies without having gone through the entire curriculum which it includes. Now the student is more free; not that these public lessons free him from all subjection to his masters: he remains under the authority of the professors and accords them the deference and respect which he owes them. But his studies are less regulated and cease to be divided into different classes. At the age of twenty the young man, having received all the instruction which is given in the school, is ready to begin higher studies: medicine, law, theology, or to decide, in the knowledge of its importance, if he wishes to devote himself to the teaching of letters.

It is evident from this how much these advanced sciences depend on the knowledge of grammar and the arts. The theologian cannot explicate religion purely, nor the jurist the laws, nor the doctor the matters of his art, without having been first instructed and exercised in letters. Magistrates and bishops are right, therefore, to welcome this instruction of letters into their cities. Without them, no good government, no public order; without them, the churches would neither be able to conserve good doctrine; nor be able to defend themselves against heresies. By means of letters families not only embellish their patrimony, but also tend to augment it by forming the character of their children with good morals. Our King has shown in what esteem he holds letters by establishing in Paris and other cities honors for those who profess them, and by designating Nîmes to become the seat of a new university. This royal example of generosity towards studies has found imitators; one of the principal ones is the bishop of Nîmes, and his prévôt Robert de la Croix, both of them ready to squander their wealth for letters, if it is squandering to employ it for the benefit of the state and the church. This liberality is such that letters and their beneficiaries will never lose the memory of it, and than which nothing is more pleasing to God. Our generous benefactors can therefore expect from God abundant graces which he promises in reward to those who do well, and from scholars affectionate gratitude, an eternal remembrance. It is hardly necessary to doubt that other bishops and other magistrates, will follow an example which again makes apparent the beauty of the enterprise. This project already has the good wishes and the sympathy of numerous inhabitants of Nîmes and of the diocese who expect thus to fulfill their duty or give a sign of their piety.

Good reasons, and most decisive ones, lead them to desire the establishment of a center of studies among us. First there are the facilities which the city presents for it. Of all the cities of Narbonne, there is none more suitable to become the home of letters. It is neither close enough to the sea to participate in the softness and corruption of maritime cities, nor far enough away to be deprived of the necessities of life. It has a multitude of other advantages well known to those who have visited there. Its inhabitants are remarkable for their modesty, their frugality, their gravity. There is no luxury or permissiveness; no exaggerated refinement of the table or of dress; none of these pleasures deadly to virtue or knowledge. These are the main reasons which have persuaded the King to make Nîmes the seat of studies and letters, and this liberality of the Sovereign moves the citizens of whom I speak to do their part in an enterprise so honorable and so beneficial. What more notable sign of esteem can a monarch give to a city than to accord it that which brings glory to his reign and benefit to his people, that which he treats, in every city, with the greatest honor.

Plato was correct to write that states will be happy when they are governed by philosophers or by princes who love philosophers and philosophy. Happy then is France! For her King is not only a philosopher himself, but full of affection and generosity for philosophy and letters, for philosophers and for the wise men who teach them. The prophet Isaiah predicted correctly that in the last days kings would be the protectors of letters and the nourishers of piety. Therein is the honor of our Prince; honor such that no age, no generation to come, shall neglect to celebrate it. For letters are neither ungrateful nor forgetful; they preserve forever the memory of benefits and respond to them with noble praises. May God keep the King in his good will for letters; may he give to those who live under his laws the desire to imitate him, to emulate him, to give him in this sphere of his enterprises the cooperation and the aid which they give him in all others!

5

Preface to Cuspinian's Chronicle

In 1537 Caspar Hedio published an edition of the Ursberger Chronicle and Philipp Melanchthon provided a foreword on the great value of history. Two years later Hedio published his translation of Johannes Cuspinian's *Caesares*, and Melanchthon included his preface once again, altered only at the beginning and end.

SOURCE: *Preface to Cuspinian's Chronicle, 1541* in Robert Stupperich: *Der unbekannte Melanchthon* (Stuttgart: W. Kohlhammer Verlag, 1961), 183-191, translated by Lewis W. Spitz, Sr.

Philipp Melanchthon wishes the reader of this chronicle God's grace through Jesus Christ our Lord and all good.

There are some learned people who are in doubt as to whether it is better and more productive to take and to pick out the best and most useful selections from the Greek authors and to translate them into Latin, or whether it is more useful to let everything in the language in which it is written. And they are concerned about this when they translate and turn into a foreign language the writings of Galen and Hippocrates, who wrote about medicine, lest they make many people lazy and indolent. As a result the Greek language, in which these writers described and published their medical art and skill, would be known and understood by very few. Or, if they do not translate them, common use of them would be understood by a very few. But one can very quickly decide about such a division of the scholars, for the first is simple and easy to answer. For anyone of an intellectually curious kind and nature will not let himself be deterred from the investigation of Greek or any other language because it has been translated into another. As Plato says: No human art or remembrance of it can possibly be attained, unless the ideas, which are secret mechanisms and forms, express them perfectly and bring them to light. In the same way no translator or commentator of any language would want to alter its form, or not let its special style and ornament remain, though he cannot reproduce it exactly and can even less improve upon it. Since matters are so arranged, then, that the useful arts and languages do not require a lazy or indolent person, and those who are industrious, diligent, and reasonable always reflect and struggle in order to acquire it better, we should not allow for common use that which is found by foreigners to be right and good. And while there are many and great things which it is necessary for all men to know, there is still nothing more necessary and useful than for a man to be knowledgeable in history and to understand it well. For no one is so wise and smart that he cannot derive some profit from reading history, since so many and various events are comprehended and stated in it.

Various excellent historians have diligently recorded how histories make us mindful in many matters, admonish to virtue, deter us from vice, protect us from injury. As Thucydides says, histories are an eternal treasure, from which all times can take examples useful for life. But Polybius, who lived at the time of Scipio the Elder and fought in wars with him, offers a very useful teaching. He says that one should not learn various examples only piecemeal, but what is much more useful, to have proper histories of governments, appended to one another, in which to see what changes took place in monarchies, lands and cities in all times, and what the causes were. Truly this thought of Polybius, a very experienced man, is a very wise one, for to take note of and to ponder such changes together with their causes and circumstances produces much by way of lofty precept and instruction. For example, Shem saw both worlds, the first before the flood and that which followed after. He heard Noah, his father, and other ancestors who lived with Adam and saw all the wondrous works of God, which happened before, and learned the lofty wisdom of the ancients. Thereafter he saw the sins because of which the flood came, and observed how after this punishment all of nature was changed and became weak. He saw how soon the world again forgot God, how Sodom was destroyed, for the holy man Shem experienced all this and did not live far from Sodom. These various examples without doubt caused him as a God-fearing and prudent man to reflect on the future mode of existence in the world and greatly strengthened his faith in God.

Therefore, as Polybius said, it is useful to have complete chronicles from beginning to end, so that we can look carefully at the world order, the beginning of our human nature, as well as of religion and kingdoms and the changes in them. For what blindness human beings would suffer, if we knew nothing of our beginning and of the origin and change of religion, and could not think back in any other way than animals do? That would be abominable blindness and darkness. One should therefore value histories highly, and especially such chronicles as guide us correctly into all times.

There can be no doubt that histories were written by the holy writers such as Moses and before for two reasons, namely for the sake of religion and of the kingdom. They were written so that one would know which religion was in all times the right one and how the world departed from it. Likewise, so that one would see how secular government was first ordained by God and due to what causes the government thereafter was chastened and changed.

Therefore, we Christians especially should seek this benefit in histories, that lead us to the beginning of religion and of the right church to confirm our faith. Thereby we also see how the world very soon despised and forgot

God's word and produced gruesome error and how ever and again God nevertheless reawakened his word and upheld it and thereafter sent the promised Redeemer, our Lord Jesus Christ, and had the gospel preached in the world. The devil raised up his might against it and roused the tyrants and stirred up other error and false doctrine.

If we view the whole course of true religion from the beginning, we find very many powerful examples which provide us with all sorts of instruction and comfort. Namely, one can see that the right church is that which held God's word pure and did not contrive any new worship of God beside it. Likewise it was at all times pure and suppressed, and had to shine forth in the world both with doctrine and great good works as with a blessed government just as Abraham, Joseph, Moses, Samuel, David, Elias, Isaiah, Daniel, Maccabeus, and thereafter Christ, the Apostles, and various holy princes besides shone forth. These examples at all times strengthen the true church, when she suffers repression and sees how small and weak she is, but nevertheless reflects that the condition of the church was always such from the beginning of the world. It also provides an example of the true worship of God. How Abraham did not live according to his own ideas, but preached God's word, going by it, and carrying out His command, He showed forth his faith in many wondrous struggles for faith. In addition he cultivated reverence for and faith in God in managing his household and ruled his own people faithfully and rejected the false worship of God, which was practiced by others.

It is furthermore very useful for refuting controversial doctrine, for one can derive much guidance from it, in that one looks at the first pure church correctly and reasonably, not as an ox stares at a gate, that is, at some external circumstances, but takes note of the witness of pure doctrine and the lofty struggle against false spirits. Thus one finds useful instruction about many important articles. For example, Gregory Nazianzen and others testify that they received this doctrine most certainly from the apostles, that there are two natures in Christ and that the WORD in the phrase "In the beginning was the WORD" means a person, namely the Son of God, who is with the Father eternally, who thereafter assumed human nature. One discovers how the devil dared to efface the truth and pushed some into abandoning the writings of the prophets and apostles and relying on their own ideas, which have a nice rational appearance, and attacked these articles, such as Samosatenus and others. Against such error it is useful to know the right evidence in the histories and the actions of the ancient church. Thus Origen writes that the baptism of children was commanded by the apostles. So also one finds that several hundred years before Gregory there was no private mass, but the church had a common communion, as Dionysius and others describe it.

Likewise, just as in these times the Anabaptists condemn secular government, property, marriage, outward preaching and doctrine, hold to enlightenment without God's word, and want to create a worldly kingdom to which only pure saints belong and no one else can be a subject, so then the Manichaeans were something like that. On the other hand, one finds how various pious and learned men who stayed with God's word, opposed this error with great earnestness, which gives us evidence now against similar blasphemy.

One can, moreover, see how ever and again blindness and confusion resulted from error. From this punishment, recorded in Psalm 68 [24], follows upon despising God's word and meddling: Their eyes shall be darkened, neither shall they see. Thus in the East Mohammed's poison was spread. For the churches were torn apart by heresies and the people were confused and impertinent, and despised God's word. Then came Mohammed and brewed all those heresies together in one pot and pretended to glossate and harmonize all opinions, and create harmony, just as the world nowadays goes around with such glossating and harmonizing. So they blundered ahead and the terrible blasphemy was strengthened. To speak of this and similar examples any further would be too long here, but the only point to be made is that we should ponder in such histories, of which there are many, the causes, circumstance and awful punishments, and should admonish ourselves to the fear of God and reverence for His word.

For it is obvious how things have gone also in the West. Since men despised God's word and the ecclesiastical rulers were concerned with possessions and power, many blasphemies gained ground, such as the abuse of the mass and unchastity. And the popes increased their power through all sorts of stratagems, which set the king and princes against each other unjustly, as when Pope Hildebrand first weakened the German empire. He held against Christian doctrine and against all the ancient canons that the emperor should have nothing to say in papal or episcopal elections. He also held that confirmation by the emperors was not to be sought as formerly the popes had been confirmed by the emperors, as by Lewis the Pious, the Ottonians and the rest.

For that reason the pope stirred up the bishops in Germany and Rudolph the duke in Swabia and Saxony against Henry. He sent Duke Rudolph an imperial crown which bore this inscription: PETRA DEDIT PETRO, PETRUS DIADEMA RODOLPHO. With this he wished to suggest that Christ had given the secular empire to Peter and the pope had the power to lend it out. With such lies the pope drew Rudolph over to his side, and when he was killed three years later, the pope still did not leave the emperor in peace, but stirred up the Guelph Duke of Bavaria and Eckhart the margrave of Meissen, and finally also the emperor's son, Henry the Fifth. In this protracted war Germany was deplorably ruined, the princedoms were changed, the great cities, Nuremberg, Augsburg, Würzburg, were torn up.

This and similar histories are to be taken note of, for in them can be seen how the papal power arose and how much abuse spread in the church.

In the third place, one cannot understand the prophets without the help of the chronicles. This reason also should inspire us to read histories with zeal. For the reasons cited it is clear that it is useful and necessary for Christians to know histories, so that they may take note of the beginning and the entire course of religion. For they can judge many controversial matters and can also understand Holy Scriptures better. A Christian finds many examples thereby which admonish him to faith and fear of God, as in truth the histories provide a frightening picture of the divine wrath and judgment against all vice. The cause of great changes in kingdoms and cities has always been their immorality, murder, unchastity, the persecution of divine truth, just as Jerusalem was destroyed for putting to death Christ and the Apostles. One can see that all Asia and Greece, where the most beautiful cities were, now are waste and wilderness, for God has punished their unchastity and other vices. These examples should remind us that God is earnestly and truly angry over sins. Jehoshaphat was punished for making an alliance with a godless person, and so Christians should not associate with persecutors and tyrants.

Furthermore, something should be said about the secular use of histories. As noted above, histories should be written first of all about the kingdoms in order to show how they followed one after the other, and to provide an example for rulers of all the dangers and plots which can occur in their government. These examples preeminently for rulers provide a reminder to all virtues for everyone in his own estate.

Since this is now very extensive, I will give an example or two, so that the inexperienced can more diligently observe how to deduce instruction and learning from the histories. For if one were to handle this subject thoroughly, one would have to repeat here all of politics and ethics. One would have to set up the rules of all the virtues and apply a correct example for every rule, as Aristotle did throughout in his *Politics*, setting up the principles and then drawing applicable examples from history. To do so would be too long here.

But I will cite very briefly one case in point of how patience and levity are a great and wholesome virtue in rulers, and how changes are thereby prevented. Thrasybulus in Athens and Scipio in Rome both provided an example of how with patience to maintain the peace and to quiet unrest with wisdom. In contrast to them, other proud and vengeful men had to express their insolence, regardless of whether the country and the people were thereby destroyed, such as Marius in Rome and Alcibiades in Athens, whose impatience brought it about that Athens was finally demolished.

In the second place, histories are useful for judging many things, for one often asks how something was done before. As when Xenophon writes of a ruler in Byzantium, who surrendered the city because of hunger. When he was accused in Sparta for having surrendered such a strong city to the enemy, he excused himself on the grounds that he did not want to see the pitiful women and children die of hunger and argued that martial law did not extend so far that these people, which the enemy, too, should spare, should be allowed by their ruler and protector to starve to death. He was spoken free. This example teaches how one should act and speak in the same situation. Thus one can find precedents for various cases. Constantine protected the Christians against Licinius, his brother-in-law and ally by treaty. He also made a law that on

pain of death no one should openly practice idolatry. That is how praiseworthy Christian rulers should act, abolishing idolatry, protecting and
maintaining correct, pure teaching.

In the third place, histories also prove that empires are God's work, as
Daniel says: God upholds and destroys empires, wherefore it also happens
that God upholds righteous governments, and when tyrants disrupt them, he
punishes them and creates other empires. Therefore it is useful to see how the
empires began, one after another, grew, flourished and fell, and to see in this
God's anger and help. This also teaches both rulers and subjects to honor
government as God's order. For the order is God's; whoever disrupts the
same, fights against God, be it subject or ruler. Thus outside the divine order,
rioters, murderers, tyrants are alike. All this should be observed in the
wonderful works of God, which are to be seen in the rising and falling of
regimes. That is enough of this for now. For daily practice teaches of itself
that in all of life, in spiritual and secular matters, in government, in common
life, in welfare, in suffering, histories provide very much instruction and
comfort to every thoughtful person. Therefore one should diligently
admonish the youth to read and learn histories, especially in matters
pertaining to Christian government.

If one holds it to be useful and good, then, to translate Greek into Latin, I
consider it to be far better to translate them both into German. There is,
nevertheless, a great difference among the translators of languages, for there
are now in our times very many unskilled commentators. But among those
who are good, Doctor Caspar Hedio, the cathedral preacher in Strassburg,
pleases me greatly. For he is keenly interested, well informed, and learned in
all histories, and through the years he has turned into German many good
histories and other books. He is a delightful, learned man, truly faithful, clear,
and good at translating into German. I was therefore very happy when I
learned that this dear man had undertaken to translate Cuspinian into
German. For Cuspinian among the modern and most recent writers of
chronicles wrote of so many wonderful events and happenings with such
utility and charm, that I do not know whether in our times anything more
perfect or copious has been published. For that reason, dear reader, I have in
good faith recommended that you read this chronicle in preference to others.

May God the Lord keep you always through Jesus Christ for the growth of
his kingdom and your salvation. Amen.

H. C. ERIK MIDELFORT

Were There Really Witches?

DURING THE LATE MIDDLE AGES Europeans began to take the threat of the devil much more seriously than ever before. The devil was blamed for plague, famine, and disastrous storms. But worse than such attacks of the devil was the fact that the devil was thought to have human assistance. From the fifteenth century onwards, men and women were found guilty of allying themselves with the Evil One, of worshipping him and seeking his aid. With the devil's help such witches could torment their neighbors, cause sexual impotence and sterility, ruin crops, and generate hatred throughout a village. Not only were these witches dangerous, but they were thought to be organized in groups which met regularly for a satanic festival, often called a sabbath. So threatening were these groups of witches that many communities in Europe reacted in panic to root out their hidden enemies. In the wake of a violent hailstorm, for example, the small town of Wiesensteig in south-western Germany executed sixty-three women as witches in 1562-1563. Similarly, when an epidemic spread through Geneva in 1544-1545, the city launched a campaign against the *bouteurs de peste*, brought at least forty-three persons to trial, and executed twenty-nine.

It is perhaps understandable that people should react to misfortune by lashing out at someone. It remains difficult to see why men of the fifteenth and sixteenth centuries should have begun a general attack on old women as the culprits. Were there perhaps actual groups of women who met for ritual purposes and who prompted the frenzied attack of their fellow citizens? Or did society single out these "witches" for other reasons? These questions lie at the root of the problem, "Were there really witches?" But before we can confront that problem directly, we need a better idea of what men in the sixteenth century thought they were doing by attacking witchcraft.

We often suppose that earlier centuries had a simple, harmonious, unified view of things. But it is extraordinary how confused men of the sixteenth century were when they tried to explain what they meant by witchcraft. Instead of being agreed on all of the basic points, Europeans seem to have disagreed at every turn. This meant that sixteenth-century witchcraft doctrines were controversial, flexible, and definitely not monolithic. Some thinkers, especially those with an inordinate reverence for the ancient world of Greece and Rome, argued that witchcraft was nothing new for Europe. The famous French jurist Jean Bodin, for example, insisted that the "witchcraft" of the ancient world was not essentially different from the current sixteenth-century variety. Both involved a rejection of all religion and all morality.

For among the pagans, those who knew the difference between good and evil spirits, not only sacrificed their own children but also committed lechery and sodomy and other abominable filthiness against the right and natural reason that God engraved in our souls, to achieve their purposes. These persons were not mere idolaters but witches as well.[1]

For men like Bodin the notable rise in witchcraft did not signify a new crime but a resurgence of atheism, skepticism, and materialism. To prove the existence of witchcraft they could point beyond the contemporary evidence of witchcraft confessions to the classical world where magic and sorcery had been common. They could argue that all peoples have known witchcraft and that all nations have punished it severely. As a fervid classicist, Jean Bodin strove to make the classics apply to the modern world, to make them "relevant" to the sixteenth century. He did so by denying real changes between the age of Rome and the age of Reformation. Although Bodin has recently been associated with a "revolution" in the writing of history, his devotion to the classics kept him from seeing that his world and its witchcraft were radically

---

[1] Bodin *De la démonomanie des sorciers* (Paris: Jacques Dupuis, 1580), p. 69.

different from that of ancient times.[2] Yet surprisingly his attitude was a common one that has asserted itself among certain historians ever since.[3]

Others in the sixteenth century emphasized not the universal existence of witchcraft but its peculiarly anti-Christian character. These thinkers argued that witchcraft involved the rejection of one's own baptism, an apostasy from the true faith. Witchcraft in this sense obviously became possible only with Christianity, and only a Christian could become a witch.[4] Pope Innocent VIII had this idea in mind when he denounced, in 1484, the witches, who, "unmindful of their own salvation and straying from the Catholic faith have abandoned themselves to devils. . . ."[5] From this point of view, witchcraft was a resurgence not merely of materialism and atheism, but also of heresy. In a century of religious war it made sense to Catholics like the learned sixteenth-century Jesuit, Martin Del Rio, that the Reformation, the greatest heresy of the age, had caused a great rise in witchcraft. Lutherans in turn could blame both Catholics and Calvinists for the new tide of evil.[6] Later scholars have agreed with one element here by noting that European witch hunting was not really possible until the late Middle Ages when notions of heresy were expanded to include magical beliefs and practices. The papal Inquisition in the fourteenth century began to argue that even simple belief in healing magic (by which one might seek to heal a sick cow, for example) displayed a gross misunderstanding of God and the devil. The use of magic became evidence for alliance with evil spirits. Speaking theologically, men in the sixteenth century saw the special horror of witchcraft as heresy, denial of God, rejection of baptism, and a pact with the devil. Speaking practically, of course, most men feared the destruction and disease which witches produced. Both fears gained force from the acute awareness that this threat of

[2] Julian Franklin, *Jean Bodin and the Sixteenth-Century Revolution in the Methodology of Law and History* (New York: Columbia University Press, 1963); Donald R. Kelley, *Foundations of Modern Historical Scholarship. Language, Law, and History in the French Renaissance* (New York: Columbia University Press, 1970).

[3] Catholic polemicists have often adopted Bodin's position in order to exculpate the Church from the charge of having invented the "witchcraft delusion."

[4] William Perkins, *Discourse of the Damned Art of Witchcraft* (Cambridge: C. Legge, 1608).

[5] In his bull, *Summis desiderantes affectibus*; reprinted in Heinrich Institoris and Jacob Sprenger, *Malleus Maleficarum*, ed. and tr. by Montague Summers (London: Rodker, 1928), p. xix.

[6] H. R. Trevor-Roper, *The Crisis of the Seventeenth Century*, p. 189.

witchcraft was something utterly new for Europe. The famous
witch hunting manual, the *Malleus Maleficarum* (Hammer of
Witches) of 1486, devoted a whole chapter to the question:
"Whence it comes that the practice of witchcraft hath so notably
increased?"[7]

Subsequently, scholars have often emphasized this realization
that witchcraft was a novel problem for the late Middle Ages and
Reformation. But unlike their predecessors of 500 years ago,
scholars have not sought explanations in the increased vigor of the
devil. Anti-ecclesiastical writers have in fact often turned this
point into an attack upon Roman Catholicism. The learned
historian George Lincoln Burr wrote:

> When ... in the thirteenth century the scholastic theology, in its love of
> logical completeness, gave new prominence to the Devil and his followers as
> the counterpart and parody of God and His church, and when, in the
> fourteenth century, the Holy Inquisition, successful in rooting out heretics,
> turned its idle hands to those viler sinners whom it believed plighted wholly
> to Satan, the terror grew.[8]

In this way the inoffensive conclusion that witch trials only began
to spread in the late Middle Ages is often turned polemically into
an attack upon the ideas and institutions of the Church.[9] Just as
scholars have sometimes adopted Jean Bodin's position to show
that witchcraft is universal, more "enlightened" researchers have
unconsciously turned the tradition of the *Malleus Maleficarum*
against itself by framing an assault on Roman Catholicism.

Yet Bodin and the *Malleus* were not the only two poles of
debate in the sixteenth century. There were other thinkers who
emphasized not the spiritual crime of witchcraft but the actual
harm produced by witches. For lawyers of this persuasion, it
mattered less whether a witch had a pact with the devil than that
real crimes were committed: murder, theft, sterility, crop failure,
storms, earthquakes, and misfortune of any unpredictable sort. In
England this view prevailed in the sixteenth century, especially
because the fantastic complications of continental demonology
and inquisitorial practice were never fully adopted there. The laws
of the sixteenth century in England punished explicitly those who
"shall use, practice or exercise any Witchecrafte, Enchantment,
Charme or Sorcerie, whereby any person shall happen to bee killed

---

[7]*Malleus Maleficarum*, Part I, Question 5.
[8]George L. Burr, *The Witch Persecutions* (Philadelphia: University of Pennsylvania
Press, 1903), p. 1.
[9]Trevor-Roper, *op. cit.*, p. 185.

or destroyed, . . . their Concellors and Aidours shall suffer paynes of Deathe as a Felon or Felons."[10] The revision of this law under James I in 1604 made injuring a person or his property by witchcraft punishable by death, and the mere intention to injure others by witchcraft was more severely punished than before. Still, it was clear that the main threat of witchcraft for Englishmen was its capacity to kill and injure.[11] On the continent we find this emphasis on *maleficium* (harmful magic) over heresy implicit in the official law of the Holy Roman Empire as late as 1532. The code promulgated by Charles V, called the *Carolina*, made it clear that "when someone harms people or brings them trouble by witchcraft, one should punish him with death. . . . When, however, someone uses witchcraft and yet does no one any harm with it, he should be punished otherwise."[12]

For lawyers trained in theology and in scholastic demonology, this law was hard to interpret. It seemed to imply that the worst Satanism was a less serious crime than the slightest harm done by non-demonic magic. As a result of this difficulty, many German legal codes in the second half of the sixteenth century were worded in such a way as to punish demonic magic (implying a pact with the devil) more severely than non-demonic or natural magic (in which no pact was evident). Men could be punished for their thoughts and intentions. But despite these changes, the traditions of both common law and Roman law, as blended into the *Carolina*, laid emphasis not on the heresy of witchcraft but on the crime of harmful magic (*maleficium*).

These three schools represent the most prevalent approaches to the crime of witchcraft in the sixteenth century. The tradition of Bodin argued that atheism was the basic crime; the *Malleus* stressed rather the pact with the devil; and a strong legal tradition emphasized the actual harm done rather than the spiritual crime of witchcraft. Yet all three traditions agreed that magical practices and the power of the devil could produce remarkable, wondrous, "supernatural" effects.[13] A fourth tradition of the sixteenth

[10] 5 Elizabeth Cap. 16; cited in Wallace Notestein, *A History of Witchcraft in England from 1558 to 1718* (New York: Russell and Russell, 1965), p. 14.

[11] For a comparison of the two statutes, see A. D. J. Macfarlane, *Witchcraft in Tudor and Stuart England*, p. 15.

[12] G. Radbruch, ed., *Die peinliche Gerichtsordnung Karls V. von 1532* (Stuttgart: Reclam, 1962), Article 109, p. 76.

[13] Not supernatural in the sense of a miracle, which only God could perform, but in the sense of events which human reason could not penetrate. Terrestrial magic could produce *mira* or wonders, but not *miracula*. Even the devil was bound by the laws of nature.

century undercut even that conclusion by insisting that magic was all a fraud perpetrated either by the devil or by infamous men, bent on deluding their neighbors. The first articulate spokesman of this viewpoint was the Rhenish physician, Johann Weyer. In 1563 he proposed that the only witches worthy of execution were those who had poisoned others. Relying on the ancient Greek version of the Old Testament he claimed that the stern injunction "Thou shalt not suffer a witch to live" (Exodus 22:18) should really be translated "Thou shalt not suffer a poisoner to live." The Bible, he said, made no mention of a pact with the devil. In a tolerant vein he argued that one should not punish men or women for their opinions and heresies, even if they did confess to copulating with the devil. Such confessions usually came from old women who were feeble, senile, and deluded. Weyer in this way concentrated on the secular crime of witchcraft and then interpreted that crime as nothing more than physical poisoning. Surprisingly enough, even this extreme position won supporters in the sixteenth and seventeenth centuries, but it never became dominant over large areas.

These four traditions summarize in fair fashion the basic positions common in the sixteenth century regarding witchcraft. Yet a vast hinterland of magical and occult practices lay behind witchcraft in the strict sense, and often seemed in danger of being subsumed into the formal concept of witchcraft. About these practices and rituals there was no less squabbling than on other points. For example, the learned Swiss physician Theophrastus Bombastus von Hohenheim, called Paracelsus, claimed that the proper use of talismans and chemicals in conjunction with the stars and planets could harness the natural cohesive energy of the universe. One could use this energy for wondrous effects on disease.[14] Obviously, Paracelsus claimed to be using forces beyond the normal understanding and perception, and yet the pompous and flamboyant medical man was never tried as a witch. Similarly, neo-Platonists like the Florentine Marsilio Ficino sang "Orphic" hymns to the heavens in an effort to commune more closely with the basic powers of the universe.[15] Alchemists of the sixteenth century tried bizarre methods of transforming base materials into more valuable ones. The English magician John Dee used magic and astrology for the benefit of the Elizabethan court. He even

---

[14] Walter Pagel, *Paracelsus. An Introduction to Philosophical Medicine in the Era of the Renaissance* (New York: Karger, 1958).

[15] D. P. Walker, *Spiritual and Demonic Magic from Ficino to Campanella*

possessed a conjuring apparatus by which he could raise spirits during special *seances*. And the Italian philosopher Giordano Bruno thought that the so-called Hermetic tradition (the spurious ideas of Hermes Trismegistus, a supposed contemporary of Moses) provided a key to the secrets of the universe.

In many ways, each of these men acted like witches, using occult powers. Yet none was punished for magic or witchcraft, although Bruno *was* executed for heresy. Recently the efforts of such men have been better understood as desperate attempts to make sense of a chaotic cosmos. [16] Convinced that cheerful rationalism, the belief in man's ability to reason, was doomed to failure, these philosophers developed strange, secret, magical ways of getting at the mysteries of the universe. They generally argued that if indeed they were using magic, it was only a "natural magic" based on a profound understanding of the ordinary forces of nature. They all resisted the allegation that such insights must really depend on the help of demons or of the devil himself. Despite the unpopularity and suspicion that haunted many of their careers, these Renaissance philosophers of magic were evidently safe enough. They were often able to convince the learned class of Europe that their bookish learning was a true descendant of the *magus* tradition of the ancient world, a tradition enshrined in Christianity by the story of the Wise Men who followed a star to Christ. These modern magi never posed a threat to the village rye crop or to the fertility of cattle. Of course there were always men who opposed these thinkers and who circulated vicious stories about them, as in the case of Agrippa of Nettesheim, a sixteenth-century German humanist who was rumored to keep a "familiar spirit" or personal demon in the shape of a black dog. But by and large Europeans made an effective distinction between such occult philosophers, buried in their ancient texts, and the village hag whose ignorant magic had a thoroughly devilish basis.

In addition to this group of Renaissance magi, there were at the village level practitioners of "white" magic, as opposed to black magic. These beneficent persons, often called "cunning men" in England, tried to help their neighbors cope with evil either by curing particular diseases or by offering advice to troubled persons regarding possible witches who could have caused their particular

---

[16] Will-Erich Peuckert, *Pansophie. Ein Versuch zur Geschichte der weissen und schwarzen Magie* (Berlin: Erich Schmidt Verlag, 1956, second edition); Charles G. Nauert, *Agrippa and the Crisis of Renaissance Thought* (Urbana: University of Illinois Press, 1965).

misfortune. [17] Such cunning men were often respected by the
local community, for whom they served as an extra-ecclesiastical
source of spiritual comfort. Often these wizards went about their
business without any trouble or disturbance. But frequently they
managed to offend either a client of theirs or some other person,
and a legal complaint might be lodged. Then, most often an
ecclesiastical court would examine the supposed white witch and
either offer a reprimand and warning or turn the hapless suspect
over to a secular court for criminal prosecution. Since the
demonologists held that anyone lifting a spell could also cast one,
many cunning men and women were brought to trial suspected of
maleficent witchcraft. But such wizards were never eliminated
completely. It has been difficult to tell just how many of these
local conjurers and magicians there were, but most estimates for
England in the late sixteenth century suggest numbers approxi-
mately equal to that of the parish clergy. We have no idea how
prevalent such wise men and women were in the rest of Europe,
but they were obviously sought out by common folk for similar
reasons. During a witch panic at Ellwangen in southwestern
Germany in the early seventeenth century, one witness described
how his father had dealt with sickness among his horses.

They went to a witch at Lusstnau named Biren Ketterin, who is now dead, to
ask advice on where this misfortune might come from. The witch came into
their house and said that such misfortune originated with evil persons. But
she could cause the evil witch in question to reveal herself. As soon as she left
their house, she said, a person would come asking for three things. If they
gave her these things, their problem with the animals would get worse than
before. Then, hardly after the witch had gone, Barbara Rieffin came into
their house and asked for a shawl, a butter box, and a cradle. But she was
refused.[18]

The horses' health had improved at once, and Barbara Rieffin was
executed as a maleficent witch. Thus the indirect testimony of
white witches and cunning women might even help convict others
of evil magic. The cunning woman was often so respected that if
charged with witchcraft she could rally her neighbors to her
defense.[19] Often she had a set fee schedule and operated on an
almost regular basis. Business could be so good that some practitioners complained of never having a moment's rest.[20] Yet their

---

[17] For the following, see Keith Thomas, *Religion and the Decline of Magic*, p. 245.
[18] This story also supports Macfarlane's contention that the persons most resented in
a village were those who made demands on its charity, pp. 172-76.
[19] Thomas, p. 251.
[20] *Ibid.*, p. 250.

reputation and prestige were usually extremely local, and they always ran the risk of being haled before the church or secular authorities and punished. If convicted of conjuring spirits or compassing someone's harm, they might even be executed.

Another form of popular magic involved no consultation of wizards but the attempt to follow the instructions or recipes of magical handbooks that guaranteed the discovery of buried treasure or the like to the careful adept. From the Middle Ages onwards certain magical books had been known to the West. Some of them rested on a neo-Platonic foundation or on the Kabala (the study of the secret meaning of the Hebrew scriptures) and formed the source of Renaissance magical philosophy. But other books prescribed rituals aimed not at profound insights into the cosmos but at the simple discovery of hidden treasure. In Germany, for example, the Faust legend inspired many men to attempt the magical route to wealth. The legend of Faust, of course, ended with the damnation of that wretched soul for selling himself to the devil. But the books of Faustian ritual that spread through Germany in the sixteenth and seventeenth centuries tried optimistically to emphasize the secret of compelling the devil to do one's bidding. So long as one made no covenant with the devil, or so long as one could escape from a pact with the devil, one was apparently safe in performing these magical rituals. We know of many attempts to put such Faustian rituals to use in raising treasure.[21] In other cases we know of men who actually signed pacts with the devil. In the seventeenth century the magical "Passau" art of protecting oneself against bullets grew in popularity, especially after the Thirty Years War. In all of these instances we can trace the corruption of high magical-philosophical ideals into popular superstitions. Yet again, we must insist, these kinds of magic almost never resulted in accusations of witchcraft.

If we return to our original question, "Were there really witches?", we can see that a careful answer is necessary. We can affirm the existence of learned magicians who claimed to practice natural magic. We know too that cunning men and women used "white" magic in the villages to help their neighbors to solve problems of love, hatred, disease, and bad luck. Again, we know of popular magical handbooks teaching the reader how to compel demons to do his bidding. We even know of men who, Faust-like, signed written pacts with the devil. And yet, none of these figures

[21] Eliza Butler, *Ritual Magic* (Cambridge: Cambridge University Press, 1949), pp. 211-13.

elicited the blind panic of witch hunting. None of these magicians and sorcerers were generally considered dangerous witches.

There remain two sorts of witchcraft whose existence is much more problematic. On the one hand we have seen that some thinkers of the sixteenth century regarded witches as those who used harmful magic. On the other hand, some men of the sixteenth century saw witches as an organized band of devil worshipers. Did witches in either of these senses really exist?

First, were there persons who used harmful magic against their neighbors? The answer is almost certainly yes. In England, for example, witches were occasionally captured with wax figures of their enemies, or with dolls pierced with needles or thorns.[22] Cursing tablets with the formulas by which one could destroy an enemy have survived as evidence that black magic was practiced in England. In Germany we know that some self-proclaimed witches performed rituals to produce rain, hail, and lightning. Part of the ceremony evidently involved throwing the contents of a witches' cauldron into the air. Necromancy, involving the magical use of corpses, was obviously practiced occasionally. As late as the eighteenth century some German towns had to warn their grave diggers not to allow anyone to steal the hair or fingernail clippings from dead children. It is also clear that many individuals accused of witchcraft were malevolent and antisocial. In some cases they were suspected of major crimes like rape, theft, and murder, and there is little reason to suppose that they would not have availed themselves of black magic if necessary. So, men and women in some numbers certainly practiced black magic across most of Europe. A recent scholar has even suggested that their magic was often effective. If one knew that an enemy had cast a spell on one, and if one believed in the efficacy of spells, the psychological pressure might well be so great as to produce an hysterical or psychosomatic response.[23] From fear of magic, magic gained its powers. Certainly, then, in this sense there really were witches.

But were there groups of witches who gathered for ritual celebration? For this the evidence is imperfect. In the early Middle Ages a famous church law denounced women who claimed to ride with Diana at night. These women, the canon said, were deluded in thinking that they or the devil could do things that only God could do. There are other similar references to secret groups

---

[22]Thomas, p. 514.
[23]Chadwick Hanson, *Witchcraft at Salem* (New York: Braziller, 1969).

worshiping pagan gods in the early Middle Ages, and it is difficult to tell what we should make of such utterances. On the one hand, there seem to have been pagan groups of Diana-worshipers. But on the other hand the Church often condemned belief in their meetings. Even later in the Middle Ages strange groups and strange practices appear. We know of several New Year's and May Day celebrations that revived at least the forms of pagan ritual. In the eleventh and twelfth centuries a number of Reformist heretics found followers and built sects that were accused of magic and heresy combined. But heretics were not only suspected of witchcraft; they often shaped the very conception of witchcraft itself.

The Catharists or Albigensians, for example, developed a powerful heresy that solved the problem of evil by positing an Evil Principle parallel to God. God in this way was spared the embarrassing responsibility for evil that orthodox theology came near to granting him, but only by depriving God of his omnipotence. Although these Christian heretics of southern France never worshiped the devil, it is obvious that they elevated him to a position of power much greater than orthodoxy allowed. It should not surprise us to find that the Catharists were accused of devil worship and firmly rooted out by ferocious crusade and zealous inquisition in the thirteenth century. Actual devil worship did emerge among the German Luciferans and the Bohemian Adamites.[24] The idea of an organized sect of devil worshipers, therefore, had a sound basis in fact, but the inquisitors came to believe that most heretics were similarly organized. During the fourteenth century organized groups of magicians were found, convicted, and executed. It is extremely difficult to tell the extent to which these groups represent (1) survivals of older heresies; (2) self-conscious groups of witches; or (3) innocent victims of inquisitorial suspicion and torture. In many early cases they must have been surviving bands of heretics, but as the Inquisition perfected its procedures, it becomes much more difficult to tell if they were finding groups of witch-heretics or simply torturing suspects into accusing their supposed accomplices. Because the courts came to assume that witches were organized, as heretics had been earlier, and because the courts could legally use torture to compel guilty men to give further information, one must treat recorded confessions with great caution. Even confessions described as "voluntary" were often extracted with the threat of

[24] Jeffrey B. Russell, *Witchcraft in the Middle Ages*, pp. 141-42.

torture. And it is possible that persons convicted of witchcraft decided to implicate their personal or political enemies. There is some evidence that rival factions in a town could use witchcraft accusations against each other. It will repay us, therefore, to scrutinize carefully the evidence that can be assembled regarding the existence of an organized witch-cult.

The first kind of evidence for the existence of a witch-cult comes from medieval descriptions of heathen survivals. English sources, for example, speak of May Day celebrations with a leader dressed in skins and a horned headdress. Since some prehistoric European religions featured a horned god, some students have suggested the survival of prehistoric cults down to the Middle Ages. According to this theory, the secret religion of medieval Europe was paganism, and the startling lack of evidence regarding this cult is due to the clerical monopoly of literacy. Since the Church was embarrassed about the pagan nature of most medieval men, it simply suppressed all reference to it. This "witch cult" supposedly survived until the Church finally mustered its strength in the fifteenth century and began to crush this fertility religion of the masses. Now it is clear that pagan rituals did survive long into Christian times. They account in part for the *Mardi Gras* and *Fasching* of France and Germany, and for the May Pole. Yet the survival of pagan ritual acts, masks, and costumes unfortunately does not demonstrate the survival of paganism. And the medieval survivals seem mostly to have been local customs, sanctioned by tradition and by the Church itself. These festivals were so thoroughly domesticated and robbed of original meaning that they can no longer be described as a cult.[25]

In modern times stories of secret meetings have also been common. The Spanish anthropologist Julio Caro Baroja, for example, tells of a secret black mass among the Basques. Riotous eating and drinking, a parody of Christian rituals, a recitation of spells and incantations, and naked dancing all took place on at least one occasion. From eyewitness accounts Caro Baroja suggests that these sorts of nocturnal festivities were precisely what the witch hunters had in mind. In this sort of evidence one could perhaps see the survival of a witch cult. Yet even Caro Baroja shrinks back from so bald an assertion, for this cult could also be of more recent origin, the offshoot of some unorthodox sect.[26]

---

[25] See Margaret A. Murray, *The God of the Witches* (London: Faber, 1952), and Elliot Rose, *A Razor for a Goat* (Toronto: University of Toronto Press, 1962).
[26] Julio Caro Baroja, *The World of the Witches*, p. 230.

Similarly the German historian Hans-Martin Decker-Hauff tells of an old forester whom he knew well and trusted.[27] In his youth the forester had once spent a night in an abandoned hunting lodge, only to be awakened by the dancing of several women, all well known to him. These women of the Black Forest were shocked and embarrassed to learn that their secret meeting had been discovered. Here too one must suspect a survival of some kind of ritual from earlier times. But there is no evidence that such groups, when they did exist, were actually as ancient as one might suppose. They could just as easily have been revivals or artificial rituals concocted by bored or spiritually deprived peasant women. With medieval and modern evidence, therefore, the same problems exist. How can one be sure that these ritual or festive activities really were the actions attacked by the witch hunters during the early modern period, 1400-1700? It seems clear that there is no real substitute for contemporary evidence.

The sixteenth-century chronicler Martin Crusius offers an example of a group of women who perhaps gathered secretly for a festival that bears all the marks of a witches' coven. As he tells it, in the year 1588 the wine steward of a tavern in Bernau in the German Southwest was unable to account for periodic shortages of wine. To get to the bottom of this mystery, the innkeeper hid in his winecellar overnight and watched with amazement as seventeen old women "poured wine for themselves and drank joyously with one another according to their established custom." When the innkeeper brought charges against them, perhaps including charges of witchcraft, they admitted that they had done this and "other such evil deeds for the past seventeen years. Therefore they were burned to death." The tale of the thirsty witches of Bernau did not end there, however. For "some of them had relatives in a village of that region, and they came to Bernau around the first of January, 1589, and set it ablaze at five places; 129 buildings burned down including the town hall and all its contents, and twenty-three persons besides."[28]

It is tempting to conclude that Crusius here describes an operating coven of witches who met for ritual celebration. As it stands, however, his account is also a clear reflection of factional tensions between town and village in the Black Forest. It may be that further documents can be found to penetrate this Bernau

[27] Personal communication.
[28] H. C. Erik Midelfort, *Witch Hunting in Southwestern Germany, 1562-1684*, pp. 186-87.

puzzle, but at present it seems possible only to conclude that a cult may have operated there. A German cultural historian has found other nebulous evidence of such secret women's groups,[29] and recently Emmanuel Le Roy Ladurie, a profound social historian, has treated French witchcraft as a form of wild rural rebellion against the urban culture of official France. In this view, the peasants of southern France were so spiritually malnourished that the devil was easily an attractive alternative. The outbursts of rural revolt in the late sixteenth century coincide often with areas of witchcraft prosecution. The same families often produced both rebels and witches.

In both phenomena, insurrection and witchcraft, we find from time to time the schema of inversion, an extension of the dream—a fictional reversal of the real world, very common in myth-making and in "primitive thought." It is not astonishing if that inversion is linked to certain types of revolts, chimerical or effective, and often desperate. To invert the world, to turn it upside down, is not to revolutionize it, not even truly to transform it; it is nevertheless to dispute it, deny it, proclaim disagreement with it in elementary fashion. Like the revolts, like popular festivals, the witchcraft of 1600 carries the systematic stamp of such a tendency.[30]

Le Roy Ladurie summons evidence from church visitation and witchcraft trial to show how common this inversion of values is among rural, "backward" people. It may well have been one of the only gratifications remaining to imagine a mass read backwards or a priest mumbling his words while upside down, or to install a beggar as mayor and a devil as god. This kind of theory would make the formation of a witch cult plausible. But the evidence cited cannot prove that a cult, an organized group of witches, actually existed.

From another angle one can detect a pharmacological explanation of witchcraft. In this theory the basic problem is how to understand the voluntary confessions of flight and witches' sabbath which seem occasionally to appear in witch trials. The answer often given is that of drug-induced hallucination. We know that witches' salves sometimes prescribed nightshade, which contains belladonna. Historians have suggested that these salves, when smeared on the body, might well produce sensations of flight. This explanation was even suggested in the sixteenth century, and a

---

[29]Will-Erich Peuckert, "Hexen- und Weiberbünde," *Kairos* 2 (1960), 101-105.

[30]Emmanuel Le Roy Ladurie, *Les Paysans de Languedoc*, as translated in E. William Monter, *European Witchcraft*, pp. 170-71

respected scholar has concluded flatly, "It is these opiates, then, and not flying brooms or animals, which carry the witch off into a world of fantasy and emotion."[31] Certainly drugs provide a better explanation than flying brooms, but again we have merely a plausible means of explaining some of the fantastic confessions of flight, dance, and demonic copulation. Proof requires more than plausibility, and pharmacology does not help prove that *groups* of women got together to induce by means of drugs a group experience. In fact, the examples from the sixteenth century indicate that use of the witches' salve was usually by individuals. After the hallucinatory state had worn off, the witch might well have tales to tell of ritual encounter with other witches. But clearly such evidence does not bolster the idea that witches actually met for a sabbath. In fact it tends to explain away and weaken even the few voluntary accounts of witches' sabbaths that have been found. So the explanation of witchcraft through drugs leads to a dead end. As with the theory of witchcraft as rural rebellion, the most we can derive is a *possible* way of understanding certain bizarre aspects of witchcraft. Without positive evidence of an actual cult or group, we are left with a few stories like Crusius's thirsty women of Bernau.

This was the status of the question down to 1966, when an imaginative Italian scholar published evidence that in at least one case the Inquisition succeeded in turning a benign fertility cult into demonic witchcraft. Carlo Ginzburg examined the archival records of inquisitorial investigations in Friuli, a Venetian province, and noted a remarkable shift between 1570 and 1650.[32] Around 1570 there is strong evidence that a group of men and women, the *benandanti* (those who walk well, do-gooders), performed annually a number of ritual battles against demons and witches. They were supposed to have special powers for this task because their amniotic membranes had been preserved after their births and were now used as magical amulets. They had to "go out" at night several times a year, while apparently asleep, to protect the fields and crops from the onslaught of witches, who caused crop failures and bad weather. These protectors of communal fertility were respected by the community until the Inquisition began to wonder how true Christians could "go out" when they

---

[31] Caro Baroja, p. 255.
[32] Carlo Ginzburg, *I Benandanti: Ricerche sulla stregoneria e sui culti agrari tra Cinquecento e Seicento*, as translated in Monter, *European Witchcraft*; esp. p. 158.

were supposedly asleep, and how witches could be combatted without the use of witchcraft. Between 1620 and 1650 the Inquisition slowly reshaped the view that the *benandanti* had of themselves. Slowly this fertility cult came to view itself as witchcraft until finally its members admitted that they were not combatting witchcraft but using it. In this process Ginzburg has isolated in a small test case a pattern which he suspects would apply to much of the rest of Europe. In his opinion, Margaret Murray's thesis of witchcraft as a surviving pagan cult turns out to have been at least partially correct. Witchcraft was the Christian interpretation of an older fertility religion. This pioneering study will force researchers to examine carefully the investigations of ecclesiastical and secular courts, instead of dismissing all such evidence as tortured and worthless. Already in England the close scrutiny of ecclesiastical records is yielding a much fuller picture of the ways magic, witchcraft, and astrology served important religious and social needs in the sixteenth and seventeenth centuries.[33] Although English evidence does not yet prove the existence of the witch cult that Ginzburg found, this kind of examination is bound to uncover much important information not to be found in criminal records.

Ginzburg's *benandanti* remain to date the only authenticated witch cult in early modern Europe. The scholar must now pose for himself the question whether Ginzburg's study represents the unique exception to the general conclusion that witchcraft as a cult did not exist in Europe. Or could such cult groups be discovered in many places once scholars know what to look for? Clearly there should be no hope of discovering that most persons convicted of witchcraft actually were guilty of some group ritual. The relentless use of torture and suggestion makes most criminal convictions easily understandable without resorting to theories of secret cults. But we now know that such secret fertility religions could survive, at least partially, into the sixteenth century. The extent of their survival may well be the next major task of witchcraft scholarship.

Witchcraft remains a subject of crucial importance for the social and intellectual history of the West. The attitudes of men toward supposed witches tell us much about the nature of science, religion, law, and social psychology during the age of the Renais-

---

[33] Macfarlane, *Witchcraft in Tudor and Stuart England*; and Thomas, *Religion and the Decline of Magic*.

sance and Reformation. We have much to learn from the persecuted outcasts of society.

FOR FURTHER READING

Baschwitz, Kurt. *Hexen und Hexenprozesse*. Munich: Rütten & Loening, 1963.

Caro Baroja, Julio. *The World of the Witches*. Chicago: University of Chicago Press, 1964.

Ginzburg, Carlo. *I benandanti. Ricerche sulla stregoneria e sui culti agrari tra Cinquecento e Seicento*. Turin: Einaudi, 1966.

Kelly, Henry A. *The Devil, Demonology and Witchcraft*. Garden City, N.Y.: Doubleday, 1968.

Macfarlane, Alan D. J. *Witchcraft in Tudor and Stuart England*. New York: Harper, 1970.

Midelfort, H. C. Erik. *Witch Hunting in Southwestern Germany, 1562-1684. The Social and Intellectual Foundations*. Stanford: Stanford University Press, 1972.

Monter, E. William. *European Witchcraft*. New York: John Wiley, 1969.

Kors, Alan C., and Edward Peters. *Witchcraft in Europe, 1100-1700. A Documentary History*. Philadelphia: University of Pennsylvania Press, 1972.

Russell, Jeffrey B. *Witchcraft in the Middle Ages*. Ithaca: Cornell University Press, 1972.

Thomas, Keith. *Religion and the Decline of Magic*. New York: Scribner, 1971.

Trevor-Roper, Hugh R. *The Crisis of the Seventeenth Century. Religion, The Reformation and Social Change*. New York: Harper, 1968.

Walker, D. P. *Spiritual and Demonic Magic from Ficino to Campanella*. London: Warburg Institute, 1958.

THE ESSAYIST'S SOURCES

1

An Early Medieval Theory of Witchcraft, The *Canon Episcopi* (906)

This canon seems really to be a Carolingian capitulary of the late ninth century. Throughout the Middle Ages, however, it was assumed to be a canon of the Council of Ancyra in 314, and it attained extraordinary authority for that reason. Although the canon demands a certain skepticism, close attention reveals that the *Canon Episcopi* condemned belief in only some kinds of witchcraft and strictly punished worship of the devil or the ascription of divine qualities to the devil. In other words this early document, apparently so damaging to any belief in witchcraft, provided a firm basis on which later thinkers could elaborate.

SOURCE: Jeffrey B. Russell, *Witchcraft in the Middle Ages* (Ithaca, N.Y.: Cornell University Press, 1972), pp. 76-77.

Bishops and their officials must labor with all their strength to uproot thoroughly from their parishes the pernicious art of sorcery and harmful magic invented by the devil, and if they find a man or woman follower of this wickedness to eject them foully disgraced from their parishes. . . . It is also not to be omitted that some wicked women perverted by the devil, seduced by illusions and phantasms of demons, believe and profess themselves, in the hours of night to ride upon certain beasts with Diana, the goddess of the pagans, and an innumerable multitude of women, and in the silence of the dead of night to traverse great spaces of earth, and to obey her commands as of their mistress, and to be summoned to her service on certain nights. But I wish it were they alone who perished in their faithlessness and did not draw many with them into the destruction of infidelity. For an innumerable multitude, deceived by this false opinion, believe this to be true and, so believing, wander from the right faith and are involved in the error of the pagans when they think that there is anything of divinity or power except the one God. Wherefore the priests throughout their churches should preach with all insistence to the people that they may know this to be in every way false and that such phantasms are imposed on the minds of infidels and not by the divine but by the malignant spirit. Thus Satan himself, who transfigures himself into an angel of light, when he has captured the mind of a miserable woman and has subjugated her to himself by infidelity and incredulity, immediately transforms himself into the species and similitudes of different personages and, deluding the mind which he holds captive and exhibiting things, joyous or mournful, and persons, known or unknown, leads it through devious ways, and while the spirit alone endures this, the faithless mind thinks these things happen not in the spirit but in the body. Who is there that is not led out of himself in dreams and nocturnal visions, and sees much when sleeping which he had never seen waking? . . . Whoever therefore believes that anything can be made, or that any creature can be changed to better or to worse or be transformed into another species or similitude, except by the creator himself who made everything and through whom all things were made, is beyond doubt an infidel.

2

A Late Medieval Theory of Witchcraft: Pope Innocent VIII, The Bull *Summis desiderantes affectibus* (1484)

Six hundred years after the *Canon Episcopi* most persons held rather different ideas about witches. By 1450 many men, including the popes, considered the powers of witchcraft real. Pope Innocent VIII was not the first pope to speak in frightened tones about witchcraft, but his bull of 1484 gained notoriety because it was widely reprinted.

SOURCE: Taken from *The Encyclopedia of Witchcraft and Demonology* by Rossell Hope Robbins, pp. 264-66. © 1959 by Crown Publishers, Inc. Used by permission of Crown Publishers, Inc. (Slight changes made after checking the original source, *Quellen und Untersuchungen zur Geschichte des Hexenwahns*

und der Hexenverfolgung im Mittelalter, by Joseph Hansen
(Bonn, 1901), pp. 24-27.

Innocent, bishop, servant of the servants of God, for an eternal remembrance.

Desiring with the most profound anxiety, even as pastoral solicitude requires, that the Catholic faith should especially in our time everywhere increase and flourish, and that all heretical depravity should be driven away from the territories of the faithful, we very gladly proclaim and even restate those particular means and methods whereby our Christian endeavor may be fulfilled; since, when all errors have been rooted out by our toil as with the hoe of a provident husbandman, a zeal for a devotion to our faith may take hold all the more strongly on the hearts of the faithful.

It has recently come to our attention, not without bitter sorrow, that in some parts of Upper Germany, as well as in the provinces, townships, territories, districts, and dioceses of Mainz, Cologne, Trier, Salzburg, and Bremen, many persons of both sexes, unmindful of their own salvation and deviating from the Catholic faith, have abused themselves with devils, incubi and succubi, and by their incantations, spells, conjurations, and other accursed superstitions and horrid charms, enormities and offenses, destroy the offspring of women and the young of cattle, blast and eradicate the fruits of the earth, the grapes of the vine and the fruits of trees; nay, men and women, beasts of burden, herd beasts, as well as animals of other kinds; also vineyards, orchards, meadows, pastures, corn, wheat, and other cereals of the earth. Furthermore, these wretches afflict and torment men and women, beasts of burden, herd beasts, as well as cattle of all other kinds, with pain and disease, both internal and external; they hinder men from generating and women from conceiving; whence neither husbands with their wives nor wives with their husbands can perform the sexual act. Above and beyond this, they blasphemously renounce that faith which they received by the sacrament of baptism, and at the instigation of the Enemy of the human race they do not shrink from committing and perpetrating the foulest abominations and excesses to the peril of their souls, whereby they offend the divine majesty and are a cause of scandal and dangerous example to very many.

And although our beloved sons Heinrich Institoris and Jacob Sprenger, professors of theology of the Order of Friars Preachers, have been by letters apostolic delegated as inquisitors of these heretical depravities, and still are inquisitors, the former in the aforesaid parts of Upper Germany, wherein are included those aforesaid provinces, townships, districts, dioceses, and other specified localities, and the latter in certain territories which border the Rhine, nevertheless not a few clerics and lay folk of those countries, seeking to know more than concerns them, since in the aforesaid delegatory letters there is no express and individual mention by name of these provinces, townships, districts, dioceses, and other specified localities; and further since the two delegates themselves and the abominations they are to encounter are not designated specifically and expressly, these persons are not ashamed to assert pertinaciously that these enormities are not practiced in these provinces, and consequently the aforesaid inquisitors have no legal right to exercise their power of inquisition in the provinces, townships, districts, dioceses, and territories, which have been rehearsed, and that the inquisitors may not proceed to punish, imprison, and correct those convicted of the offenses and wickednesses set forth. Accordingly, in the aforesaid provinces, townships, districts and dioceses, the abominations and enormities in question remain unpunished not without evident danger to their souls and loss of eternal salvation.

Wherefore we, as is our duty, desirous to remove all hindrances and obstacles whatsoever by which the work of the inquisitors may be impeded, as also to apply potent remedies to prevent the disease of heresy and other turpitudes diffusing their poison to the destruction of other innocent souls, as our position demands and marked by the greatest zeal for the faith, lest the provinces, townships, dioceses, districts and territories of those parts of Upper Germany, which we have specified, be deprived of the benefits of the Holy Office of the Inquisition thereto assigned, by the tenor of these presents by our apostolic authority, we decree and enjoin that the aforesaid inquisitors be empowered to proceed to the correction, imprisonment, and punishment of any persons for the said abominations and enormities, without let or hindrance, in every way as if the provinces, townships, dioceses, districts, territories, yea, even the persons and their crimes in this kind were named and specifically designated in our letters.

Moreover, for greater surety we extend these letters deputing this authority to cover all the aforesaid provinces, townships, dioceses, districts, and territories, and also persons, and crimes newly rehearsed, and we grant permission to the aforesaid inquisitors, to each separately or to both, as also to our dear son John Gremper, priest of the diocese of Constance, Master of Arts, their notary, or to any other public notary, who shall be by them or by one of them temporarily delegated to these provinces, townships, dioceses, districts, and aforesaid territories, to proceed according to the regulations of the Inquisition against such persons of whatsoever rank and high estate they may be, and to correct, punish, imprison, and beat, as their crimes merit, those whom they have found guilty.

Moreover, they shall enjoy a full and perfect faculty of expounding and preaching the word of God to the faithful, so often as opportunity may offer and it may seem good to them in each and every parish church of the said provinces, and they shall freely and legally perform any rites or execute any business which may appear advisable in the aforesaid cases. By our supreme authority we grant them once again full and complete faculties. . . .

Let no obstacle whatever be set against these apostolic letters and ordinances. Let no man therefore in any way rashly oppose this page contrary to this declaration extending our authority and injunction. But if any man dare do so, let him know that on him will fall the wrath of God almighty and the blessed apostles Peter and Paul.

Given at Rome, at St. Peter's, on December 5 of the year of the incarnation of our Lord one thousand four hundred eighty-four, in the first year of our pontificate.

3

The Witchcraft Law of the Holy Roman Empire, Article 109 of the *Carolina* (1532)

In 1532 the Emperor Charles V promulgated a criminal code for the Holy Roman Empire. Witchcraft was among the crimes treated. It is worth emphasizing the *Carolina's* distinction between harmful and harmless witches, a distinction very common in the sixteenth century.

SOURCE: Gustav Radbruch, ed., *Die peinliche Gerichtsordnung Karls V. von 1532 (Carolina)* (Stuttgart: Reclam, 1962), p. 76.

Item, when someone harms people or brings them trouble by witchcraft, one should punish him with death, and one should use the punishment of death by fire. When, however, someone uses witchcraft and yet does no one any harm with it, he should be punished otherwise, according to the custom of the case; and the judges should take counsel as is described later regarding legal consultations.

4

The Spread of Witchcraft Ideas
Among the Common People (1580)

Complex scholastic and legal theories often filtered down to the village in the form of rough newspapers or sensationalist pamphlets. An example of this literature helps to recapture the mood of terror which witchcraft inspired among common folk. The original is in crude verse. The title translates as "Two New Reports: The Witches Who Have Been Burned from the 7th of February to the 20th of July, 1580, and Where and What They Confessed. The other, On the Terrible Rage of the Turks." (The second report is not translated here.)

SOURCE: *Zwo Newe Zeittung. Was man für Hexen oder Unholden verbrendt hat, von dem siebenden Hornung an biss auff den zwentzigsten Höwmonat diss MDLXXX. Jars, auch darbey angezeigt, an was ohrt und enden, auch was sie bekendt haben, etc. Die ander, Von der grausammen Wüterey des Türcken...* (Hof, 1580).

Hear Oh Christians, what is now sung to you; listen eagerly to what has recently happened—great misery and a miracle! Behold an evil deed, this year, as I will show. They executed many witch-women, as I will shortly show, and what they did; behold the great wonder.

In 1580 I was amazed that on 7 February in Wurzach nine witches were executed. They confessed to many miserable deeds, as I will explain. At Biberach, I tell you, they burned five of them at the same time. At Kirch they burned four all at once without hesitation; they were all old and very rich, and had caused much misery, as I will describe later. In Allgäu I must report that they burned nine at once openly at Wanga, and three more at Isny. And at Fissach they burned eleven at the end of the same month. Three fled to Lindau thinking they would be safe there. At Rottenburg on the Neckar and at Horb they burned nine. And at Dreiburg on the Walde and at Rottweil they burned a goodly number of witches, nearly thirty in all, who had wretchedly killed many small children. Constance on Lake Constance burned two on the 6th of May, who confessed an evil crime. At Überlingen they burned three who with great sorrow confessed many crimes, as I will tell later.

Mr. Lazarus von Schwendi burned many of them. At Kuppenen they burned six and three more nearby. In the Wanzenau in the city of Keisersberg they burned one on St. Vitus Day and others still lie in prison. At Burgau on the day after St. John's Day they burned six. They could not refrain from burning an unrepentant man-witch and another woman. At Rastatt they burned seven and five in Baden, who had done strange things to men, women, and children with magic and poison. And in the Margravate Baden they took away the wife of a tile maker, carrying her magically through the air together with a child. They found her on the second day at Gersbach, miserably bound to the child. She had lost her wits; her reason was taken from her along with the child. At Rastatt, as I said, they were busy burning. A rain and thunderstorm brought misery and wretchedness to that place, and it sounded as if armored men and horses were up there. Furthermore I must tell what they confessed; I cannot remain silent.

Listen Oh men and women! Three hundred plainly came together in the Black Forest and they resolved on a crime by which they should cause frost throughout the land on Holy Pentecost. They prayed to the devil for help and counsel. At once they buried three pails of corn, wine, and grain in three places. There was a young maid there from Wurzach, who was the daughter of a witch. They looked and found the pails deep in the woods, full of all kinds of fruit. They seized her at once and said the devil had taught her to harm man, woman, and child. They then confessed how the witches come together; I cannot keep from telling you this. The devil came to them quickly and told them to make a storm so that no one would bring sickles to the fields for thirty German miles around.

And they said that they wanted it to start in that place on the day of Christ's Ascension. But God used his power to protect so that the storm went no farther than five German miles, starting in the Black Forest and having a width of one-half mile. It destroyed most of the grain in the fields at Biberach. Finally they confessed openly that with their own hands they had ruined the fruit of the trees at Breisach and a great many grapes at Kestenholtz. May God have mercy, for they quickly confessed how they had harmed 200 children, both rich and poor, and had made them dumb; and they had killed many poor men's cattle in their stalls.

Afterward they confessed that on a Saturday night the devil held an assembly at a castle high on a mountain one German mile from Colmar. Large and small came together there. Nearly 500 persons came from many lands and from far away, riding on cats and on calves. Many of them were dead, and yet they too had strange adventures at that place. They danced and jumped over sticks and stones. And each one brought along his lover-demon, who had strange names. I must tell you what these lovers commanded them to do. They told them to make a huge storm. With their strange help it could happen. So they tried five times to make a hail which was to wreak destruction. They couldn't make a storm as large as they wanted, but a rainstorm came that did much harm to houses, mills, grain, and corn, which drowned in the fields of many pious folk. Shortly afterward they confessed that if they hadn't been caught so quickly, they would have made a storm for forty German miles around, that would have caused much more damage. They would have ruined so much grain and wine so far around that no pious upright man could have made even half a measure of wine or brought even half a bushel of grain into his barn. And whatever cattle and men were in the fields would have been hit with hail stones weighing five or even seven pounds. They were indeed so angry that they went crazy, and no one knew what they might have gone on to freeze with frost: corn, wine, and fruit in the fields. But the frost was prevented at Villingen.

So throughout you have heard how 114 witches in all were convicted and executed, who confessed such things as they did in many a place. Oh God, grant us a pious magistracy who may truly root out such godless folk at any time, and grant us eternal salvation.

5

On Hailstorms: A Sermon by Johann Brenz (1539)

To calm the terror and to combat the vulgar errors of common folk many learned preachers insisted that the physical threat of witchcraft had been exaggerated. In effect, they harked back to the attitude of the *Canon Episcopi*. Johann Brenz (1499-1570) is best known as the Protestant Reformer of Schwäbisch Hall and of the Duchy of Württemberg, but he preached eloquently on the false fear of witchcraft as well.

SOURCE: Johann Brenz, "Ein Predig von dem Hagel und Ungewitter," in *Evangelien der fürnembsten Fest–und Feyertagen* (Frankfurt, 1558).

Beloved in Christ, since faithlessness and idolatry are not simple but complex and of many varieties among mankind, and since they are no small cause of the corruption of body and soul, it is necessary that we recognize and avoid both kinds of corruption and piously live our life in our calling and walk in the fear of the Lord. First of all we must see that this pertains not only to the unbelieving heathen who invoke, pray to, and honor images, gods, and so forth; but that all those who grant or ascribe to witches, the devil's followers, and to magicians what pertains and belongs only to God's majesty, are guilty of idolatry too. It is even idolatry when a man falls into misfortune and despairs of God's help and does not believe that God could help him in time of need, and so seeks help elsewhere. Oh, would God that our idolatry would disappear as that of the heathen did. But idolatry changed only its name, as we know by experience, and men continued with an idolatrous life. Many of that pitiable sort are to be found. That this is true is sufficiently proved by the horrible event which recently occurred and which we saw ourselves. For God the Lord has so thoroughly punished and visited us with very destructive cold weather, frosts, hail and storms from heaven that we might recognize and learn that he is father and still rules and governs, and that if he wanted to use his power, he could destroy us in a moment. But how do we react? We do nothing extraordinary. The majority, when they see that wine, fruit, and other things necessary for nourishing the body are destroyed by hail and storms, complain vehemently and act so indecently and so dejectedly that, in their great impatience, they seem to think that God himself has died and cannot help. Others are of the opinion that hail and storms come not from God but from magicians and witches. Therefore they begin to scold, curse, and grumble against them and to wish that all the witches could be burned at once. But such persons would do better to remember their own sins and many misdeeds, which they do very rarely because they never muddy their own waters and think that in the sight of God they are innocent. Truly this is blatant, heathen idolatry and myth. For whoever doubts God's help in time of need and does not call on God the Lord and does not trust him acts just as if there is no longer a God who can and will help.

Still others think that hail and storms, which God sends us because of our sins, actually are the work and business of the devil and his followers. Such persons really have not one spark of Christian faith in their hearts and neither know nor understand what the true faith is. In the first article of our Christian creed we confess openly that we have a gracious, good, and almighty God. And we pray and ask in the fourth part of the Lord's Prayer that dear God not withhold from us our daily bread, but that he graciously give and share it. Moreover the First Commandment warns us to avoid strange gods and pray to and honor only the one God. Now what are *we* to make of that? Some of us are just like the Marcionite heretics, who believed in, or made, two gods, one from whom good came, and the other from whom evil came. They make the devil himself into a God. Surely this is the greatest idolatry of all.

That this matter may be properly understood, I should like to insert at this time a short report concerning the origin of thunder, hail and storms, to the end that our terror and fright may be diminished. For we should learn and observe how we should properly react to thunder, storms, and other misfortunes. If we know and understand the true character of thunder, then we will be surer that God the Father and his beloved Son, Jesus Christ, are still completely in control even if the earth has been smitten and destroyed by hail. And the more certain we are of that, the better we will learn and understand our catechism, the creed, the Lord's Prayer, and the Ten Commandments, and the more reason we will have to walk in the fear of God.

First of all, beloved in the Lord, you should note that here I am not speaking about hail and its properties in a natural way, but I bring explanations from the true Word of God. The scientists assert that hail originates when the sun draws up the humidity or moisture out of the earth and carries it through the air to the clouds. There it is turned into clouds because of the great cold of the air, but later, when it is warmed by the sun again, it is turned into rain or hail, especially during the summer. And the rain falls unless the drops freeze again because of the freezing cold air, and they coalesce. This freezing and coalescing are the origin of hail as explained by the scientists and naturalists. Yet the significance of hail is taught us by the Word of God, for God is the true, natural, and almighty inventor, creator, and distributor of hail. His Word tells us also how he governs and for what reasons he ordains hailstorms. For men too are conceived naturally in their mothers' wombs, but the greatest and most important fact is that the dear God creates, supports, nourishes and supplements this natural order, for without God's help no man can be born into this vale of tears. It is the same with hail, which begins in a natural way but is ordered and regulated by God the Lord, the true and right author, according to his desire. The unbelieving and godless are certain that thunder, hail, and storms come from none other than the devil and from his followers, the magicians and witches. And if the wine and fruits of the field are ruined or beaten down, they blame only the witches. But we are taught completely different things by God's Word, i.e., that God the Lord makes the hail in order to punish the godless, the faithless, and the unjust, and thereby bring them to a recognition of their sins and turn them to repentance and improvement. And the pious, god-fearing people are tested by a hailstorm to see whether they will stand firm in the true faith and confession of God. This is clearly proved by the testimony of Holy Scripture, as in Exodus 9, where we read that God ordered Moses to stretch out his hand and release a huge hailstorm over Egypt, over men and cattle alike. This is an obvious proof that God the Lord is the author and founder of hail and that He releases it over men and beasts to punish the godless. And in Job 38 it is written that God said to Job, "Have you been where the snow comes from or have you seen the storehouses of the hail which I have reserved for the time of trouble, for the day of battle and war?" Here we hear that God himself claims that hail is sent by Him and only Him. I must insert one more example from Joshua, where it is written that the Lord allowed a great hail to fall from heaven among the enemy of the people of Israel, and that more died from the hail than from the sword of the children of Israel. And in Haggai, the second chapter, God says, "I have smitten you with drought, mildewed grain, and hail in all your labors, and yet you still do not turn to me, says the

Lord." Here .he prophet shows us two things. First that hail comes from God the Lord. Second, that it is sent in order to punish the godless and to warn or drive them to repent. Here someone could conclude "I have heard that neither the devil nor witches can make hail." To which I would agree that God the Lord, and not the devil, is the author and founder of hail and storms, and they give evidence, as shown above, of his ruling pleasure and will.

But in addition, it is the devil's principal and highest task to bring harm to men both in material or temporal matters and in spiritual concerns. Without God's permission and decree he cannot begin or finish the task, as is clear in Job. For the will and purpose of the devil were totally directed at corruption of righteous Job and bringing him to utter ruin. Yet without God's permission and decree he could not harm or rumple a hair on his head. Similarly he could not seduce or deceive the prophets of King Ahab without God's command, just as he couldn't enter the herd of swine without Christ's permission. And he was unable to attack and tempt Christ's disciples without the permission of the Lord Christ, as is clear in Luke 22, where Christ says to Peter, "The devil demanded to have you that he might sift you like wheat, but I have prayed for you that your faith may not fail." From these examples we should learn, and console ourselves too, that when we hear of the devil as a forceful, powerful, sworn enemy of the human race who sneaks about day and night to devour us, yet we should not give up since he has no power or strength to harm us without the decree of God. Thus the devil is not so powerful that at his own pleasure he can change and transform the air. Even less can the witches and sorcerers do such things.

How then does it happen that the Imperial [Roman] law punishes witches? For it is written in the law that there are many who take up evil arts and use them to enchant and disturb the air and the elements, not even sparing the life of the innocent, but causing them great harm. Such persons, because they are enemies and attackers of nature, should be given their reasonable and well-deserved punishment. Thus we also read in Exodus 22 that God said to Moses, "You shall not allow the witch among you to live." Now if no witch can interfere in the working of nature, and if it is not in her power to make hail, why are they punished according to Imperial laws and edicts and especially by the command and law of Moses, which originated in the Holy Spirit? Here one must observe that the witches and sorcerers are punished by Imperial laws and mandates and by command of Moses not because they caused or made hail and storms of their own power and will, but because they gave themselves to the devil and have drunk so deeply of Satan's spirit that they desire only what their captain, the devil, desires; namely, the corruption and ruin of mankind. This they seek with all their strength. And they believe that they have produced the evil, which, however, only the devil causes by using the decree and permission of God. For when the devil is allowed by God the Lord to awaken or cause a hailstorm, he at once turns to his tools, the witches, and encourages them to use their magic and to attack their neighbors by causing misfortune. And when the hail begins to fall, it comes not from the power or strength of the witches but from the devil, to whom God gave control and permission. In this way the witches are deluded and deceived by the devil into thinking that it was their work whenever evil things happen, when actually it is the devil alone who causes such things with God's decree. Thus witches are punished by the magistrates because they are without fear of God, lead a godless and un-Christian life, give themselves entirely to the devil to corrupt and harm mankind, and not because they actually cause any harm, as they think they do; for they cannot harm.

Why then does God permit the devil to ruin and lay waste the wine and fruit of the field? On the causes of this I have taught and shown above that God causes hail and allows it to fall in order to test thereby the faith of the faithful and to punish the godless as they deserve, bring them to recognition of their sins, and encourage true repentance. I will say no more about it here.

How, and with what means, can hailstorms and punishments be avoided? This I will try to show with God's help. Here there are many recent errors, for some take blessed or consecrated herbs and throw them into the fire in the belief that they will in that way drive the devil out of the air. This is pure magic and idolatry. For the devils, who are purely spirits, cannot be driven off with such delusions and with physical materials. For that reason I regard such persons who use smoke rituals to drive off the devil, displaying thereby an utter faithlessness, as worse than the infamous magicians and witches. They ought to be punished no less severely than the witches. Some people blow horns and ring bells in the opinion that the hail and storm will be driven off by the noise, a practice which I wish to expand on. The pious and god-fearing have their own useful customs relating to bells, but the godless are all of the firm opinion that the clang of a baptized bell has such powers that the devil is frightened and driven from the air, and that thereby hail and storms can be avoided or controlled. That is a horrible and gruesome idolatry, first, because baptism is given to bells, and second, because these men attribute to the clang of bells what belongs to God alone. Yet the pious turn bells to their own use in two ways, as I said, namely in a temporal and in a spiritual way. First, the pious, and especially the weak and fainthearted are given some courage by the ringing of bells, for they note that men are still around. Secondly, the careless, lazy, and negligent persons are reminded by the ringing bells of God's wrath that they may turn more zealously to prayer and ask God for grace. For the sound of bells warns us to call out to merciful God and ask him to forgive our sins. If a storm is coming, therefore, we ought first to go to church and pray from the heart that God graciously turn away from wrath. Since man is not accustomed at such times to run to church, however, our dear ancestors ordained and recommended that bells be rung and sounded at such times to remind everyone at home to turn to thoughtful and heartfelt prayer in his house as if he were in church. And such bell ringing would still be tolerable and permissible except that bells are merely rung, or they are baptized by the suffragan in order to drive away the devil and thereby prevent storms and hail, as if they could claim such power and strength. This is certainly the greatest and most terrible idolatry for the bells can do nothing in such cases.

On the other hand there are others who think that there is no other way of avoiding hail and storms than by burning witches. Although the magistrate must indeed punish the witches according to the laws described above, yet he must not rely on their confession but only when their deed is proved and undeniable. Why is that? Even·if all witches were burned to ashes, still hail, thunder, and storms would not on that account cease, for all of them are sent by God, as I said. But then in what way can we turn aside hail and storms? Above we have said that God the Lord is author and administrator, governor and ruler of the hail, and that he decrees and allows the devil to act when he wants to unleash a hailstorm on account of our sins. Now what sort of sins are they for which God releases the devil? Oh, dear God! Who could list all of these sins one after the other? Yet I will describe and explain a few of them briefly. The law teaches that God usually punishes us in those things with which we offend him, as is written: "An eye for an eye, a hand for a hand, tooth for tooth, foot for foot." We misuse the gifts of God, like wine, grain, and other things; therefore God punishes us in the same way. Here both rich and poor are guilty, for the rich hoard everything as if they were always in want and were about to starve to death. And when they grow even wealthier, and have stuffed their barns, kitchens, and cellars, and have filled their purses, then the gluttony, swilling, and gaming are almost without pause. And among those who have many goods, the trick is common in which the lord whom one owes money, fruits, and tithes is a master of deceit and gives himself the advantage of saying how much should be his portion. But the punishment is not long in coming, as the prophet Amos said, "Hear this word, you who are on the mountain of Samaria, who oppress the poor, who crush the needy," etc. Therefore have I allowed it to rain on one town and not on another; one field gets rained on, and the other, which receives no rain, dries up. And in Haggai, chapter 1, it is written "Now thus speaks the Lord of hosts, Consider how you have fared. You have sown much and harvested little; you eat, but you never have enough; you drink, but you never have your fill," etc. And why is this? For this reason, the Lord says, "that my house lies in ruins, and everyone busies himself with his own house. Therefore the heavens above you have withheld the dew and the earth has withheld its produce. And I have called for a drought upon the land and the hills, upon the grain, the new wine, the oil, upon what the ground brings forth, upon men and cattle, and upon all the work of their hands." And further he says, "I smote you with drought, mildewed grain, and hail, and all the products of your toil." And why? "Because my house is not yet built, says the Lord." God says the same thing through the prophet Malachi, saying, "Since you have cheated me in your tithes and offerings, so be cursed that everything will flow through your hands." Yet how many servants gladly pay their debts without deceit? When they bring money or tithes or pay whatever is appropriate, they cry out and say, "May it all go to the devil," which is truly a sign of a godless character and mind.

Since therefore both poor and rich lead an immoderate and impudent life, and misuse the gifts of God, such as wine and fruit, God the Lord will send us hail and storms to ruin the wine and grain. He has good cause. Thus men should not immediately seek and shout for the burning of witches, for with such a cry we condemn ourselves to the fire. But since some are stubborn and insist on executing and burning witches, tell me rather where will one find fire enough, and who would be safe? Truly neither magistrate nor subject, neither lord nor servant would be able to protect himself or escape such a misfortune or remain safe. Whoever would seek to avoid the harm and ruin of thunder and hail, let him learn his own sins, do true penance, and turn his heart to the Lord, and work in his office or calling with a zealous fear of God. If even then you encounter some misfortune, the dear God will richly restore everything to you through his grace and blessing, for the sake of Jesus Christ, His beloved Son. To whom be laud, honor and praise, together with the Father and the Holy Spirit, now and forever. Amen.

6

Debate on the Nature of Witchcraft: Correspondence Between Johann Weyer and Johann Brenz (1565)

Johann Weyer (1515?-1588) was a physician at the court of Jülich-Cleves who concluded that most witches were silly, deluded, melancholy old women who deserved sympathy rather than punishment. The only physically dangerous witches, he thought, were those who used poisons. Naturally, he read Brenz's sermon (Source 5) with great interest and wrote to him enlisting his aid. Brenz responded with appreciation for Weyer's efforts on behalf of the innocent, but he insisted that real witches, even if harmless, must be severely punished. This exchange reveals clearly the importance of accurate biblical interpretation in the sixteenth century and helps explain why even humane and reasonable men could believe in witchcraft. The debate also provides evidence for a number of different kinds of witchcraft and distinguishes carefully the kinds of punishment appropriate for each.

SOURCE: Johann Weyer, *De Praestigiis Daemonum* (Frankfurt, 1586), pp. 491-99.

Johann Weyer to Dr. Johann Brenz, Doctor of Sacred Scripture and Provost at Stuttgart:

I wish you happiness, grace, and good fortune together with my friendly greeting, worthy Brenz, through Him who loved us and with His blood cleansed all who deny themselves, receive Christ and walk in His footsteps and follow Him.

For good reasons I have always regarded you highly and held you in highest honor for the great energy, skill, and fear of God which you have displayed in your efforts to rid the church of idolatry and to cleanse it of false teaching. But now even more should you be praised and honored on account of a wonderfully learned and pious sermon which you recently delivered and had printed. For in that sermon you teach elegantly and truly that idolatry should not be held to be the sin of heathen alone, when they make gods and pray to them, but also the sin of men who attribute what belongs to God alone to the devil and his horde, the magicians, witches, and covenanters with the devil. As when men, after an accident or misfortune, neglect God's help, as if there were no longer a God who could help, and fall away from God, no longer calling on Him in need; but seek elsewhere for help and salvation, with the devil or his followers. This too is a shameful and cursed idolatry. Therefore, you were rightfully angry about the people in the Duchy of Württemberg whose wine and fruit were destroyed by a terrible hail. In their stubborn faithlessness, instead of coming to recognize their own sins through such punishments, and instead of truly repenting and reforming their lives and living according to God's word, they fell into superstition. They hold that such misfortunes come not from the Lord God on account of their sins, but from witches, whom they wish burned. Rightly have you punished and thumped these fellows. Verily you instructed and taught your congregation and dear flock rightly by displaying witnesses from Holy Scripture and also by showing the natural causes of hail so that it is in no way a work or creation of the devil or of his followers, the witches and magicians, but that it is God the true author and ruler's creation and work, and that he sends such things to mankind that the godless may thereby be punished, led to recognize their sins, and encouraged to repentance and improvement of life. But also that the pious may be tested through such hail and storms whether they will remain steadfast in the true faith. I say truly that your teaching of how men should react to such evils in certainty and with a good conscience, and how they may avoid misfortune, is not poor or despicable advice but true and godly. I understand your teaching and opinion very well, dear Brenz, and I do not doubt that you serve the Christian congregation best with such a glorious and consoling sermon.

The seriousness and industry that suffuse your work are especially needed in this area of great darkness and confusion, for the conjurers blind the eyes of many, especially those who praise the gospel most highly, including great lords and nobles as well as the common man, but even more importantly those like you whose office and calling require them to teach healthy, pure doctrine to others. They have made much confusion. But the good and gracious God, who leaves no pious man unrewarded, will reward you richly.

As to the first part of your sermon, I must confess that it seems sufficient to me (for which I thank you very much). As to the second part, however, I have a criticism and objection at a point in which we do not agree. Therefore I could not omit explaining myself and describing my position briefly so that if you teach me that I have erred anywhere, I can improve and change my opinions, which are contained for all to see in my *Six Books on the Delusions of Demons* (*De praestigiis daemonum*), and especially in Book Six. Witches have no power to make hail, storms, and other evil things, but they are deceived by the devil. For when the devil, with the permission and decree of God, can make hail and storms, he goes to his witches and urges them to use their magic and charms, so that when the trouble and punishment come, the witches are convinced that they and the devil have caused it. Thus the witches cannot make hail and other things, but they are deluded and blinded by the devil himself to whom they have given themselves. In this way they think that they have made hail and storms. Not on that account but for their godless lives should they be punished severely. All of this you teach openly. And to confirm and strengthen your position you also cite the Imperial Law with these words: "There are many who practice evil arts to disturb and poison the elements. And they spare not the life of innocent persons but cause them great harm. Therefore when such people oppose nature they should be punished with death." You also confirmed and strengthened your teaching with the law of Moses, by which, as Moses said: "Thou shalt not suffer a witch to live" (Exodus 22:18).

Now, dear Brenz, so that the truth may appear openly from a friendly comparison, I ask that I may present freely my opinions. Do not take offense at this or blame me, for I will not present anything willful, unreasonable, frivolous, immoderate, or outrageous (as God is my witness, who knows everything). First you admit that witches have no power at all to cause hail or storms, even though their senses are so deluded by the devil that they believe and confess that they have awakened or caused storms and other such evils. The law, however, does not speak of those who cannot work such magic, but of those who do use the evil magical arts, which our witches cannot learn or understand because they are stupid, uneducated, dull, foolish, and crazy, and also because of their age and sex. And the law states clearly that it has those in mind who disturb and poison the air, which again our witches cannot do, as you explicitly teach. For no one can do that. Thus such witches are not referred to in this law for they cannot harm human life. I argued this extensively in my book. Since I find that you agree sufficiently with me in your sermon, I do not wish to explain myself at length or use a lot of words.

For if witches could physically harm someone or be dangerous, then they are not simply witches or sorcerers, and they should be called poisoners instead. And they deserve the punishment meted out by Moses, Imperial law, and common law. Yet just because there is no agreement in that matter, one should not on that account conclude that Imperial law teaches or confirms that our witches must be punished. Indeed the law says not one word about them. Our witches have been corrupted in their phantasy by the devil and imagine often that they have done evil things that didn't even happen or caused natural occurrences that actually did not take place. In their confessions, especially under torture, they admit to doing and causing many things which are impossible for them and for anyone. One should not believe them when they confess that they have bound themselves to the devil, given themselves to his will, promised to follow his evil goals, just as we do not believe their confession that they make hail and storms, disturb and poison the air, and other impossible deeds. For both are confessed by one man at the same time and in the same way. Why should we believe such ridiculous confessions, brought us by the devil, more than others? Why approve a confession which is totally false and deluded, especially when made by an old, feeble, and captive woman, who is not to be trusted anyway? Therefore put no trust in such false and unfounded confessions, for they are started and fostered by the devil who is a liar and a father of lies. A person who is driven by the devil and almost always possessed by him confesses whatever the devil forcefully impresses on her senses, and she believes thoroughly whatever she confesses and says. Yes the devil always rules the tongues of witches so that they say much that they did not intend, which can be seen in women possessed by the devil, who, when released from the devil's bondage, are reminded of what they said earlier, and they are ashamed. I saw this the first time in a nun who lay sick in the hospital; when she came to her senses, she confessed to me the same horrible deeds that others confess with torture and torment. She had been plagued by the devil in this way in her cloister. She was later sacrificed, despite the fact that she was possessed by the devil, and despite the law's insistence that in criminal cases proof must be as bright and clear as the noonday sun. Even if an old woman, in deep depression, gives herself to the devil, one should not immediately condemn her to the fire but instead have regard for her confused, burdened, and depressed spirits and use all possible energy to convert her that she may avoid evil, and give herself to Christ. In this way we may bring her to her senses again, win her soul, and save her from death, as St. James teaches. For every man who sins, or is unjust, or hates his brother, is not of God but of the devil, as St. John says. And the fornicators, adulterers, idolaters, voluptuaries, drunkards, calumniators, and slanderers, and the avaricious will not inherit or possess the Kingdom of God. When such persons devote themselves criminally to the devil's service, and are unfaithful to God the Lord, they are not condemned to flames at once, even if they have seduced other persons into taking part in their evil deeds, thereby sinning more grievously. They fully deserve God's revenge and punishment, which is much harder and stricter than temporal punishment; nor can they escape it unless they repent and cordially convert. For then they are released from pain and punishment, just as those whom Paul described, who abandon the faith in the last times, and follow seductive spirits and devil's doctrine. I would say the same concerning heretics, who are seduced by the devil's false words and persuasions, and who are unjust to God and to others. At the Last Judgment they will not be severely punished if they repent, confess their error, and abandon it. That such persons should be sharply restrained in some cases I do not deny; nor would I oppose it. But clearly it is even more imperative for magistrates not to proceed too harshly or too quickly with the many old women who are naturally feeble and silly and are deceived, seduced, and sometimes even possessed by the devil; for they are considered witches although they are harmless. Those who kill these poor, duped, crazy, but innocent women anger God most of all. I do not doubt that they will have to suffer harsh punishment from Christ for the gruesome cruelty and tyranny that they exercise against these women, like the bloodthirstiest hangmen, unless they do true penance and obtain a merciful God. A vice or sin, committed or conceived in the heart, is punished by God the Lord, who is a searcher of men's hearts and who knows our thoughts. For a man who desires the wife of another is an adulterer in his heart and cannot escape the punishment of God. But the magistrate must not punish him as an adulterer even if he confesses openly his deepest will and thoughts, for the sword is not entrusted to the magistracy for such cases.

Now, if a troublemaker or quarreler is to be punished, as the will and consensus of mankind agree, it is first necessary and required that he really deserve punishment by displaying a reasonable and understanding human will. He must have intentionally planned, with will, mind, and spirit, to commit some crime or heinous deed against the commonwealth; and he must have been able to do the deed; and he must have begun to commit at least part of the crime, or have made an attempt. It were well to distinguish clearly such men from those who, in the weakness of their mind, imagine that they are committing some evil or believe that they have already completed some deed which actually never occurred and was impossible to do. Otherwise one would have to attribute criminal will and consent to fools, children, and the mentally ill, who often persuade themselves that they have done evil and in their folly confess that they are guilty of crimes. What have witches done in consenting to and applauding the plans of the devil for causing trouble and misfortune (at God's decree)? Nothing more than people who, when in trouble, wickedly and jealously wish bad luck to others, and who rejoice and are happy, with willing and consenting minds, when misfortune occurs, as we often see. The secular laws occasionally deal with this matter, teaching that all other things being equal, women sin less than men in doing certain crimes because their mind and understanding are weak. Therefore, they ought also to be less severely punished, as I demonstrate in Book Six, Chapter Ten. And God specially commanded that poor widows be faithfully protected and cared for, because they are old women, as Holy Scripture testifies. I know of no better or more secure way of punishing and chastising the witches than having them taught the law of God's Word by a true and pious teacher, so that they may withstand the devil and his deeds, and his blandishments, and if repentant thus find the free acceptance of the whole community again. Yet because they did give in to the devil and did not completely oppose him, some argue that they have earned and indeed deserve a sharper punishment; in that case then send them for a while into miserable exile or fine them according to the gravity of their crime and sin; but spare their lives.

Regarding the law of Moses in Exodus 22, which you apply to this case, I answer that in the Hebrew text the word is *Mechasepha* which the Seventy Translators [the editors of the Septuagint] rendered as *pharmakous ou peribiósete*, that is, thou shalt not suffer the poisoner (as the Hebrews called it) to live or to survive; and in this way the Seventy Translators interpreted and explained the intent and meaning of the law. And the word *Casaph*, and other words with that as a root, can hardly be interpreted in the Greek translation as meaning anything other than poisoning. Therefore this decree does not concern our witches, who poison no one and use no poisons in their business. They cannot be punished on that basis. Yet others foolishly persuade themselves that the witches should be killed and burned because this word *Mechasepha*, in the Old Testament, is translated into German as sorceress. Here one should note the teaching of Josephus, who was a born Jew. He interpreted the law this way: "No Israelite should possess anything deadly or poisonous, prepared for harmful use. Those who are found with such things should be killed and thus suffer what they planned to do to others, and the prepared poison should be exhibited."

For this reason no one will easily convince me that anyone at the time of Moses had ever seen or heard of the kind of diabolical nonsense and delusion with which our witches have long been troubled and fooled. Moses and the books of the Old Testament actually speak of only four kinds of sorcery and magic. The first were the diviners or tricksters of Pharaoh, who dazzled the eyes of the king with their devil's art, and could make a fog before his eyes so that he believed certain things existed which actually did not. Our witches cannot bring such things to pass, and do not want to. Moses called them *Hartumim*, if I remember correctly, for I am at the hunting lodge Betsburg, fifteen miles from my library at Cleves, and cannot consult a Hebrew Bible. Secondly, there are the *Mechasepha* or poisoners, who kill or otherwise grievously harm men and cattle, using perhaps poison or other evil medicines. Third are those who practice all kinds of divination, and they are called by various names: *Kasam* (Deut. 15; Jeremiah 17), *Onen* (Deut. 18; 2 Chron. 31; Jeremiah 17; Micha 5), *Nahas* (Deut. 18; 2 Chron. 33), *Ob* (Deut. *18;* Isaiah 19; 1 Kings 28; 4 Kings 23; and elsewhere), *Jidoni* (Deut. 18; Levit. 19 & 20; 4 Kings 23; Isaiah 19). [Fourthly] the Hebrews used the word *Habar* for magicians who mumble secret words which supposedly contain great mystery and power. David uses this word and also *Lahas* (Psalm 58) when he speaks of the adders that stop their ears against the voice of the charmer. Whatever the meaning of these words, they do not imply the kind of foolishness employed by our old women. When the decree of Moses is rightly used against poisoners, they really ought to be punished according to its terms. And I have never defended those whom the *Lex Cornelia de sicariis et veneficis* condemns (*Digest*, Book 46, Title 8).

I have been glad to send you my opinion, dear Brenz, because I trust that you will respond to my writing with a favorable answer. May the merciful God give grace and spirit that you may follow faithfully your Christian calling, for the honor of God, the building of his Church, and so that souls may be saved.

Betsburg, 10 October 1565

RESPONSE OF JOHANN BRENZ TO JOHANN WEYER

[Brenz praises Weyer's work but insists on one point of disagreement.]

Yet it must be noted clearly that these persons who have broken the laws deserve a dreadful punishment and are reasonably and rightly condemned. Regarding the imperial law, I see very well that it uses language like this: "Whoever uses evil and inappropriate arts to infect or disturb the elements," etc. And I insist now as before that it is not within the ability of the devil himself or of any man to cause the disturbance of the elements. It is in God's power alone. Yet I do not doubt that the said law only uses the language of the common man and simply expresses the opinion which magicians and witches also have regarding themselves. For they are persuaded by the devil that they can disturb the elements with their arts. To this I can hear your response that in this case the law is punishing only an intention and a false persuasion. But this is not so, for the law "regards the completed and certain attempt as equivalent to the crime itself." For these poor, wretched women do not only intend to disturb the elements with their cooking and other arts, but they do all they can with the greatest energy, collecting herbs, cooking them with their charms over a fire, and all those things that they learned from the devil and his followers. Here the law is right in punishing the "completed attempt" as I indicated. . . . [Brenz gives several examples in which attempted murder and attempted fornication are punished.] Thus one can conclude that regardless of whether witches and sorcerers can disturb the elements or cause harm to men with their charms and magic, yet their intentions do not remain only evil thoughts and desires, but produce a full attempt at the crime itself. For this reason the stern seriousness of the law should not be rejected or discarded in this case. And I believe also that the law of Moses in Exodus 22 has the same meaning. It is true, of course, that the word *Casaph* is translated as *pharmakos* or poison. But the *pharmakos* is not only a person who gives someone a poisoned drink, but also he who by mistake gives a safe drink to a person for whom he had prepared a poisoned drink. Thus when the witches and magicians thoroughly intend and plan to harm the fruits, meadow, cattle, or other persons by using either poison or other illicit means, they cannot be held guiltless. . . .

It is, however, necessary to know that one has to have really thorough knowledge and sound witnesses in these cases so that one does not go too far in accusing and punishing those who break these laws. If the matter is understood rightly, one has to distinguish, as you correctly say, between the evil-minded, impudent, willful knaves and the melancholy or mentally ill, or those who err solely from simplicity or superstition. For who could be so merciless and stubborn that he would want to prosecute these last-mentioned persons? . . . It is a great virtue and sign of virtue to take care of the poor orphans, to sympathize with them and have mercy on them. May the dear Lord further you in your new calling and office since you desire that the poor, troubled women should be taken from the hangman and saved from fiery punishment either through your medical healing or through my theological healing. . . . Stuttgart, on the day of the holy martyr Stephen, 1565.

7

Scholarly Attack on the Positions of Brenz and Weyer: Jean Bodin, *On the Demonic Madness of Witches* (1580)

Jean Bodin (1529?-1596) was one of the greatest French thinkers of the sixteenth century. His historical and constitutional principles were widely influential. His ideas on witchcraft were also persuasive. He states that he was skeptical of witchcraft until he witnessed several cases including voluntary confessions. They convinced him that witchcraft was a major threat to the well-being of Christendom and that soft-hearted men like Brenz and Weyer must be strenuously refuted. His legal mind may be seen at work in the careful definition of witchcraft with which he works. Despite his erudition, however, it is questionable how successful Bodin's arguments were, even in sixteenth-century terms. Like most witchcraft books, the *Démonomanie* was placed on the Catholic Index of Prohibited Books.

SOURCE: Jean Bodin, *De la démonomanie des sorciers* (Paris, 1580), Preface, sigs. aiii recto-verso, bii verso-biii verso, biv recto; fols. 1, 68-69, 79, 226-27.

PREFACE

The judgment which was passed against a witch in a case to which I was called on the last day of April, 1578, gave me occasion to take up my pen in order to clarify the subject of witches—persons who seem strange and wondrous to everyone and incredible to many. The witch whom I refer to was named Jeanne Harvillier, a native of Verbery near Compiegne. She was accused of having murdered many men and beasts, as she herself confessed without questioning or torture, although she at first stubbornly denied the charges and changed her story often. She also confessed that her mother presented her at the age of twelve years to the devil, disguised as a tall black man, larger than most men and clothed in black. The mother told him that as soon as her daughter was born she had promised her to him, whom she called the devil. He in turn promised to treat her well and to make her happy. And from then on she had renounced God and promised to serve the devil. And at that instant she had had carnal copulation with the devil, which she had continued to the age of fifty, or thereabouts, when she was captured. She said also that the devil presented himself to her when she wished, always dressed as he had been the first time, booted and spurred, with a sword at his side and his horse at the door. And no one saw him but her. He even fornicated with her often without her husband noticing although he lay at her side. Now because she was widely rumored to be an infamous witch, it was almost impossible to keep the peasants from taking the law into their own hands and burning her, fearful that she might escape. For it was ordered before proceeding to a definite judgment that an enquiry be made at Verbery, where she had been born, to find out about her life, and in the other villages where she had lived. It was found that thirty years earlier she had been whipped for the same crime and that her mother had been condemned to be burned alive by an edict of the Court of Parlement, confirming the sentence of the judge of Senlis. And it was learned that she was used to changing her name and residence to hide these facts. In all of these ways she was suspected as a witch. Finding herself convicted, she begged pardon, appeared to repent, and constantly denied many of the crimes which she had committed and confessed earlier. But she persisted in her confession of the latest murder, saying that she had thrown certain powders, prepared for her by the devil, into the path of the man who had struck her daughter. Instead, another man passed by whom she wished no ill, and at once he felt a sharp pain throughout his whole body. And all the neighbors had seen him enter the place where she had cast the spell, and on the same day they had seen the man burned by the sudden malady and crying out that she had enchanted him. She promised to cure him, and in fact she nursed the patient during his illness and confessed that the Wednesday before being taken prisoner she had prayed that the devil cure him. But he had responded that this was impossible. . . . And two days later the man died.

. . . .

Now even Aristotle was astonished at the many things whose cause he did not know and said that one who calls in question what he sees is no better than other people. For we see that Orpheus, who lived about 1200 years before Jesus Christ, and before him, Homer, men who were the first authors among the pagans, described sorcerers, necromancers, and charms which are still performed today. One sees in the Law of God, published more than two years before Orpheus, that the sorcerers of Pharaoh counterfeited the works of God. One sees the sorcerer of Saul calling up spirits and making them speak. The Law of God forbids going to diviners, witches, fortune-tellers, and specifies all the kinds of sorcery and divination. God declares that it was on their account that he exterminated the Amorrheans and Chananeans from the face of the earth. And for such sorceries Jehu gave Queen Jezebel to the dogs after throwing her from his palace. One also sees the punishments established against witches in the Twelve Tables [of Roman Law], which the ambassadors of the Romans had extracted from the Greek laws. One sees again the very cruel punishments set up for witches in all of the constitutions of the Roman emperors which called them enemies of nature, enemies of the human race, and maleficent witches on account of the great evils which they work. And the horrid imprecations of the laws are not found in any place but against them, whom (the law says) a cruel plague should destroy and consume. One sees the histories of Greeks and Latins, of ancients and moderns, of all countries and all peoples, which describe the things done by witches, and the same effects in diverse countries: the rapture of the soul, the transport in body and soul of witches to distant places conducted by evil spirits who later return them in the briefest time. All witches confess the same things as one can see the books of Germans, Italians, French, and other nations. What Plutarch described concerning Aristeus Proconesus and Cleomedes Astypalaia; or what Herodotus said of a philosophic atheist; or Pliny of Hermes Clazomenae; Philostratus of Appolonius Tyana; and what all the Romans said of Romulus, who was carried through the air before the whole army. As we read in our chronicles, this happened also to a Count of Mascon. And, as is discovered in an infinite number of trials, many do as the witches and find themselves transported in a short time 100 or 200 leagues from their homes. When they see the assembly of witches, they have called on God for help. And then, just as fast, the evil spirits and witches vanish, and they find themselves alone and return the long journey home. In brief we see the trials against the witches of Germany, France, Italy, and Spain, in which we have written evidence and every day we see an infinite number of witnesses, the recollections, confrontations, convictions, confessions, in which some who are executed persist right up to their deaths. These persons are mostly completely ignorant, or old women who never heard of Herodotus, Philostratus, or the laws of other peoples; nor have they ever spoken to the witches of Germany and Italy that they should agree so well in all of these matters and at all points as they do. They never read St. Augustine's Fifteenth Book of the *City of God* where he says that there can be no doubt and it would be shameless to deny that demons and evil spirits have carnal copulation with women, whom the Greeks for that reason called Ephialtes and Hyphialtes; the Latins, Incubi and Succubi and Sylvans; the French, Dusios (this is the word used by St. Augustine). These spirits appear in the guise either of a man or a woman. This copulation, all witches agree, occurs not while they sleep but while awake, which shows that it is not the "oppression" of which the physicians speak, for they all agree that that never occurs unless one is asleep.

. . . .

The ignorant think that it is impossible. The atheists and those who pretend to be wise do not want to admit that they see what they cannot explain, so that they will not look ignorant. . . . But men who fear God, after seeing the stories of witches and contemplating the wonders of God in the whole earth, and having read His Law and the sacred histories, will not call in question things which seem incredible to human sense. For they judge that if many natural things are incredible and some of them incomprehensible, how much more incomprehensible are the powers of supernatural intelligences and the actions of spirits. We do see strange things in nature which are nonetheless ordinary, like the circling of the earth and the sea, which our merchants do, or running upside down, which seemed ridiculous to Lactantius and to St. Augustine. Those men denied that there were antipodes, a fact which is now as certain and as firmly demonstrated as the brightness of the sun. And those who say that it is impossible that an evil spirit carry a man 100 or 200 leagues from his house have not considered the fact that the heavens and all the great celestial bodies make their movement [around the earth] in twenty-four hours, that is to say, 245,791,440 leagues at 2000 paces to the league, as I will demonstrate in the last chapter. If they say that one sees that action every day and that one must judge with one's senses, they confess therefore that one has to believe and pay attention to the actions of spirits against the course of nature even though we cannot understand the marvels of nature which we see regularly before our eyes.

CHAPTER 1: DEFINITION OF THE WITCH

A witch is someone who by diabolical means consciously tries to accomplish something. I have set up a definition here which is necessary not only for understanding this treatise but also for the judgments which must be made against the witches. This definition has been omitted up to now by all who have written on witches, but nevertheless it is the foundation on which this treatise must be built. Let us examine our definition in detail. First, I say "consciously" because error cannot imply any consent, as the law says. Such is the case with a sick man, who uses in good faith a diabolical recipe given to him by a witch whom he considers an honest person. Such a person is not a witch for he has a just plea of ignorance. But not if the witch tells him or if he invokes evil spirits in his presence, as happens sometimes. . . .

BOOK II, CHAPTER 3: ON EXPLICIT INVOCATIONS OF EVIL SPIRITS

Those who in seeking to do good invoke the evil spirit for advice and counsel, or for aid and comfort, thinking that he is God, in the way that many still do in the West and as the ancient pagans did, are no more witches than those who worship the sun and the moon, and other creatures. One could well say that they are idolaters. To enquire if God approves of their good intentions I leave to the judgment of God. For it infringes too closely on the secrets of God to ask how those who have been damned to eternal damnation like Socrates, Phocion, and Aristides the Just, merit the same punishment as the most detestable witches. The Law of God says that one must differentiate punishments, having regard for the gravity of the crime. But among the pagans those who knew the difference between good and evil spirits and not only sacrificed their own children but also committed lecheries and sodomies and other abominable filthinesses against the right reason which God engraved on our souls to attain their designs were not merely idolaters but also witches. And all the philosophers and legislators have condemned such men. God told his people that this was why he had uprooted the land of the Amorrheans and other peoples who gave themselves to such witchcraft. And also by edict of the Roman Senate the Bacchanales were banned from Rome and all of Italy on account of the horrid witchcraft which was committed during the night. Satan does all in his power to enslave men and draw them from the true worship of the true God. And since God is invisible, men see the admirable beauty of the sun and the course of the celestial bodies, their virtue and their strange movement, and easily fall into praise or worship of the sun, moon, or even Jupiter and other celestial bodies. And instead of following Noah's advice to his children to sacrifice to God in all places, men found it easy to turn their eyes to the sun and the moon and other celestial bodies. . . .

Witchcraft distinct from idolatry

The differences among witches are very noteworthy and must be taken into account in the difficult judgments which have to be made. The most hateful witches, however, are those who renounce God and his service, or, if they do not worship the true God, then those who, having some superstitious religion, renounce it in order to give themselves to the devil by an explicit pact. For there is no religion so superstitious that it does not restrain men somewhat within the barriers of the law of nature, urging men to obey their fathers and mothers and the magistrates, and instilling a fear of hurting anyone. Yet Satan wants to uproot from the heart of men all fear of sin. And as for the explicit pact, sometimes she gives her word verbally and without writing; but occasionally Satan, to secure his people before granting their demands, makes them write out their obligations, if they know how to write, and sign the agreement, sometimes with their own blood as the ancients used to do to guarantee their oaths and friendships. Just as we read in the second book of Titus Livy and in Tacitus regarding the kings of Armenia, so Satan with his own.

Are the witches mentally ill or melancholy?
Refutation of the opinions of Johann Weyer

Hippocrates, in the first book of common diseases, and Galen, in the same book, hold that women generally are healthier than men because of their menstrual flow, which guards them from a thousand illnesses. Hippocrates says that women never have gout, pulmonary ulcers (according to Galen), epilepsy, apoplexy, raving madness, lethargy, convulsions, or trembling so long as they have their menstrual period. And although Hippocrates describes as natural the falling sickness and the disease of those who are possessed by demons (which is called the sacred disease), nevertheless he holds that the disease attacks only the phlegmatic and not the bilious. This is a fact which Johann Weyer, being a doctor, cannot ignore.

Now we have shown that ordinarily women are possessed by demons more often than men and that witches are often transported bodily but also often ravished in an ecstasy, the soul having separated itself from the body, by diabolical means, leaving the body insensible and stupid. Thus it is completely ridiculous to say that the illness of the witches originates in melancholy, especially since the diseases coming from melancholy are always dangerous. Nonetheless, one finds witches who have practiced their trade forty or fifty years, from the age of twelve years on, as with Jeanne Harvillier, who was burned alive the 29th of April 1578, and with Magdaleine de la Croix, Abbess of Cordova in Spain, in 1545. They had ordinary acquaintance and copulation with the devil over a period of forty years for the former and thirty years in the latter case. Thus Weyer must admit that there is a remarkable incongruity for one who is a doctor, and a gross example of ignorance (but it is not ignorance) to attribute to women melancholy diseases which are as little appropriate for them as are the praiseworthy effects of a tempered melancholy humor. This humor makes a man wise, sober, and contemplative (as all of the ancient philosophers and physicians remark), which are qualities as incompatible with women as fire with water. And even Solomon, who as a

man of the world knew well the humor of women, said that he had seen a
wise man for every thousand men, but that he had never seen a wise woman.
Let us therefore abandon the fanatic error of those who make women into
melancholics.

8

The Different Kinds of Magic:
Martin Delrio, *Six Books of Discourse on Magicians* (1599)

Although the Catholic Index forbade most witchcraft books, it
never banned the careful and scholarly writings of Martin Delrio
(1551-1608), a member of the Jesuit Order. Perhaps the reason
for Delrio's success came from the theological care with which he
dissected the various kinds of magic. His discussion of "harmless"
witchcraft merits comparison with the views of Brenz, Weyer, and
Bodin.

SOURCE: Martin Delrio, *Disquisitionum Magicarum Libri Sex*
(Venice, 1616; original edition, 1599), pp. 3, 738, 740.

I define magic as a whole in the broadest terms as an *art or means for
producing, with created (not supernatural) forces, certain strange wonders
whose cause is beyond the understanding and common capacity of man.* I
have used such broad limits because I see that great men, following Fr.
Victoria, by surrounding the subject with a tighter wall, have excluded both
artificial and natural magic. I called it an *art* or *means* for producing any
information or action, and this art clearly comprehends those that produce
knowledge and those that do not, the liberal as well as the mechanical arts,
the true as well as the false, the artificial as well as those free of artifice, the
superstitious as well as those free of vice. I use the word *producing* for all
functions of mind, soul, sense, or members. I understand the *force* of things
used or of the person using it to be of course human or demonic. I used the
words *created (not supernatural)* in order to exclude true miracles, which are

the work of God alone. For that reason I prefer to speak of wonders (*mira*) rather than miracles (*miracula*). Finally, I mention the *common understanding and capacity* because the cause of many magical effects is only understood by the wiser men, who in any age are always few. Thus broadly there is a division of the whole of magic into final and efficient causes also. With the efficient the division is said to be into natural, artificial, and diabolical, for its whole effect is to be ascribed either to things of inborn nature or of human diligence or of the malice of evil demons. With the final cause, we can rightly divide [magic] into *good* if it uses licit means with a good intention (which includes only artificial and natural magic); and into bad, whose goals or means, of course, are evil. *This is the characteristic of prohibited magic, which we can call tacit idolatry and a type of superstition.* Prohibited magic can be described, therefore, as a means or art, using a pact with demons, by which certain wonders are produced which exceed the common understanding of man. I said *using a pact* because all the force of this magic depends on a tacit or express pact, as I will show in the proper place. The theologians call it *tacit idolatry* because the magicians (at least most of them) do not worship creatures as if they were God, but rather offer their cult as if to some generous benefactor from whom they may obtain something. This intention produces four kinds of tacit idolatry, or prohibited magic, by reason of the variety of its objects: (1) Special magic; (2) Divination; (3) Harmful magic; (4) Empty observances.

SHOULD HARMLESS WITCHES BE EXECUTED?

In conclusion witches are to be executed even if they have not killed any person with poison and even if they have not harmed crops or animals, and even if they did not commit necromancy; for this reason alone, that they stand out as confederates of the devil, take part in their customary meetings, and are drilled there. . .

From the Laws of Charles V (the *Carolina*) it is objected that the ruling Article 109 is that "if they cause anyone harm by witchcraft or by sorcery, they are to be punished with death by fire. But if they cause no one any harm they are to suffer punishments according to the quantity and quality of the crime." I answer that the quality and quantity of this crime are always clearly such that if they were in league with the devil, if they did in meetings those things that are usually done, they should be punished with death. Strictly speaking, therefore, this law decrees that magical poisoners are always to be punished with fire, but others, if they are not magical poisoners, are to be punished sometimes with fire but sometimes with another penalty.

ELIZABETH L. EISENSTEIN

The Advent of Printing and the Protestant Revolt: A New Approach to the Disruption of Western Christendom

Between 1517 and 1520, Luther's thirty publications probably sold well over 300,000 copies. . . . Altogether in relation to the spread of religious ideas it seems difficult to exaggerate the significance of the Press, without which a revolution of this magnitude could scarcely have been consummated. Unlike the Wycliffite and Waldensian heresies, Lutheranism was from the first the child of the printed book, and through this vehicle Luther was able to make exact, standardized and ineradicable impressions on the mind of Europe. For the first time in human history a great reading public judged the validity of revolutionary ideas through a mass-medium which used the vernacular languages together with the arts of the journalist and the cartoonist.[1]

As this citation suggests, the impact of print, which is often overlooked in discussions of the Renaissance, is less likely to go unnoted in Reformation studies. In this latter field, historians confront a movement that was shaped at the very outset (and in large part ushered in) by the new powers of the press. Protestan-

Reprinted with permission from *Annales Economies, Sociétés, Civilisations* Vol. 26, No. 6, 1971, pp. 1355-1382.

This is an abridged version of a much longer chapter for a forthcoming book. Most of the middle section of the chapter has been eliminated, with a few excerpts presented in summary form beginning with first new paragraph on p. 243 and ending with first new paragraph on p. 250.

[1] Arthur G. Dickens, *Reformation and Society in Sixteenth Century Europe*, p. 51.

tism was the first religious movement to take full advantage of these powers. It was also the first movement of any kind to exploit the new medium for the purpose of propaganda and agitation on a mass scale. By pamphleteering directed at arousing popular support and aimed at readers who were unversed in Latin, the reformers unwittingly pioneered in mass communication techniques. They also left "ineradicable impressions" in the form of broadsides and caricatures. Designed to catch the attention and arouse the passions of sixteenth-century readers, their anti-papist cartoons still have a strong impact when encountered in history books today. By its very nature then, the exploitation of the new medium by Protestants is highly visible to modern scholars.

Moreover the reformers were aware that the printing press was useful to their cause and they acknowledged its importance in their writings. Luther, himself, described printing as "God's highest and extremest act of grace, whereby the business of the Gospel is driven forward." It was typical of the Protestant outlook that he also regarded it as "the last flame before the extinction of the world."[2] Not until later, after man's future on earth had been indefinitely prolonged, would the invention be associated (by Condorcet and others) with progressive enlightenment. Luther believed, on the contrary, that the forward movement of history was soon to be terminated by the day of judgment. Moreover Protestants, like humanists, still looked back and not ahead when seeking to overcome Gothic darkness and move toward an age of light. When John Foxe heralded "the excellent arte of printing most happily of late found out . . . to the singular benefite of Christe's Church" he was thinking about the restoration of "the lost light of knowledge to these blynde times" and "the reneuing of holsome and auncient writers whose doinges and teachinges otherwise had lyen in oblivion."[3] Nevertheless, the epoch-making role assigned printing in Protestant schemes marked a departure from previous historiography. By associating Gutenberg's invention with a decisive break with Rome and Elizabethan statecraft, Foxe and his co-religionists pointed the way to later trends.[4]

[2] Luther's remarks cited by M. H. Black, "The Printed Bible," in *The Cambridge History of the Bible*, vol. III (hereafter C.H.B. III), p. 432.

[3] John Foxe, Preface to collection of Protestant texts (1572) cited by Margaret Aston, "Lollardy and the Reformation: Survival or Revival," *History* 49(1964): 169. See also her "John Wycliffe's Reformation Reputation," *Past and Present*, no. 30 (April 1965), pp. 23-52, for an account of how Foxe followed "where John Bale had led" and of early use of "luminary metaphors" by eulogists of Wycliffe.

[4] The invention was first heralded in German humanist circles on patriotic grounds as

Although Protestant divines diverged from Enlightened philoso-
phes on most issues, both viewed printing as a providential device
which ended forever a priestly monopoly of learning, overcame
ignorance and pushed back the dark forces commanded by Italian
Popes.[5]

The Lord began to work for His Church not with sword and target to subdue
His exalted adversary, but with printing, writing and reading . . . How many
presses there be in the world, so many block-houses there be against the high
castle of St. Angelo, so that either the pope must abolish knowledge and
printing or printing must at length root him out.[6]

Printing and Protestantism seem to go together naturally as
printing and the Renaissance do not, partly because vestiges of
early historical schemes are carried over into present accounts. The
new presses were not developed until after Petrarch's death and
had no bearing on early concepts of a "rinascita," whereas they
were in full operation before Luther was born and did enter into
his views of a religious reformation. In the latter case, moreover,
they affected events as well as ideas and actually presided over the
initial act of revolt.

When Luther proposed debate over his Ninety-Five Theses his
action was not in and of itself revolutionary. It was entirely
conventional for professors of theology to hold disputations over an
issue such as indulgences and "church doors were the customary
place for medieval publicity."[7] But these particular theses did not
stay tacked to the church door (if indeed they were ever really
placed there).[8] To a sixteenth-century Lutheran chronicler, "it

---

a unique contribution to cultural revival and as a German achievement that rivalled
Italian accomplishments. (See e.g. Lewis Spitz, *The Religious Renaissance of the German
Humanists,* pp. 84-85.) This patriotic theme was interwoven with antipapist propaganda,
carried over to England and ultimately to the American colonies.

[5] Foxe's world historical scheme which stresses printing is discussed by W. Ferguson,
The Renaissance in Historical Thought: Five Centuries of Interpretation (Cambridge,
Mass., 1948), pp. 54; 97. The important position of printing in ideas of progress and
Enlightenment thought requires a separate study. It is touched on by Roy S. Wolper,
"The Rhetoric of Gunpowder and the Idea of Progress," *Journal of the History of Ideas*
31 (Oct.-Dec. 1970): 589-98.

[6] Cited from Foxe's *Book of Martyrs* by William Haller, *The Elect Nation,* p. 110.

[7] Geoffrey R. Elton, *Reformation Europe 1517-1559,* p. 15.

[8] Erwin Iserloh, *The Theses Were Not Posted,* does not prove the event did not occur
but shows there is no reliable contemporary evidence that it did occur. Heinrich Grimm,
"Luther's 'Ablassthesen' und die Gegenthesen von Tetzel-Wimpina in der Sicht der
Druck- und Buchgeschichte," *Gutenberg Jahrbuch,* 1968, pp. 139-50, believes a
hand-copied text was nailed on the church door but in mid-November rather than
October 31. Harold J. Grimm, Introduction to Ninety-Five Theses, *Career of the*

almost appeared as if the angels themselves had been their
messengers and brought them before the eyes of all the people."[9]
Luther himself expressed puzzlement, when addressing Pope Leo
X six months after the initial event:

> It is a mystery to me how my theses, more so than my other writings, indeed,
> those of other professors were spread to so many places. They were meant
> exclusively for our academic circle here. . . . they were written in such a
> language that the common people could hardly understand them.
> They . . . use academic categories. . . .[10]

According to a modern scholar, it is still "one of the mysteries of
Reformation history how this proposal for academic disputation,
written in Latin, could have kindled such enthusiastic support and
thereby have such far reaching impact."[11] Precisely when were
Luther's theses first printed outside Wittenberg? Just who was
responsible for their being translated into German at first and then
into other vernaculars? How did it happen that, soon after being
printed in a handful of towns, such as Nuremberg, Leipzig, and
Basel, copies were multiplied in such quantities and distributed so
widely that the Theses won top billing throughout central
Europe—competing for space with news of the Turkish threat in
printshop, bookstall, and country fair?[12] These questions cannot
be answered in detail here.[13] I have posed them simply to direct

---

Reformer, 3 vols. (*Luther's Works*, vols. 31, 32, & 34, H. T. Lehman, ed. [Philadelphia:
Fortress, 1957]), I, 22-23, states that the text was printed before being nailed. That the
last word on whether the theses were nailed or mailed has not been spoken is noted by
Robert L. McNally, "The Ninety-Five Theses of Martin Luther," *Theological Studies*
28(1967):461n. I imagine the same point applies to whether they were first duplicated by
hand or in print.

[9] Friedrich Myconius, selection from *Historia Reformationis* in Hans Hillerbrand, ed.
and tr., *The Reformation: A Narrative History Related by Contemporary Observers and
Participants* (New York, 1964), p. 47.

[10] Luther, letter of 30 May 1518 in Hillerbrand, p. 54. See also insistence by Bainton
that "Luther took no steps to spread his theses among the people . . . " and "General
dissemination was not in Luther's mind when he posted the theses." Ronald Bainton,
Here I Stand, pp. 63-64.

[11] Hillerbrand, p. 32.

[12] The rapid distribution of news about Luther's protest throughout central Europe is
discussed by Max Kortepeter, "German Zeitung Literature in the Sixteenth Century," in
Editing Sixteenth Century Texts, R. J. Schoeck, ed. (Toronto, 1966), p. 155.

[13] According to Harold J. Grimm, *op. cit.*, the first printing was done by Johann
Grunenberg of Wittenberg. Heinrich Grimm, *op. cit.*, p. 142, discounts this possibility,
somewhat arbitrarily, I think. He deprecates Grunenberg and Wittenberg printing in
contradiction to an essay by Maria Grossman, "Wittenberg Printing, Early Sixteenth
Century," in *Sixteenth Century Essays and Studies* (St. Louis, Mo.: Foundation for
Reformation Research, 1970), I:54-74, who notes Grunenberg's 1517 edition of
Luther's *Die Sieben Busspsalmen* as well as his earlier Greek and Latin press work. There

attention to the important intermediate stages between the academic proposal and the popular acclaim. The mystery, in other words, is primarily the result of skipping over the process whereby a message ostensibly directed at a few could be made accessible to the many. If we want to dispel it, instead of jumping directly from church door to public clamor, we should move more cautiously, a step at a time, looking at the activities of the printers, translators, and distributors, who acted as agents of the change.

In addition to investigating just how the message was spread, however, we also need to look more carefully at the so-called "academic circle" to which it was first addressed. In this regard, the conventional medieval format of Luther's proposal is somewhat deceptive. By 1517, the audience for learned disputation had been extended far beyond earshot of pulpit or lectern. The educated elite who could understand Latin and theological debate was no longer composed only of churchmen and professors. The scholar printer who presided over the new centers of erudition was usually a layman and rarely had a university degree. Although it was closer to commercial crossroads than to cloistered precincts, the printer's workshop attracted the most learned and disputatious scholars of the day. His products made it possible for academic argument to be followed from afar. Whether or not the theses were actually tacked on the door of the castle church in Wittenberg on All Hallows Eve, they were initially read by a small group of learned laymen who were less likely to gather on the church steps than in urban workshops where town and gown met to exchange gossip and news, peer over editors' shoulders, check copy, and read proof.[14] There, also, new schemes for promoting best sellers were being tried out. Given access to presses and booksellers' routes, it required only a small following in a handful of towns to create an unprecedented stir in the early sixteenth century.

---

is agreement at least that editions were issued by three separate printers—Hölzel of Nuremberg, Thanner (or Herbipolensis) of Leipzig, and Petri of Basel—by December 1517. The likelihood that a single directing hand guided this triple publication is noted by Heinrich Grimm (p. 145). The important role played by the "Sodalitas Staupitziana" in Nuremberg—especially by Christoph Scheurl and Kaspar Nutzel—in getting the Theses printed, in German as well as Latin, is noted by several authorities. See also Gerald Strauss, *Nuremberg in the Sixteenth Century* (New York, 1966), pp. 160ff.

[14] A good view of Erasmus at work in Froben's press room in Basel surrounded by a boisterous group who read what he set down and responded to it on the spot is offered by James D. Tracy, "Erasmus Becomes a German," *Renaissance Quarterly* 21 (1968):288.

A letter from Beatus Rhenanus to Zwingli in 1519 suggests how the tactics employed by the small Latin-reading audience, whom Luther addressed, might produce distant repercussions in a short time. "He will sell more of Luther's tracts if he has no other to offer," Zwingli was told by Beatus in a letter recommending a book peddler. The peddler should go from town to town, village to village, house to house, offering nothing but Luther's writings for sale. "This will virtually force the people to buy them, which would not be the case if there were a wide selection."[15] The linking of concern about salvation with shrewd business tactics and what we would nowadays call a "hard sell" seems to have been no less pronounced in the early sixteenth century than among Bible salesmen today. Deliberate exploitation of the new medium helps to explain the paradox, which is noted in many Reformation studies, that a return to early Christian Church traditions somehow served to usher in modern times.

"Rarely has one invention had more decisive influence than that of printing on the Reformation." Luther "had invited a public disputation and nobody had come to dispute." Then "by a stroke of magic he found himself addressing the whole world."[16] Here is an example of revolutionary causation where normally useful distinctions between precondition and precipitant are difficult to maintain.[17] For there seems to be general agreement that Luther's act in 1517 *did* precipitate the Protestant Revolt. October 31 "continues to be celebrated in Lutheran countries as the anniversary of the Reformation and justly so. The controversy over indulgences brought together the man and the occasion: it signalled the end of the medieval Church."[18] To understand how Luther's theses served as such a signal, we cannot afford to stand at the door of the Castle Church in Wittenberg looking for something tacked there. If we stay at the Wittenberg church with Luther we will miss seeing the historical significance of the event. It was largely because traditional forms of theological disputation had been transformed by entirely new publicity techniques that the act of the German monk had such a far-reaching effect.

---

[15] Letter of 2 July 1519 from Beatus to Zwingli in Hillerbrand, p. 125. (See also pp. 123ff. for correspondence pertaining to distribution of the Ninety-Five Theses.)

[16] Gordon Rupp, *Luther's Progress to the Diet of Worms, 1521* (Chicago, 1951), p. 54.

[17] Lawrence Stone, *Social Change and Revolution in England 1540-1640*, Problems and Perspectives in History, H. F. Kearney, Ed. (London, 1966), p. xxii.

[18] Elton, p. 15.

The theses . . . were said to be known throughout Germany in a fortnight and throughout Europe in a month. . . . Printing was recognized as a new power and publicity came into its own. In doing for Luther what the copyists had done for Wycliffe, the printing presses transformed the field of communications and fathered an international revolt. It was a revolution.[19]

The advent of printing was an important precondition for the Protestant Reformation taken as a whole; for without it one could not implement a "priesthood of all believers." At the same time, however, the new medium also acted as a precipitant. It provided "the stroke of magic" by which an obscure theologian in Wittenberg managed to shake Saint Peter's throne.

In this respect, the contrast, drawn by several authorities between the fate of Luther who had the new vehicle at his disposal and that of the Lollards and Waldensians who did not is worth more extended discussion.[20] How did the advent of printing affect the heresies that were current during the later Middle Ages? The problem calls for much more thought and study than can be given here.[21] Previous discussion of the problem of the Renaissance however, points to a line of analysis that might be worth pursuing further.[22] It may be helpful, in other words, to keep typographical fixity in mind when comparing the sixteenth century upheaval

[19] Margaret Aston, *The Fifteenth Century: The Prospect of Europe* (London, 1968), p. 76.

[20] That Hus and Wycliffe were separated from Luther by a technical discovery as well as by time, circumstance, and conviction is noted by Aston, *op. cit.*, p. 50. Apart from works mentioned above (see notes 19 and 1 on pages 241 and 235), see also more extended treatment in Arthur G. Dickens, *The English Reformation* Chap. 2, Henri Hauser, *La Naissance du Protestantisme*, G. Dumezil, ed. (Paris, 1962), pp. 51ff., and Louise W. Holborn, "Printing and the Growth of a Protestant Movement in Germany from 1517-1524," *Church History* 11 (June, 1942): 1-15.

[21] According to Gordon Leff, *Heresy in the Later Middle Ages: The Relation of Heterodoxy to Dissent c. 1250-1450* 2 vols. (Manchester, 1967), I, 47, the heresies were defined within the context of a Catholic Church that was co-extensive with Western Christendom and could only exist within that context. After the Protestant revolt, they came to an end, almost by definition, along with the medieval church. Just how they "passed into the Reformation," however, is left open by Leff. The Lollard revival, undertaken by Foxe and others who fully exploited print, retrieved texts, and wrote eulogies, is documented by Aston, "Lollardy and the Reformation," *passim.* How the Waldensians (by contributing to the printing of Olivetan's French translation of the Bible, for example) entered into Calvinist developments might be worth more study. A program for studying the effect of print on Italian heresies is outlined by Carlo de Frede, "Per la Storia della Stampa nel Cinquecento in Rapporto con la Diffusione della Riforma in Italia," *Gutenberg Jahrbuch*, 1964, pp. 175-84. I lack the background to comment on studies concerning Hussite survival and revival in central European Protestant movements.

[22] Elizabeth L. Eisenstein, "The Advent of Printing and the Problem of the Renaissance," *Past and Present*, no. 45 (November 1969), pp. 27ff.

with previous religious developments. Thus medieval heresies can be distinguished from the Protestant Revolt in much the same manner as medieval revivals from the Italian Renaissance. In both instances, localized transitory effects were superseded by widespread permanent ones. Partly because religious dissent was implemented by print, it could leave a much more indelible and far-reaching impression than dissent had ever left before.

For example, there had been many schisms within the Western Church. Popes had often been at odds with emperors and kings, with church councils, and with rival claimants to the throne. But no episode that occurred from Canossa to Constance—not even a contest between three rival popes—shattered the unity of the Church as decisively or permanently as did the contested divorce case of a sixteenth-century English king. Thomas Cromwell proved to be as skillful as Luther's German friends in mobilizing propagandists and attracting a large public by vernacular translations.[23] When implemented by new techniques, divisions once traced were etched ever more deeply and could not be easily erased. Sixteenth-century heresy and schism shattered Christendom so completely that even after religious warfare had ended, ecumenical movements led by men of goodwill could not put all the pieces together again. Not only were there too many splinter groups, separatists, and independent sects who regarded a central Church government as incompatible with true faith, but the main lines of cleavage had been extended across continents and carried overseas along with Bibles and breviaries. Colonists who crossed a great ocean to arrive safely in the new world offered prayers to the same God much as had medieval pilgrims or crusaders. But the sign of the cross had become divisive. The forms of worship shared by congregations in New England markedly diverged from those of fellow Christians who attended mass in the Baroque churches of New Spain. Within a few generations, the gap between Protestant and Catholic had widened sufficiently to give rise to contrasting literary cultures and life styles. Long after theology had ceased to provoke wars, Christians on both continents were separated from each other by invisible barriers that are still with us today.

The lasting establishment of antipapist churches and the continuous propagation of heterodox faiths were of enormous con-

---

[23] Many studies note the exploitation of print by Cromwell, who had a hand in promoting English Bibles as well as various tracts. A group biography of the printers, publicists, and hired hands whom he mobilized might be worth while. See Geoffrey Elton's recent study, *Policy and Police*, Chapter 2.

sequence to Western civilization. But the impact of print on Western Christendom was by no means confined to the implementation of protest or the perpetuation of heterodoxy. Orthodox beliefs and institutions were also affected in ways that should be taken into account. The Christian tradition, like the classical heritage, had been shaped by scribal transmission. It does not seem plausible that it would continue unchanged after methods of transmission had been completely transformed. In this respect, Reformation studies, while they do make room for printing, almost always say too little and bring the topic in too late. It is thus in connection with the spread of Luther's ideas that Dickens finds it "difficult to exaggerate the significance of the Press" and it is almost always when discussing the dissemination of Protestant views that historians pause over printing at all.

Actually, church traditions were already being affected by the advent of printing, well before Martin Luther had come of age. When fixed in a new format and presented in a new way, orthodox views were inevitably transformed.[24] Much of the religious turbulence of the early modern era may be traced to the fact that the writings of church fathers and the scriptures themselves could not continue to be transmitted in traditional ways. As a sacred heritage, Christianity could be protected against most forms of change. As a heritage that was transmitted by texts and that involved the "spreading of glad tidings," Christianity was peculiarly vulnerable to the revolutionary effects of typography. Heralded on all sides as a "peaceful art," Gutenberg's invention probably contributed more to destroying Christian concord and enflaming religious warfare than any of the so-called arts of war ever did.

Processing texts in new workshops was, to be sure, a peaceful activity undertaken by pacific urban craftsmen and merchants. Nevertheless it brought into focus many troublesome issues which had always been blurred, or glossed over, before. Oral testimony, for example, could be distinguished much more clearly from written testimony when poets no longer composed their works in the course of chanting or reciting them and reading out loud no longer signified the publication of a work. Accordingly, questions were more likely to arise about the transmission of teachings that

---

[24]Thus, a new chapter in the history of Thomism commenced. See e.g. P. O. Kristeller, *Le Thomisme et la Pensée Italienne de la Renaissance* (Montreal, 1967), pp. 36-39. Similarly, Spanish mysticism was transformed. See Arthur G. Dickens, *The Counter Reformation* (London, 1969), pp. 25-26.

came from the lips of Christ or from a dictation of the Holy Spirit
to the Apostles.[25] The traditional mediating role of the priesthood
also became less secure after lay grammarians and philologists had
been summoned by scholar printers to help with the task of
editing old texts. The priest might claim the sacred office of
mediating between God and man; when it came to scriptural
exegesis many printers decided that Greek and Hebrew scholars
were better equipped for the task.

With typographical fixity, moreover, positions once taken were
more difficult to reverse. Polemical disputes developed a momentum of their own; passions were enflamed as Protestant and Papist
saw the devil at work in the enemy camp. It soon became
impossible to play down provocative issues; too many pens were
being employed in playing them up.

That a clash of warring faiths eventually dethroned theology
and undermined confidence in Christianity itself has often been
noted. My point is not that disputes between rival churches paved
the way for later views but rather that printing (by revolutionizing
all processes of transmission) made it necessary for churchmen to
depart from earlier views and set them at odds with each other.
Given the new technology, it was quite impossible to preserve the
status quo and hence some kind of disruption was inevitable.

A specific illustration of this point is provided by the status of
the Holy Writ itself. Whatever position a sixteenth-century church-
man might take on questions pertaining to the Gospel was bound
to mark a departure from precedent because the terms of all such
questions had changed along with the format of the Gospel itself.

The character of Bible study had been affected by the new
technology even before Protestant doctrines had emerged. By
introducing new methods of editing biblical texts, the establishment of printers' workshops forced a division between scholars
and obscurantists. This division not only preceded the Lutheran
Revolt; it never became entirely congruent with the Protestant-
Catholic split. For dogmatic Protestants were no less hostile than
dogmatic Catholics to the scholar printers' research. At the same
time, however, it is necessary to distinguish between Bible study in
the sense of scholarly exegesis and Bible study in the sense of lay

---

[25] R. Preus, *The Inspiration of Scripture* (Edinburgh, 1957) and George H. Tavard,
Holy Writ or Holy Church: The Crisis of the Protestant Reformation (London, 1959)
offer pertinent data. Howard M. Teeple, "The Oral Tradition That Never Existed,"
Journal of Biblical Literature 89 (March 1970):56-69, shows the issue is still controversial.

Bible reading. In this latter field, Protestant-Catholic contrasts did become extremely important.[26] Thus during the second century of printing, vernacular Bibles were rarely authorized by Catholic rulers. Their publication frequently led to persecution and imprisonment, and they were generally handled under foreign or heterodox auspices.[27] During the same period, Protestant policy moved in the opposite direction. Vernacular Bibles, and prayer books and catechisms, were adopted by all reforming churches. Sooner or later, they were officially authorized by all rulers who broke with Rome and entered into the mainstream of national literary culture in Protestant lands.

This sixteenth-century division over the question of Bible translation had long-range implications and the relationship between Protestantism and nationalism might be clarified if they were explored. In view of their far-reaching consequences, I am inclined to agree with Dickens that the decisions made at Trent "have attracted too little attention":

The divided Fathers failed ... to establish any priority for Biblical studies or ... to encourage the laity to read the Scriptures, or to prepare the Scripturally-orientated catechism for laymen which the humanist group had ... planned. This great refusal of 1546 had permanent effects.... At no stage did the spirit of Erasmus and Lefèvre suffer a more catastrophic defeat and in no field did the fear of Protestantism leave deeper marks upon the development of Catholic religion.[28]

But, in my view, something that ran even deeper than fear of Protestantism was at stake in the "great refusal of 1546." This refusal was also designed to counteract forces which had begun to subvert the medieval church before Luther was born and which continued to menace Roman Catholicism long after Protestant zeal

[26] Opposing positions taken by seventeenth-century Catholics and Lutherans over "the right of the Laity to read Scripture" are delineated by Preus, pp. 164ff.

[27] Spanish translations were thus printed in Geneva, Basel, Amsterdam, and on a Jewish press in Ferrara; the Protestant Diodati had his celebrated Italian translation printed in Geneva; French translations were produced in Antwerp, Geneva, Louvain, and Amsterdam. Even the (Rheims-Douai) Anglo-Catholic translation was produced outside England. See *C.H.B. III*, 112, 114, 126-28; Henri Martin, *Livre, Pouvoirs, et Société à Paris au XVIIe Siècle (1598-1701)* 2 vols., (Geneva, 1969), I, 102-4. The successful opposition to a temporary authorization by Louis XIII is described in II, 610-11.

[28] Dickens, *Counter Reformation*, p. 115. This (Protestant) interpretation is quite different from the (Catholic) one by F. J. Crehan, S.J., "The Bible in the Roman Catholic Church from Trent to the Present Day," *C.H.B. III*, 203. The latter asserts that "the Christian humanists at the Council" swept aside "conservative arguments in arranging for lectureship in Scripture" and says nothing about other more substantive issues.

had ebbed.[29] Regardless of what happened in Wittenberg or Zurich, regardless of other issues taken up at Trent, sooner or later the Church would have had to come to terms with the effect on the Bible of copy-editing on the one hand and expanding book markets on the other.

As these remarks suggest, the fate of the medieval *Vulgate* was closely intertwined with that of the medieval church. By examining the effects of print on Jerome's version one might also illuminate the forces that disrupted Latin Christendom.[30] In summary form, one could say that printing subjected the *Vulgate* to a two-pronged attack. It was threatened by Greek and Hebrew studies on the one hand and by vernacular translation on the other. Distrusted as an inferior translation by humanist scholars, Jerome's version was also discarded as too esoteric by evangelical reformers. Although they were not entirely discrete, it is necessary to keep the two prongs of the attack separate; for vernacular translators often worked at cross purposes with classical scholars.[31] By reinforcing linguistic barriers they undermined a cosmopolitan commonwealth of learning which collaboration on polyglot Bibles helped to construct. In the form of the Lutheran Bible or the King James version, the sacred book of Western civilization became more insular as it grew more popular. It is no accident that nationalism and mass literacy have developed

---

[29] That the suppression of Protestantism by the Roman Curia was incidental to the containment of other more basic and more long-range forces is also argued by William J. Bouwsma, *Venice and the Defense of Republican Liberty*, pp. 293-95. Whereas he associates the threat with "Renaissance values" and sees Rome's "primary adversaries . . . symbolized by Florence and Venice rather than by Wittenberg and Geneva," (p. 294) I think the threat was posed by forces unleashed by print. In my view, both Venice and Geneva, as important printing centers, represented "primary adversaries" of sixteenth-century Rome. (Unfortunately, discussion of Catholic censorship and the creation of the Index, despite its relevance, cannot be undertaken here.)

[30] The fate of the medieval *Corpus Juris* (also described as the "legal *Vulgate*") was somewhat analogous to that of Jerome's version of the Scriptures. See Julian Franklin, *Jean Bodin and the Sixteenth Century Revolution in the Methodology of Law and History* (New York, 1963), pp. 7-10. It would be useful to study the impact of print on the medieval legal textual tradition as well as the medieval scriptural one.

[31] The English translation movement is well covered by R. F. Jones, *The Triumph of the English Language* (London, 1953); J. G. Ebel, "Translation and Cultural Nationalism in the Reign of Elizabeth," *Journal of the History of Ideas* 30 (Oct.-Dec. 1969):593-602; H. J. Graham, " 'Our Tongue Maternall Marvelously Amendyd and Augmentyd': The First Englishing and Printing of the Medieval Statutes at Large 1530-1533," *U.C.L.A. Law Bulletin* 13 (Nov. 1965):58-98: Eleanor Rosenberg, *Leicester: Patron of Letters* (New York, 1955). A comparative study of sixteenth-century translation movements would be useful since they occurred in different areas at more or less the same time. See e.g. Paul F. Grendler, "Francesco Sansovino and Italian Popular History 1560-1600," *Studies in the Renaissance* 16(1969):141.

together. The two processes have been linked ever since Europeans ceased to speak the same language when citing their scriptures or saying their prayers. Outside Catholic Europe, a scriptural faith penetrated deeply into all social strata and provided the foundation for some sort of "common culture." But although a Bible Belt left permanent marks across many lands, the "old-time religion" was abruptly arrested at new linguistic frontiers.

It is worth noting in this regard that the Bible Belt is the product of the same forces that produced the Index. It is a mistake to couple Biblical fundamentalism with Aristotelianism as "obsolescent habits of thought" which seemed in retreat in the age of Erasmus, before religious warfare revived them.[32] The capacity of like-minded men to cite the same chapter and verse and to govern their daily lives accordingly hinged on their access to identical copies of whole Bibles and hence on the output of sizable standard editions. Scribal compendia which mingled excerpts from the Bible with other matter did not lend themselves to the same cast of mind.[33]

Thus, the same process which encouraged the development of the higher criticism and modernism also led to literal fundamentalism and Bible societies. Vernacular Bible translation took advantage of humanist scholarship only in order to undermine it by fostering patriotic and populist tendencies. It has to be distinguished from scholarly attacks on the *Vulgate* because it was connected with so many non-scholarly anti-intellectual trends.

By considering the vernacular translation movement that was fostered by printers, one might illuminate the relationship between Protestantism and nationalism. Similarly, by stressing other effects of the shift from script to print, one might throw new light on the relationship between Protestantism and a new "spirit" of capitalism.

To keep his firm solvent and stay ahead of his creditors, the printer could not learn much from advice proffered by Thomas à Kempis or Thomas Aquinas. Moreover, his ideas about Christian

---

[32] Hugh Trevor-Roper, *The Crisis of the Seventeenth Century*, p. 161. The same sort of error is made by Richard Altick, *The English Common Reader*, p. 38, when he speaks of the Bible as providing "immemorial fare" in English cottages!

[33] The "rarity of Bibles in clerical possession" and "the rare use made of them even in the services" before the Reformation is noted by Peter Heath, *The English Parish Clergy on the Eve of the Reformation* (London, 1969), pp. 74-75. Preacher's manuals before print are described by Beryl Smalley, *English Friars and Antiquity in the Early Fourteenth Century* (Oxford, 1960) and by G. R. Owst, *Literature and Pulpit in Medieval England* (Oxford, 1966).

virtue rarely agreed with those of monks. He not only shared with fellow urban entrepreneurs a natural antipathy for members of the begging orders; he had more reason than most business men to feel keen contempt for monkish learning; and he was uniquely well situated to make his view known. Although he fed the demand for religious literature and contributed to its vastly increased circulation, he was, himself, better at charting courses in this world than in any other. By turning out guidebooks, tables, and charts he also encouraged the reading public to resort more to planning and less to prayer in order to achieve earthly goals.[34] Moreover, the printer not only helped to shape a competing utilitarian ethic; he also made possible a fuller orchestration of all the old anticlerical themes. With the transfer of book production to lay urban milieus and the replacement of hand illumination by woodcuts and engravings, anticlerical forces were provided with organs of publicity that had not been at their disposal before.

A sociologist discussing "underdeveloped regions" today notes that "Literacy is the basic personal skill that underlies the whole modernizing sequence."[35] This point is also relevant to many of the historical problems that preoccupied Max Weber. The prevalence of Protestants among "higher technically and commercially trained personnel"[36] becomes less puzzling when one considers that the premium placed on learning to read was much higher among Protestants than among Catholics[37] and that, therefore,

---

[34] See Cosmo Gordon, "Books on Accountancy 1494-1600," *Transactions of the Bibliographical Society* 13: 145-70; Kenneth Charlton, *Education in Renaissance England* (London, 1965); Mark Curtis, "Education and Apprenticeship," *Shakespeare Survey–XVII*, A. Nicholl, ed. (Cambridge, 1964), pp. 68-70; Louis B. Wright, *Middle Class Culture in Elizabethan England* (Chapel Hill, N.C., 1935). A most illuminating study of how commercial transactions were divorced from moral and religious contexts and presented as neutral problems in how to maximize gain is offered by Natalie Z. Davis, "Sixteenth Century French Arithmetics on the Business Life," *Journal of the History of Ideas*, 21 (1960): 18-48.

[35] Daniel Lerner, "Toward a Communication Theory of Modernization," (1963 Essay) reprinted in *Comparative Perspectives on Social Changes*, Shmuel N. Eisenstadt, ed. (Boston, 1968), p. 145.

[36] Max Weber, *The Protestant Ethic and the Spirit of Capitalism*, tr. Talcott Parsons (London, 1948), p. 35. A striking example of high literacy rates is given in a recent study of Latin American Protestant minorities: E. Willems, "Cultural Change and the Rise of Protestantism in Brazil and Chile," in *The Protestant Ethic and Modernization*, Shmuel N. Eisenstadt, ed., p. 198. This entire volume incidentally passes over the advent of printing despite its apparent relevance to all the issues covered.

[37] In Tudor England, "religious instruction and exhortations to read went hand in hand—as is evident from the Injunctions of 1538, 1547, and 1559"—Margaret Aston, Review of Charlton and Simon, *Shakespeare Studies* 4 (1968):388. In Scotland, an act of Parliament imposed fines for failure to purchase the Geneva Bible—Lloyd Berry,

religious affiliation had a direct bearing on literacy rates. Catholic policy after Trent stressed lay obedience and, in the words of an admittedly biased Protestant scholar, resulted in a Church where "the priest reads for all."[38] Once an incentive to learn to read was eliminated among Catholics and reinforced among Protestants, book markets were likely to expand at different rates. Because Bible printing became a special privilege, its extinction in Catholic centers directly affected a relatively small group of printers.[39] The entire industry, however, suffered a glancing blow from the suppression of the large potential market represented by a Catholic lay Bible-reading public. Furthermore, vernacular Bibles were by no means the only best-sellers that were barred to Catholic readers after the Council of Trent.

The expansion of the printing industry probably affected the rate of development of many other enterprises—not merely because type-founding is related to metallurgy, paper mills to textile manufacture, publicity and advertising to sales, but also because the rate of technological innovation and supplies of skilled labor were likely to develop most rapidly in regions where printers also flourished and book-markets were growing. After the mid-sixteenth century, these regions were likely to be Protestant. In general, the movement of printing industries seems marked enough to be correlated with other developments.

Given the convergence of interests among printers and Protestants, given the way the new media implemented older evangelical goals, it seems pointless to argue whether material or spiritual, socioeconomic or religious "factors" were more important in transforming Western Christianity. Not only are such dichotomies based on spurious categories but they also seem irrelevant to the distinctive amalgam which resulted from collaboration between diverse pressure groups. It is by no means pointless, however, to insist that printing be assigned a prominent position when enumerating "factors" or analyzing causes. To leave the interests and outlook of printers out of the amalgam (as most accounts do) is to lose a chance of explaining how Protestant-Catholic divisions related to other concurrent developments that were transforming European society. Not all changes ushered in by print were

---

Introduction, *The Geneva Bible A Facsimile of the 1560 Edition* (Madison, Wis., 1969) p. 21.

[38] Hauser, p. 58.

[39] The relocation of continental Bible printing centers after Venetian activities were halted is described by Black, "The Printed Bible," *C.H.B. III*, 440-51.

compatible with the cause of religious reform; many were irrelevant to that cause; some, antipathetical to it. Nevertheless, Protestants and printers had more in common than Catholics and printers did. Religious divisions were of critical importance to the future development of European society partly because of the way they interacted with other new forces released by print. If Protestants seem to be more closely affiliated with certain modernizing trends than do Catholics, it is largely because reformers did less to check these new forces and more to reinforce them at the start.

That Protestantism was above all a "book religion" has certainly been noted repeatedly.[40] But this could be more fully exploited in comparative studies if it were related to other unevenly phased changes set in motion by printing. Given a clearly defined incentive to learn to read that was present among Protestants *qua* Protestants and not among Catholics *qua* Catholics, for example, one might expect to find a deeper social penetration of literacy among the former than among the latter during the second century of printing. Earlier lines dividing literate from unlettered social strata—magistrates, merchants, or masters from journeymen artisans or yeomen—might grow fainter in Protestant regions and more indelible in Catholic ones between the 1550s and 1650s. This, in turn, would encourage the pooling of talents drawn from more varied social sectors among Protestants. Distinctions between Latin reading elites and vernacular reading publics would also be less sharp where clergy and laity shared in common vernacular prayer books and Bibles. Where scholars were accustomed to reading in the vernacular and artisans were encouraged to master letters, there were greater opportunities for a cross-fertilization of ideas. If seventeenth-century scientific activity was promoted more effectively in Protestant regions, this may have been partly because a livelier interchange between artisan-authors and closet philosophers could occur there.[41]

The variation in literacy rates during the centuries of Bible reading has important implications not only for the history of

---

[40] See references in Altick, pp. 24-45. Long before Gutenberg, of course, Christians (as well as Jews) were being described as "people of the Book." The phrase appears in the *Koran*. See H. I. Marrou, *A History of Education in Antiquity*, tr. George Lamb (New York, 1956), pp. xiv-xv.

[41] A few aspects of the science-Protestantism controversy are noted in Elizabeth L. Eisenstein, "Some Conjectures about the Impact of Printing on Western Society and Thought," *Journal of Modern History* 40 (March 1968):46-50.

science or of ideas. It affected the phasing of political and social developments as well. It thus entered into the shaping of new kinds of group identity and new forms of political consciousness. Access to printed materials encouraged adherence to causes that lay beyond immediate local interests. It made possible vicarious participation in more distant events. It weakened a traditional nexus of loyalties (and antipathies) which bound countrymen to local lords, burghers and guildsmen to their own town halls, gossiping congregations to their parish church steps. It encouraged the formation of larger collective units and more uniform linguistic groupings. It forced a more clear-cut division between provincial dialects and national languages and between private and public zones of life. It helps to account for the appearance of the "articulate citizen in Elizabethan England,"[42] the greater impersonality of political discourse in seventeenth-century France,[43] and the growth of "Leviathan States," swarming with officials and bureaucrats, everywhere in ancien régime Europe.

Changes affecting political consciousness and group identity came at a very uneven rate to the vast majority of European people. As long as they belonged to a "hearing public" they were bound by the older nexus of loyalties and were relatively impervious to the new. The social penetration of literacy, which was linked with Bible reading, thus affected the timing of "revolutions of rising expectations." Because it was associated with the expansion of printing industries and access to printed materials, religious affiliation entered into the patterning of social agitation and mobility, political cleavage and cohesion.

Possibly the most fundamental divergence between Catholic and Protestant cultures may be found closest to home. The absence or presence of family prayers and family Bibles is a matter of some consequence to all social historians. Where functions previously assigned only to priests in the Church were also entrusted to parents at home, a patriarchical ethic was reinforced.

---

[42] Arthur B. Ferguson, *The Articulate Citizen and the English Renaissance* (Durham, N.C., 1965), *passim.*

[43] Vicarious participation in major public events, especially royal campaigns and court festivities, was greatly facilitated by the printed propaganda of Valois and Bourbons, described by Martin, *Livre à Paris* I, 261ff. The impact of duplicating images and portraits of royal personages (which reached a climax in Napoleon's day) has yet to be assessed by political scientists. The increasing impersonality of political discourse in seventeenth-century France, noted by Lionel Rothkrug, *Opposition to Louis XIV: Political and Social Origins of the French Enlightenment* (Princeton, N.J., 1965), pp. 458-59, needs to be balanced against the heightened "visibility" of the features and activities of individual rulers.

Since the Reformation the family had become the ... most essential unit of government in the Church. The head of the household was required to see that his subordinates attended services and that children and servants were sent to be catechized. He was expected, moreover, particularly by Puritans, to conduct daily worship at home and to see to the general welfare of all his household. ... The master was both king and priest to his household. ...[44]

Concepts of the family were probably also transformed where the Holy Spirit was domesticated.

Religion is for the Puritan, family religion. Divine worship is, not incidentally but primarily, family worship.
... the home was deliberately and not illogically transformed into a church. It was no longer that the family went to the temple, rather the temple came to the family and fashioned it anew.[45]

The character of family life, to be sure, was changed by various Protestant policies which had little to do with typography. The abandonment of matrimony as a sacrament which paved the way for divorce and the sanctioning of clerical marriage which helped to dignify the matrimonial state are two examples that come to mind. Nevertheless, "the temple" entered the family circle in the form of a printed Bible.[46] Boundaries between priesthood and laity, altar and hearthside, were effectively blurred by bringing Bibles and prayer books within reach of every God-fearing householder. Here again, the printer was quick to encourage self-help: "To help guide him, the father could rely on the numerous pocket-size manuals that came off the printing presses, such as *A Werke for Householders* (1530). ..."[47] or "Godly private prayers for householders to meditate upon and to say in their families (1576)."[48]

---

[44] Keith Thomas, "Women and Civil War Sects," in *Crisis in Europe 1560-1660*, Trevor Aston, ed., p. 333. See also Michael Walzer, *The Revolution of the Saints*, p. 190, on duties assumed by the Puritan father.

[45] Levin L. Schücking, *The Puritan Family*, tr. Brian Battershaw (London, 1969), pp. 56-57. Schücking also contrasts the situation in Piers Plowman's day where lack of widespread educational facilities made home-services impossible (p. 65).

[46] For a richly documented description of English developments in this field, see Christopher Hill, *Society and Puritanism in Pre-Revolutionary England*, 2d ed. (New York, 1967), Chapter 13. The title of this chapter—"The Spiritualization of the Household"—and that of the preceding one—"The Secularization of the Parish"—suggest some of the multiple transformations printed Bibles produced in Protestant lands.

[47] Charlton, *Education in Renaissance England*, p. 201. See also Peter Laslett, *The World We Have Lost* (New York, 1965), p. 241, n. 3, for other references.

[48] Cited by Wright, *Middle-Class Culture*, p. 245, along with many other relevant titles.

Through prayer and meditation, models for which they could find in scores of books, the draper, the butcher . . . soon learned to approach God without ecclesiastical assistance. . . . The London citizen learned to hold worship in his own household. . . . the private citizen had become articulate in the presence of the Deity. . . .[49]

Puritan tradesmen who had learned to talk to God in the presence of their apprentices, wives, and children were already on their way to self-government.[50] However low they were ranked among parishioners in church[51] they could find at home satisfying acknowledgment of their own dignity and worth.[52]   Catholic tradesmen and businessmen left religious affairs to the priest and could not play the role of "king and priest" at home.[53] Was the French bourgeois perhaps more likely to spend his money to enhance his prestige by buying land or office (or by employing dancing masters) partly because the stigma associated with being in trade was not counterbalanced by religious offices performed in the home?[54] One might also speculate that Puritan English

---

[49] *Ibid.*, pp. 239-41.

[50] Haller, *The Elect Nation*, pp. 182-83, stresses Bible-reading as a source of new self-assertion on the part of "free born Englishmen." That a politically aggressive Puritan ministry contained a large proportion of auto-didacts and that Gospel-reading was the key element in creating a sense of fellowship is noted by Walzer, pp. 135; 120-21, but unlike Haller he is not explicit about the role of the printed word in the formation of his Puritan "new man" (p. 4).

[51] Laslett, p. 30, cites Sir Thomas Smith in the 1560s as testimony of the very low rank assigned "merchants and retailers . . . tailors, shoemakers" etc. who "have no free land . . . no voice nor authority in their commonwealth."

[52] This seems to contradict Walzer's discussion (pp. 248-49) of an "uneasy literature of self-enhancement" composed by English merchants in response to status anxiety stimulated by the increased output of books on heraldry. He also cites books aimed specifically at "would-be gentlemen" (p. 250). How printers helped to sharpen social divisions by prefaces distinguishing among markets needs more analysis. Although they may have shared much in common with other tradesmen, I still think Puritans did exhibit a new self-respect which owed much to their newly elevated position at home. See Laslett's discussion of how men got to be addressed as "*worshipful*," p. 27.

[53] A Catholic cardinal warning the laity against reading Scripture put it well: "You should *not* be your owne masters"—Reginald Pole, "Speech to the citizens of London on behalf of religious houses," cited by J. W. Blench, *Preaching in England in the late Fifteenth and Sixteenth Centuries* (Oxford, 1964), pp. 50-51. How Counter Reformation policy discouraged "household religion" is described by John Bossy, "The Counter Reformation and the People of Catholic Europe," *Past and Present* no. 47, (May, 1970), pp. 68-69. The notion that Bible-reading was a layman's duty was condemned as a Jansenist proposition by the Bull Unigenitus, see Crehan, "Bible in Catholic Church," *C.H.B.* III, 222. The similarity between sober Jansenist and Puritan life-styles, and their common antipathy for dancing masters, is worth further thought. Too often it is handled by invoking the "rising middle class."

[54] To forestall misunderstanding, please mentally underline "partly." Before

householders would feel particularly keen hostility to the threat of
a Catholic restoration. After becoming accustomed to functioning
as priest in one's home, much was at stake in keeping papists off
the throne.

The transformation of the home into a church and of the
householder into a priest, at all events, seems to bear out Weber's
suggestion that:

The Reformation meant not the elimination of the Church's control over
daily life, but rather the substitution of a new form of control for the
previous one. It meant the repudiation of a control that was very lax . . . in
favor of a regulation of the whole of conduct which, penetrating to all
departments of private and public life was infinitely burdensome and
earnestly enforced.[55]

I think it is possible, however, to be more specific about the
difference between controls implied in the above passage. Instead
of merely contrasting laxity with strictness, one might compare
the effects of listening to a Gospel passage read from the pulpit
with reading the same passage at home for oneself. In the first
instance, the Word comes from a priest who is at a distance and on
high; in the second it almost seems to come from a silent voice
that is within. The "deep penetration of new controls" to all
departments of life becomes more explicable when we note that
printed books are more portable than pulpits, more numerous
than priests, and the messages they contain are more easily
internalized.

The formation of a distinctive ethos within Puritan households
may be partly explained by the fact that Puritans exploited most
fully the new possibility of "going by the book." To understand
the control over daily life exerted by Calvinist churches, it is
worth looking more closely at certain examples of early book-
learning. In particular it is worth pausing over domestic manuals
and household guides (such as one issued "For the ordering of
Private Families according to the direction of God's word")[56]

---

comparing social mobility in France and England many factors have to be considered.
For example, it is easier to enter and harder to exit the ranks of the nobility in France
than in England, as Betty Behrens points out in "Nobles, Privileges and Taxes in France
at the End of the Ancien Regime," *Economic History Review* 15, no. 3(1963): 455.
Many equally important issues have to be noted. My point is merely that variation in
religious role-playing at home *may* be relevant to this complex comparative problem.

[55]Weber, *Protestant Ethic*, p. 36.

[56]Wright, *Middle-Class Culture*, p. 211, cites this subtitle of a book by Robert Weaver
(1598).

while recalling, once again, new features introduced by typography.

With regard to books on "household government" and "domesticall duties" some previous observations seem particularly cogent. Here, in particular, the superficial observer will see only evidence suggesting that printing contributed to cultural inertia. The domestic advice that was issued after print seems to vary not at all from that which was issued in the age of scribes. Those who look for novel views in sixteenth- and seventeenth-century conduct books are likely to be disappointed. The same ancient wisdom is cited, the same cautions issued, the same morals drawn by one generation after another.[57] In this one instance, I must reluctantly admit that McLuhan's bold formula does seem to apply: It was not a new message but a new medium that changed the character of domestic life most profoundly. Along with cookbooks and herbals, domestic books were written in the age of scribes. They had not been duplicated in sizable quantities, however. Views of how family life should be conducted in a well-ordered household were relatively casual and amorphous as long as reliance on unwritten recipes prevailed. Elizabethans who purchased domestic guides and marriage manuals were not being given new advice. But they were receiving old advice in a new way and in a format that made it much more difficult to evade. A much more limited and standardized repertoire of roles was extended to them than had been extended to householders before. Instead of a cross fire of gossip conveying random impressions about what was expected, or haphazard interpretations of what a sermon meant, came books that set forth (with all the i's dotted and all the t's crossed) precise codes for behavior that godly householders should observe. These codes were known to others—to relatives and neighbors—as well as to oneself. Insofar as they were internalized by silent and solitary readers, the voice of individual conscience was strengthened. But insofar as they were duplicated in a standardized format, conveyed by an impersonal medium to a "lonely crowd" of many readers, a collective morality was also simultaneously created. Type-casting in printers' workshops thus contributed to new kinds of role-playing at home. A "middle-class" morality which looked back to

---

[57]See *ibid.*, pp. 226-27, for comment on "strange sameness" of domestic guidance offered to a burgher in 1558 and to his grandson in 1640. The tendency to stress cultural inertia in assessing the impact of print is noted in Eisenstein, "Some Conjectures," p. 53, n.151, and "Printing and the Renaissance," pp. 25, n.15; 70, n. 140.

Xenophon and the Bible was fixed in a seemingly permanent mold.

In dealing with altered concepts of the family and the roles performed within it, we need then to consider the sort of cultural differentiation that came in the wake of the printing press. Early book learning among Protestants was more homely, perhaps, and less courtly than among Catholics.[58] In all regions, however, primers and grammars, arithmetic books and writing manuals became both more uniform and more abundant at more or less the same time.[59] Domestic and educational institutions were transformed in a manner that affected well-nurtured youths of *all* faiths. The sort of changes that affected family life between the fifteenth and eighteenth century have been illuminated by Ariès' pioneering study of French society.[60] Studies based on other regions are needed to supplement his findings. But new theories are also needed if we wish to understand how and why the changes he describes occurred when they did. "The family ceased to be simply an institution for the transmission of a name and an estate," it assumed moral and spiritual functions, it "moulded bodies and soul." How and why this happened remains to be explored. In setting out to do this, a revival "of an interest in education" seems to me the wrong place to begin. Why not consider, first of all, how child-rearing and schooling were affected by the printed book?

Possibly no social revolution in European history is as fundamental as that which saw book learning (previously assigned to old men and monks) gradually become the focus of daily life during childhood, adolescence, and early manhood. Ariès has described the early phases of this vast transformation: "The solicitude of family, Church, moralists and administrators deprived the child of the freedom he had hitherto enjoyed among adults." The school

---

[58] See Wright, *op. cit.*, p. 203, n. 3, on limited vogue in England for translations of Castiglione's *Courtier* and other aristocratic guidebooks.

[59] How print implemented the drive to achieve a standardized and uniform system of education is well illustrated by Walter Ong, *Ramus*, p. 314. Ong mentions a pedagogy based on the schoolmaster's ability to say, "Look at p. 7, line 3, the 4th word." It is also illustrated by William Lily's introduction to his Grammar: *An Introduction of the Eyght Partes of Speeche* (1542) as cited by T. W. Baldwin, *William Shakespere's Small Latine & Lesse Greeke*, I, 179-80. (See also Baldwin's discussion of uniformity of Elizabethan curricula, I, 492-93.) Is there any vernacular French equivalent to Henry VIII's authorized primer of 1545? Or must one wait for Napoleon before French education becomes standardized as it was in Tudor England?

[60] Philippe Ariès, *Centuries of Childhood, passim.*

"was utterly transformed" into "an instrument of strict discipline."[61] I would argue that such changes are probably related to the shift from "learning by doing" to "learning by reading." Surely some sort of new discipline was required to keep healthy youngsters at their desks during daylight hours. Some sort of new profession—that of tutor, schoolmaster, or governess—was required to keep them there.[62] And some sort of new attitude on the part of parents was probably also apt to result. A new "concept of childhood" indeed might owe much to the widened gap between literate and oral cultures. The more adult activities were governed by conscious deliberation or going by the book, the more striking the contrast offered by the spontaneous and impulsive behavior of young offspring[63] and the more strenuous the effort required to remould young "bodies and souls." It was "to gain a start on the devil" that the Puritan child "was given the Bible to read at an early stage."[64]

It may be partly because spontaneous and impulsive behavior had to be more sternly repressed that Satanic forces appeared more threatening in the Age of the Reformation. It is often noted that Protestants repudiated Mariolatry, attacked the cult of saints and scholastic angelology, even while swallowing completely the views of Dominican friars on demonology. Belief in the Devil was shared in common by churchmen who were divided on many other doctrinal issues. Of course, religious warfare itself fostered preoccupation with Satan, who was assigned a commanding role in the enemy camp. But the forces of evil probably also loomed larger when efforts were bent to enforce a stricter, closer "walk with God." The new moral rigorism, shared by Catholics and Protestants alike, made particularly heavy demands on the clergy. Whether the duty of lay obedience or that of lay Bible reading was stressed, sixteenth-century churchmen in all regions were subject to the stricter discipline that was associated with "going by the book." It is more than coincidence, I think, that the same interval saw the most prolonged and intensive witchhunt Western Christendom had ever known.

---

[61] *Ibid*, pp. 412-13.

[62] On the growing importance of these new occupations, after the need for scribal bookhands had ended, see Curt Bühler, *The Fifteenth Century Book*, pp. 28-29.

[63] As already noted in my "Conjectures," p. 41, n.110, it seems likely that a redefinition of *la folie* went together with that of *L'Enfant*. Foucault's analysis of madness and civilization would be enhanced by considering the effect of print.

[64] Schücking, *Puritan Family*, p. 68.

The relationship between the shift from script to print and the incidence of witchcraft trials is, however, a much more complicated issue than the above paragraph suggests. This many-faceted topic deserves a whole book of its own and cannot be handled adequately here. Let me simply underline the need for such a study in view of the cavalier treatments the topic currently receives. A recent celebrated essay by Hugh Trevor-Roper provides a good case in point. Having reduced the effects of print to the "mere multiplication of evidence," the author confidently dismisses them as too trivial to account for the growth pattern he observes. "Whatever allowance we may make for the mere multiplication of the evidence after the discovery of printing, there can be no doubt that the witch craze grew, and grew terribly after the Renaissance."[65] The topic is not mentioned again, despite its relevance to all the speculations which follow as to why "organized systematic demonology" acquired a "terrible momentum" during the sixteenth and seventeenth centuries.

The topic receives somewhat more attention in a recent review article by Pierre Chaunu, partly because the book under review (a study of French magistrates by Robert Mandrou) is exceptional in taking some aspects of the impact of print into account.[66] Thus something is said about the shift from the oral transmission of witchcraft lore to its codification in printed form. The contribution of publicity to the spread of the mania; the effect of law-printing and standardization on demonology, in general, and French trials, in particular, are also discussed. Finally, the eventual replacement of credulity by scepticism which results in changing the legal definition of sorcery (so that witches are linked with crooks and charlatans instead of demons by an edict of 1632) receives considerable attention. The problems posed by this significant change in attitudes (raised many years ago by Lucien Febvre)[67] are handled, however, in a disappointing and conventional way. Cartesian rationalism is stressed, while the effects of a new publicity system on old forms of secrecy and on the position of sorcerers go unnoted.[68] Chaunu is prepared to agree with

---

[65] Trevor-Roper, *Crisis of the Seventeenth Century*, p. 91.

[66] Pierre Chaunu, "Sur la Fin des Sorciers au XVII⁰ Siècle," *Annales* 24, no. 4 (July-Aug. 1969): 895-911.

[67] Lucien Febvre, "Sorcellerie, Sottise ou Révolution Mentale?", *Annales* 3, no. 1 (Jan.-March, 1948):9-15.

[68] Speculations about the effect of print on occult lore and the position of sorcerers are offered by Eisenstein, "Printing and the Renaissance," pp. 78-79.

Mandrou that more efficient judicial machinery helped to increase the number of cases brought to trial. He also agrees that the authority conferred by the printed word and the diffusion of learned treatises helps to explain the increased preoccupation with the threat posed by witches. But in the end he decides (much as Trevor-Roper does) that mere duplication is too trivial to account for such a massive movement. "Small cause, great effect?" he asks and concludes: "One must search further."[69]

Chaunu's further search takes him away from law courts and book readers into the same rugged backwoods territory that Trevor-Roper and others have also profitably explored. I found his journey unusually rewarding partly because it suggests how much sixteenth-century missionary "mopping up" operations (designed to complete the Christianization of the barbarian peoples in Europe) owed to printed catechisms and service books and also because it provides a fascinating preview of later clashes between the Western powers and native cultures. His vivid portrayal of the conflict provoked between clergymen with their intrusive civilizing mission and the insular resistant folk culture clinging to familiar procedures seemed analogous to me to more recent developments such as the revival of Mau Mau in Kenya or the resurgence of Voodoo in Haiti. He argues convincingly that stubborn resistance to "rigueurs Puritanes"—particularly to the attack on rituals designed to protect fertility—accounts for much of the data that entered the dossiers compiled by witchhunters. When stern black-robed clergymen forced their way into secluded communities in the Scottish highlands or Vosges mountains and demanded the abandonment of age-old rituals in the name of Christ, they threatened practices associated with birth, copulation, and death—with community preservation, in brief. That deep anxieties were aroused by the priestly intruders, that some midwives or herbalists refused to accept their authority or partake of their sacraments and instead furiously attacked Christian symbols and clung to their unwritten recipes, does not seem surprising. Nor does it seem unnatural that missionaries and magistrates would regard obdurate, blasphemous old women who spit on the cross as servants of Satan.[70]

[69] Chaunu, "La Fin des Sorciers," p. 906
[70] Chaunu stresses the Christian marriage ceremony as a focus of conflict because it interfered with rites designed to guard against sterility and ensure a fruitful match. I think it likely that anxieties would also be aroused by any move that weakened the authority of midwives who presided over childbirth itself or that of herbalists entrusted with power to kill or cure.

Although it is not explicitly concerned with the advent of printing, Chaunu's discussion illuminates an aspect of the topic. The suppression of community practices based on oral transmission by a missionary movement implemented by print and backed by law courts and magistrates was (I think) associated with the same historic process as the repression of impulsive, spontaneous behavior among sixteenth-century Europeans at home—or at work and at school. Chaunu's sympathetic treatment of the deep anxieties the intrusive missionaries aroused is at all events more enlightening than Trevor-Roper's contemptuous reference to "the mental rubbish of peasant credulity and feminine hysteria."

... the Hammerers of Witches built up their systematic mythology of Satan's kingdom and Satan's accomplices out of the mental rubbish of peasant credulity and feminine hysteria; and the ... mythology once launched acquired a momentum of its own. It became an established folklore generating its own evidence and applicable far outside its original home. ...[71]

Because the contribution of the new medium to the launching of the myths and to the momentum they acquired is left out of account, the timing of the witch-craze becomes unnecessarily perplexing:

The duration of the witch-craze is certainly surprising. ... In the fourteenth century, that century of plague and depression and social dislocation, the mental climate might be congenial; but the later fifteenth century which saw the craze formally launched was the beginning of a period of new European expansion. ....Besides, the Witch Bull and the Malleus appeared in an age of enlightened criticism. ... of Renaissance humanism. ... At a time when the older forgeries of the Church were being exposed and the text of scripture critically examined, why should the new absurdities escape scrutiny?[72]

Once we realize that "formally launched" means to appear in print, the questions posed become somewhat easier to answer. In 1486, the first edition of the *Malleus Maleficarum*, an encyclopedia of demonology compiled by two Dominican inquisitors, was published. It contained the papal bull of 1484, which called for the extirpation of witches in Germany and thus helped to promote the Dominicans' book sales as well as their cause. "What the

---

[71] Trevor-Roper, *Crisis of the Seventeenth Century*, p. 116. E. William Monter, "Chronique: Trois Historians Actuels de la Sorcellerie," *Bibliothèque d'humanisme et Renaissance* 31 (1969): 205-13, also finds Trevor-Roper's display of "aristocratic disdain" objectionable (p. 209).

[72] Trevor-Roper, *Crisis of the Seventeenth Century* pp. 128-29.

Dominicans had been doing hitherto was local. . . . From now on a general mandate was given or implied . . . the persecution which had been sporadic. . . . was made general."[73] To ask why diffusion by means of print did not occur in the age of scribes is a waste of scholarly energy. Speculation about a "congenial mental climate" provided by the plague-ridden fourteenth century is beside the point. The invention of print and not the outbreak of plague accounts for the timing of an event which "advertised to all Europe . . . the new epidemic of witchcraft and the authority . . . given . . . to suppress it."[74]

If more attention was paid to the effects of print, moreover, one would not be surprised that humanist scholarship coexisted with efforts to codify demonology or increased concern about pacts with the Devil. As I have already noted, data inherited from the age of scribes came to sixteenth-century scholars in scrambled form and time was required to unscramble them.[75] Mystification as well as enlightenment also resulted from the output of early printers. Renaissance scholarship was by no means incompatible with belief in a spirit world. It entailed the acceptance of many "forgeries" and false texts. It encompassed the hieroglyphics of "Horapollo," alchemy, astrology, and learned treatises on the Cabala. Moreover, the expanded horizons of Renaissance bookworms contributed to suspicions of pacts with the Devil.

The sort of book learning that was cultivated by Doctor Faustus was correctly perceived as unchristian by orthodox theologians and this was increasingly true as time went on. For the more the scriptural tradition was reconstituted and purified by textual analysis, the more pagan and Christian elements which had coexisted for millennia were seen to be in sharper conflict, and the larger the share of an ancient, Latin and barbarian, heritage that got consigned to the Devil. Although Trevor-Roper strangely exempts belief in the hermetic texts from his category of "new absurdities," the hermetic vogue was no less vulnerable to critical textual analysis than Dominican demonology.[76] By present stan-

[73] *Ibid.*, p. 102.
[74] *Ibid.*, p. 101.
[75] Eisenstein, "Printing and the Renaissance," pp. 35;71.
[76] Platonism and "Hermetic mysticism" are associated by Trevor-Roper with the advancement of science and arbitrarily detached from "vulgar," "ridiculous," and "crude" forms of "witch belief," *Crisis of the Seventeenth Century*, pp. 132-33. Again, I agree with Monter, "Chronique," that there is no basis for exempting Hermeticism from other kinds of sixteenth-century credulity. Not until the seventeenth century did Isaac

dards, sixteenth-century scholars exhibited a similar credulity in both cases. Hermeticists who boasted of their magical power may have, on occasion, attacked witchhunters. But they certainly did not help to dispel fears of the demonic. On the contrary, every new treatise on the occult that appeared spread more alarm about traffic with the Devil.

When all due allowance is made for backwoods resistance to Christianization there is still much that remains to be said about tensions within the academic community, about the mentality of Renaissance scholars and the battles of books in which they were engaged. It is well to remember in any case that peasants have no monopoly on credulity nor women on hysteria—particularly in periods of intellectual dislocation, monks and professors are well supplied with both.

In dealing with sixteenth-century demonology, Trevor-Roper seems to make the same basic error that I have noted above in connection with literal fundamentalism. Indeed he couples them both—the "dying witch-craze" with "biblical fundamentalism"—in his list of "obsolescent habits of thought" that were "in retreat in the age of Erasmus."[77] As already noted, however, literal fundamentalism was a postprint phenomenon. I think the monster trials, which followed publication of the *Malleus*, were too.

> The recrudescence of the absurd demonology of the *Malleus* was not the logical consequence of any religious idea. . . . Perhaps on the eve of the Reformation the mythology was on its way out. Who can say what might have happened if Erasmus had triumphed instead of Luther and Loyola? Then the Renaissance might have led direct to the Enlightenment and the witch-craze have been remembered as a purely medieval lunacy.[78]

But the witch-craze that was "formally launched" with the *Malleus* could never have been remembered as "purely medieval." Like literal fundamentalism and Erasmus's career, it would not have preceded Gutenberg's invention. To imagine that Bible

---

Casaubon and Louis Cappel undermine belief in Hermetic and cabalistic texts; before then erudite scholars, such as Reuchlin, had enthusiastically supported the occult tradition.

[77] See p. 247 above, also n. 32. The two phenomena *are* coupled in the sense that the command in *Exodus* XXII.18, "Thou shalt not suffer a witch to live," was impressed upon many more readers' minds after Bible-printing got underway. The case of a Lutheran witchhunter who "read the Bible from cover to cover 53 times . . . and procured the death of 20,000 persons," is cited by Trevor-Roper, *Crisis of the Seventeenth Century*, p. 159.

[78] *Ibid.*, p. 140.

reading and witch burning were on their way out on the "eve of the Reformation" is to overlook the very forces which propelled them—to overlook the same forces, be it noted, that shaped Erasmus's career and produced an expanding Republic of Letters.

The basic error is to pattern developments as straight line trends so that we are given to understand there is a direct route from Renaissance to Enlightenment that only fools and fanatics failed to take. Movements that do not point in the designated direction are classified as retrograde, obsolescent, or anomalous. Calvinism is thus dismissed as an "obscurantist deviation," Bible-reading relegated to the age of hand-written books, and the persistence of fundamentalism into the age of Darwin or the holding of a Scopes trial in the age of Ford become almost completely inexplicable.

One of the advantages of considering the effects produced by printing is that we can come to terms with the coexistence of incompatible views and the persistence of contradictory movements without treating any as anomalous and without forcing them into oversimple grand designs. The many changes introduced by the new technology (as I have noted already) far from synchronizing smoothly or pointing in one direction, contributed to disjunctions, worked at cross purposes, and operated out of phase with each other. For example, religious, dynastic, and linguistic frontiers were fixed more permanently by the same wholesale industry that operated most profitably by tapping cosmopolitan markets and was naturally antagonistic to all the old frontiers. Similarly the presses helped to fan the flames of religious controversy even while creating a new vested interest in free thought, ecumenical concord, and toleration.[79]

J. H. Hexter has pointed to the fallacy of assuming that an increase in secularism meant a decrease in religiosity. Both were intensified during the sixteenth century, he suggests, because the more furious the battles between religious zealots, the more concerned statesmen became about securing a stable civil order.[80] This interpretation is helpful. Like many clear and logical schemes, however, it has the defects of its virtues. Opposing factions are lined up so neatly—with secular-minded *politiques* set against fanatical *ligueurs*—that one looks in vain for run-of-the-mill, ambivalent, inconsistent human beings. Fickle printers "who ran

---

[79] Whereas Henry Kamen attributes *The Rise of Toleration* to the burghers of Zurich and the landed aristocrats of England, I think we should look first to early printers and their expanding book-trade.

[80] J. H. Hexter, *Reappraisals in History* (Evanston, 1961), p. 42.

with the hares and hunted with the hounds,"[81] who turned out prayer books and Jesuit tracts for one market, atlases and travel books for another, suggest that conflict between two groups might mean opportunity for yet a third. To understand the forces that drove Christians apart and brought worldly men together, it is not enough, in any case, to list sixteenth-century polarities. One must look beyond the immediate issues to the more general process of polarization that was at work. After the advent of printing (as we have seen), incompatible elements within the Christian tradition became more difficult to reconcile and decisions were forced on churchmen and policy makers that could be avoided or glossed over before. A more careful investigation of the effects of the new medium should make it possible to explain a variety of cross currents during the early modern era without resorting to dialectical schemes or oversimplifying the conflicting trends.

To illustrate this point, one more look at Bible printing is in order. By the mid-sixteenth century, as already noted, it was proceeding apace in Protestant regions while being arrested in Catholic ones with consequences unforeseen by all. Even with hindsight, no simple formula can be applied to these consequences. Not only did Protestant and Catholic cultures move apart, but, within Protestant regions, contrary tendencies were encouraged. The new mode of production had a different impact on printers and publishers than it had on purchasers or consumers. Men who saw copy through the stages of publication looked at texts differently than did those who received the finished products. To be enabled to read the holy words of God in one's own tongue was probably an awesome experience for a devout sixteenth-century reader. It seems quite likely that new forms of sect-type Christianity and literal fundamentalism resulted from an increased consumption of vernacular Bibles. On the other hand, in worskhops where texts got processed and copy-edited and among

---

[81] Elizabeth Armstrong, *Robert Estienne, Royal Printer* (Cambridge, 1954), pp. 13-14, uses the phrase in connection with Colines who published works by Lefèvre d'Etaples and attacks on those works by Sorbonnistes. Hexter's scheme also overlooks groups who advocated toleration on religious, not political, grounds as shown by debates between Justus Lipsius who took a "politique" position and Dirk Coornhert who believed that forced conversion was displeasing to God. (D. W. Jellema, Review of *Das Toleranz-Problem, The American Historical Review* 75, no. 4 [April 1970]; 1143-44.) The existence of a "third force" which was neither "politique" nor incredulous but adhered to belief in heavenly harmony and the futility of earthly quarrels is also discussed by Leon Voet, *The Golden Compasses* 2 vols., (Amsterdam, 1969) I, 29-30, in connection with Plantin's circle. Coornhert's connection with this circle is also noted, I, 385.

booksellers seeking new markets, the scriptures probably inspired less awe than ever before. One might compare the devotional attitudes of the monastic scribe, who worked over the pages of one copy, for remission of his sins, with that of an early printer:

... The first Strasbourg printer Johann Mentelin ... was a careless printer but obviously a smart business man. His first publication was a Bible, issued in 1460-1 in direct competition with Mainz; but whereas the 42-line Bible occupied 1,286 pages, Mentelin succeeded in squeezing the work into 850 pages, thus saving almost a third of the paper. His next book again shows his sound commercial instinct. It was the first Bible printed in German or in any vernacular and, although full of school-boy howlers, it nevertheless remained the standard text of all German Bibles before Luther.[82]

There were, of course, many printers who were deeply devout; who took particular pains over holy books and considered their Bibles as the crowning glory of their career. The book trade, moreover, contributed many martyrs to the antipapist cause who laid down their lives for their faith. But even the most pious printer was persuaded that God's words could be spread further by printing than by preaching. For this purpose, markets had to be gauged, financing secured, privileges sought, Catholic officials evaded, compositors supervised, distribution organized. What appeared to the devout reader in a quasi-miraculous guise involved an exercise in processing texts, shrewd politicking, and practical problem-solving for the equally devout producer. Mammon as well as Caesar necessarily entered into the latter's calculations. So, too, did variant readings of the same sacred words.

Moreover, printers themselves did not share a "common mind" and hence were diversely affected by involvement in a new mode of production. Some were fiery apostles wholly committed to serving one true church or one "elect nation." But others were not and tried to serve many. Genevan printers surreptitiously turned out books for populous Catholic markets in France. The same Antwerp firm won a privileged position from Catholic Spain under Philip II, but served Calvinist Holland and Jewish communities as well. Even as Henri IV felt Paris worth a mass or Cardinal Richelieu that "raison d'état" dictated alliance with infidel Turks, so too did a Manutius, an Estienne, or a Plantin keep family firms solvent and presses in operation by alliances with Protestants, Catholics, Jews, Spaniards, Dutchmen, and all shades of French-

[82] Sigfrid H. Steinberg, *Five Hundred Years of Printing* (Bristol, 1961), p. 47.

men alike. The formation of syndicates of heterodox businessmen and printers linked to far-flung distribution networks indicates how the new industry encouraged informal social groupings that cut across traditional frontiers and encompassed varied faiths.

In Plantin and his creditors we have uncovered a group which resembles in miniature the . . . longer lasting group of financiers . . . known as "la banque protestante" . . . and recently studied . . . by Herbert Luthy. . . . And perhaps we should conclude, as did Luthy, that the primary forces binding people of this sort together in . . . financial combines are ties of blood and friendship. However, it seems to me that one can go further and find connections more analogous to those which . . . Max Weber sought. . . . I would suggest that the beliefs of the members of the "House of Love" were a positive economic advantage to businessmen operating in situations . . . ridden with ideological tensions . . . A set of beliefs, which were secret, "nicodemite," and empha-sized brotherly love, permitted its members to avoid the disasters which could overtake any businessman, particularly any printer . . . so committed . . . to a dogmatic position . . . that he could not accommodate himself to a . . . regime enforcing an opposite point of view.[83]

To forestall misunderstanding, we may assume that Kingdon does not mean Plantin chose his beliefs with their economic advantages in mind—a faith so rationally selected being almost a contradiction in terms. He is, instead, suggesting that business men, particularly printers, with antidogmatic views, were most likely to prosper amid the shifting fortunes of religious warfare and that a tolerant outlook helped to attract foreign financial support. The point is valid but needs to be supplemented by other considerations. The cosmopolitan and ecumenical outlook of many early printers was not only related to their position as capitalist entrepreneurs. It was also related to the nature of the products they manufactured. Plantin's merchandise set him apart from other businessmen and tradesmen. It encouraged him to feel more at ease with strange scholars, bibliophiles, and literati than with neighbors or relatives in his own home town. The prospering printer had to know as much about books and intellectual trends as cloth merchants did about drygoods and dress fashions; he needed to develop a connoisseur's expertise about typestyles, book catalogues, and library sales. He often found it useful to master many languages, to handle variant texts, to investigate antiquities and old inscrip-tions along with new maps and calendars. If emigrés or aliens were

---

[83] R. M. Kingdon, "Christopher Plantin and His Backers 1575-1590," *Mélanges d'Histoire Economique et Sociale* (Geneva, 1963), p. 315.

welcome in his workshop, this was rarely because of ties of blood
or friendship; nor was it only because foreign financing, new
market outlets, patrons, or privileges were being sought. Foreign
experts were also needed as editors, translators, correctors, and
type designers. In these capacities they were welcomed into homes
as well as shops. They were offered room and board by their
employers. They were admitted into the printer's family circle as
well.[84]

Once again Bible printing enters the picture; for "belief in the
sacred scriptures as an ultimate source of truth" was not only an
important element in the rise of printing industries, as Kingdon
points out. It also contributed to the establishment of polyglot
households by sixteenth-century scholar printers. Representatives
of ten different nationalities sat around the table of Robert
Estienne and Perrette Badius. According to their son, Henri, even
the Estiennes' servants picked up a smattering of Latin, the only
tongue shared in common by all.[85] Similar heterodox and cosmopolitan circles were formed around the "New Academy" of Aldus
Manutius in Venice and Christopher Plantin's "House of Love" in
the Netherlands.[86] To account for the Philhellenic sympathies
associated with Aldus' circle, or for the even broader, philanthro-
pic ones of Plantin's group, it is a mistake to stop short with
positive economic advantages. The need to preserve domestic
peace in actual households also played a part in the advocacy of
doctrines pertaining to brotherly love and in the organization of
semisecret societies designed to propagate these doctrines. In the
late sixteenth century, for the first time in the history of any civilization, the concept of a *Concordia Mundi* was being developed on a
truly global scale and the "family of man" being extended to
encompass all the peoples of the world. To understand how this
happened, there is no better place to begin than with the

---

[84] See "The Plantin House as a Humanist Center," in Voet, I, 362-395, for data.

[85] Armstrong, *Robert Estienne*, p. 15.

[86] An interesting link between these two groups is provided by the printer Daniel
Bomberg (or Bomberghen) who pioneered in Hebrew Bible printing in Venice but came
from Antwerp and had sons and nephews who inherited his types and allied themselves
with Plantin. See Voet, I, 44 ff. Also Colin Clair, *Christopher Plantin* (London, 1960),
David W. Davies, *The World of the Elseviers 1580-1712* (The Hague, 1954); J. A. Van
Dorsten, *Thomas Basson 1555-1613 English Printer at Leiden* (Leiden, 1961). On Aldus
a new monograph is needed. Deno John Geanakoplos, *Greek Scholars in Venice*
(Cambridge, Mass., 1962) provides only a limited view of his circle. How his "Accademia
dei Filleleni" was linked with the Pléiade is noted by Frances Yates, *The French
Academies of the Sixteenth Century* (London, 1947), p. 6

hospitality extended by printers who plied their trade during the religious wars.[87]

Here again, I think Trevor-Roper is misguided when he overlooks printers' workshops and envisages three periods of peace, in order to explain the growth of attitudes encouraging theological reconciliation.[88] However armistice intervals are juggled, the fact remains that syncretic, irenic creeds were being quietly shaped and persistently advocated throughout a century and a half of religious warfare. The problem of understanding the religious origins of the Enlightenment cannot be resolved by carving out an "age of Erasmus" or an "age of Bacon" to serve as a sanctuary for peace-loving philosophers. By taking into consideration the possibility that Bible reading could intensify dogmatism even while Bible printing might encourage toleration, the problem becomes somewhat easier to handle. The same approach may be helpful when dealing with other, similar problems relating to contradictory attitudes manifested during the Reformation.

On the whole, it seems safe to conclude that all problems associated with the disruption of Western Christendom will become less baffling if we approach them by respecting the order of events and put the advent of printing ahead of the Protestant revolt.

FOR FURTHER READING

Altick, Richard D. *The English Common Reader: A Social History of the Mass Reading Public, 1800-1900.* Chicago: University of Chicago Press, Phoenix Books, 1963.

Ariès, Philippe. *Centuries of Childhood: A Social History of Family Life*, tr. by R. Baldick. New York: Knopf, 1962.

---

[87]The "global scale" is provided by Ortelius, the pioneer atlas publisher, whose affiliations with Plantin's circle are noted by René Boumans, "The Religious Views of Abraham Ortelius," *Journal of the Warburg and Courtauld Institutes* 17(July-Dec 1954): 374-77. For an expanded view of the "Family of Man," see William Bouwsma, *Concordia Mundi.* Postel was a self-taught, low-born Norman scholar who mastered Greek, Hebrew, Arabic, and other exotic tongues. He worked with Bomberg in Venice and Oporinus in Basel. His correspondence with Plantin and Ortelius included letters in which he mentioned the "family of love," and described printing as "the lance and sword of Christ's victory," pp. 240-42. Plantin asked his advice on designing Syriac types. Apart from his friendship with Ortelius and Postel, Plantin also helped Mercator. His multifarious connections are suggested by Voet, I, 367-69, 383ff.

[88]Trevor-Roper, *Crisis of the Seventeenth Century,* pp. 200-202, describes three periods: an age of Erasmus, of Bacon, and of Newton, as "phases of light," as intervals of "cosmopolitan intellectual correspondence" which were immune from "ideological war" whether "hot or cold."

Armstrong, Elizabeth. *Robert Estienne, Royal Printer*. New York: Cambridge University Press, 1954.

Aston, Margaret. *The Fifteenth Century: The Prospect of Europe*. (History of European Civilization Library.) New York: Harcourt Brace & World, 1968.

Aston, Trevor, ed. *Crisis in Europe, 1560-1600*. New York: Basic Books, 1965.

Bainton, Roland. *Here I Stand: A Life of Martin Luther*. New York: Mentor Books, 1950.

Baldwin, T. W. *William Shakespere's Small Latine & Lesse Greeke*. 2 vols. Urbana, Ill.: University of Illinois Press, 1944.

Blench, J. W. *Preaching in England in the Late Fifteenth and Sixteenth Centuries*. New York: Barnes & Noble, 1964.

Bouwsma, William J. *Concordia Mundi: The Career and Thought of Guillaume Postel, 1510-1581*. Historical Monograph Series. Cambridge, Mass: Harvard University Press, 1957.

Bouwsma, William J. *Venice and the Defense of Republican Liberty: Renaissance Values in the Age of the Counter Reformation*. Berkeley: University of California Press, 1968.

Bühler, Curt. *The Fifteenth Century Book*. Philadelphia: University of Pennsylvania Press, 1960.

Charlton, Kenneth. *Education in Renaissance England*. Toronto: University of Toronto Press, 1965.

Davies, David W. *The World of the Elseviers 1580-1712*. Reprint of 1954 text. Westport, Conn.: Greenwood Press, 1971.

Dickens, Arthur G. *Reformation and Society in Sixteenth Century Europe*. New York: Harcourt Brace & World, 1968.

Dickens, Arthur G. *Thomas Cromwell and the English Reformation*. New York: Harper & Row, 1969.

Dickens, Arthur G. *The Counter Reformation*. History of European Civilization Library. New York: Harcourt Brace & World, 1969.

Dickens, Arthur G. *The English Reformation*. New York: Schocken, 1964.

Eisenstadt, Shmuel N., ed. *Comparative Perspectives on Social Change*. Comparative Perspectives in Sociology Series, Boston: Little, Brown, 1968.

Eisenstadt, Shmuel N., ed. *The Protestant Ethic and Modernization: A Comparative View*. New York: Basic Books, 1968

Elton, Geoffrey R. *Reformation Europe 1517-1559*. New York: Harper & Row, 1966.

Elton, Geoffrey R. *Policy and Police: The Enforcement of the Reformation in the Age of Thomas Cromwell*. Cambridge: Cambridge University Press, 1972.

Ferguson, W. *The Renaissance in Historical Thought: Five Centuries of Interpretation*. Boston: Houghton Mifflin, 1948.

Franklin, Julian H. *Jean Bodin and the Sixteenth-Century Revolution in the Methodology of Law and History*. New York: Columbia University Press, 1963.

Greenslade, S. L., ed. *The Cambridge History of the Bible*. Vol. III. *The West from the Reformation to the Present Day*. Cambridge: Cambridge University Press, 1963.

Haller, William. *The Elect Nation: The Meaning and Relevance of Foxe's Book of Martyrs*. New York: Harper & Row, 1963.

Heath, Peter. *English Parish Clergy on the Eve of the Reformation*. Studies in Social History Series. Toronto: University of Toronto Press, 1969.

Hexter, Jack H. *Reappraisals in History*. Evanston, Ill.: Northwestern University Press, 1961.

Hill, Christopher. *Intellectual Origins of the Puritan Revolution*. Oxford: Oxford University Press, 1965.

Iserloh, Erwin. *The Theses Were Not Posted: Luther Between Reform and Reformation*. Boston: Beacon Press, 1968.

Kamen, Henry A. *The Rise of Toleration*. New York: McGraw-Hill, 1967.

Kingdon, Robert M. "Patronage, Piety and Printing in Sixteenth-Century Europe," in *A Festschrift for Frederick B. Artz*, eds. David W. Pinkney and Theodore Ropp. Durham, N.C.: Duke University Press, 1964.

Laslett, Peter. *The World We Have Lost*. New York: Scribner, 1965.

Leff, Gordon. *Heresy in the Later Middle Ages: The Relation of Heterodoxy to Dissent, c.1250-1450*. 2 vols. New York: Barnes & Noble, 1967.

Marrou, Henri I. *A History of Education in Antiquity*. New York: New American Library, Mentor Books, 1964.

Ong, Walter. *Ramus: Method and the Decay of Dialogue*. Cambridge, Mass.: Harvard University Press, 1958.

Ong, Walter, *The Presence of the Word*. New Haven: Yale University Press, 1967.

Owst, Gerald R. *Literature and the Pulpit in Medieval England*. 2d rev. ed. New York: Barnes & Noble, 1961.

Rupp, Gordon. *Luther's Progress to the Diet of Worms, 1521*. New York: Harper & Row, Torchbooks, 1951.

Schoeck, R. J., ed. *Editing Sixteenth Century Texts*. Toronto: University of Toronto Press, 1966.

Schücking, Levin L. *The Puritan Family: A Social Study from the Literary Sources*, tr. B. Battershaw. New York: Schocken, 1970.

Spitz, Lewis. *The Religious Renaissance of the German Humanists*. Cambridge, Mass.: Harvard University Press, 1963.

Steinberg, Sigfrid H. *Five Hundred Years of Printing*, rev. ed. Baltimore: Penguin, 1962.

Stone, Lawrence. *Social Change and Revolution in England 1540-1640*. Problems and Perspectives in History Series. New York: Barnes & Noble, 1965.

Trevor-Roper, H. R. *The Crisis of the Seventeenth Century: Religion, the Reformation, and Social Change*. New York: Harper & Row, 1968.

Van Dorsten, J. A. *Thomas Basson 1555-1613: English Printer at Leiden*. New York: Oxford University Press, 1961.

Voet, Leon. *The Golden Compasses*. 2 vols. Amsterdam: Vangendt & Co., 1969.

Walzer, Michael. *The Revolution of the Saints: A Study in Origins of Radical Politics*. New York: Atheneum, 1968.

Wright, Louis B. *Middle-Class Culture in Elizabethan England*. Ithaca, N.Y.: Cornell University Press, 1958.

Index

Acknowledgments: My warm thanks to Raymond A. Mentzer, Jr., now of Montana State University, for assistance in assembling some of the typescript for this book and in preparing the indicated source translations, and also to Kate Frost, of the University of Texas, for assistance in preparing the Index.—R.M.K.

271